Designing with Light

Designing with Light

The Art, Science, and Practice of
Architectural Lighting Design

Jason Livingston, IALD, LC

Cover Design by Wiley
Cover Photographs: Left top and left center: R2Architects; Left bottom: Ella Bromblin; Right: Jason Livingston

This book is printed on acid-free paper. ♾

Copyright © 2014 by Jason Livingston. All rights reserved.

Published by John Wiley & Sons, Inc., Hoboken, New Jersey.
Published simultaneously in Canada.

For general information about our other products and services, please contact our Customer Care Department within the United States at (800) 762-2974, outside the United States at (317) 572-3993 or fax (317) 572-4002.

Wiley publishes in a variety of print and electronic formats and by print-on-demand. Some material included with standard print versions of this book may not be included in e-books or in print-on-demand. If this book refers to media such as a CD or DVD that is not included in the version you purchased, you may download this material at http://booksupport.wiley.com. For more information about Wiley products, visit www.wiley.com.

Library of Congress Cataloging-in-Publication Data:

Livingston, Jason, 1965-
  Designing with light : the art, science, and practice of architectural lighting design / Jason Livingston.
    pages cm
  Includes index.
    ISBN 978-1-118-74047-7 (paperback); ISBN 978-1-118-74039-2 (ebk.); ISBN 978-1-118-74040-8 (ebk.)
  1. Lighting, Architectural and decorative. 2. Light in architecture. I. Title.
  NK2115.5.L5L58 2014
  729'.28—dc23

Printed in the United States of America   2014002868

SKY10027162_051821

To My Parents, who have given me so much

Contents

Additional resources for students and instructors are available on the book's companion website at www.wiley.com/go/designingwithlight. The following icon is used throughout the text to indicate content for which a related resource is available on the site:

Preface

Perhaps more than any other design discipline, lighting design is a combination of art, science, and technology. Lighting designers need to understand a wide range of architectural and interior design styles, so that our work supports the aesthetic goals of the owner and the design team. We need to know how light affects vision and perception, and understand the interplay between light and materials so we can extend and reinforce the viewer's response to a space. We need to understand the lamp technologies, lighting hardware, and control systems that will bring our vision of a project to fruition. It sounds like a lot, and it is. The wonderful thing about lighting design is that there is a wide range of projects with room for many types of designers. Some practitioners have a science, math, and numbers orientation. Some lean toward art, aesthetics, and intuition. Most designers fall somewhere in the middle. If you're bright, talented, and have a discerning eye there's a good chance you can have a career as in lighting design. I hope that encourages you.

I came to the practice of architectural lighting design after two decades as a theatrical lighting designer. As a result my design approach, and the emphasis of this book, focuses on aesthetics and design. I outline several approaches to the process of working through a design and present case studies of my own work, walking you through the design from start to finish so you can see how it was done. However, one cannot practice lighting design without a firm grasp of the technical side of the profession. That fact is becoming truer every year. After several decades of relative stagnation, so much of the lighting industry is changing that it's sometimes hard to keep up. New energy legislation, phasing out of old technology, introduction of new technology, and expansion of the body of knowledge that a designer must master are keeping all of us on our toes these days. I've devoted chapters to all of these issues, from lamps and luminaires to controls and codes.

Most books are a reflection of the author, and this one is no different. First, I love history, and I always want to know how things were discovered, not just the outcome of the discovery. As a result, you'll see that I often start with some history on the scientists and researchers responsible for important discoveries to give you some background on the concepts that are covered here. Second, I'm fascinated by science, and try to present some of the dryer material with a sense of excitement and wonder. I hope that comes through. Finally, I love this profession and I have fun at work (almost) every day. I take this material very seriously, and I strive for perfection in my work, but I'm not dour about it. I hope my joy for design and my excitement at solving design challenges comes through, and I hope that encourages you, too.

Acknowledgments

This book would not have made the journey from idea to manuscript to published work without the support and assistance of many wonderful people. My good friends Paul Bartlett and Ed McCarthy generously provided photographs and assistance. Lenore Doxsee gave me thoughtful feedback that clarified the text, and Sabra Zacharias and Lisa Cohen were sources of unfailing support and encouragement. I also want to thank Paul Drougas at Wiley for believing that there was room in the world for another book on lighting design, and that this should be the one.

Architects and manufacturers I've had the pleasure of working with over the years supplied many of the drawings and photographs. I want to especially thank David Rudzensky and John Ruiz of R2Architects, Frank Moya of Matthews Moya Architects, Emma Price of Edison Price, Michael Hewitt and Carolyn Kerr of Philips, and Wendy Luedtke of Rosco Laboratories.

Finally, I want to thank my students whose questions and engagement in class have made teaching both a challenge and a joy, and who have helped me to clarify my own ideas about light, design, and education.

About the Author

Jason Livingston IALD, LC, MIES, LEED Green Associate is the principal of Studio T+L, LLC a lighting design and theatre consulting firm based in New York City.

The first two decades of his career were spent as a theatrical lighting designer before he transitioned to architectural lighting design and theatre consulting. As an architectural lighting designer his projects have included residences, high end retail, corporate offices, restaurants, places of worship, and theatres. He was awarded a 2012 IES Illumination Award of Merit for the Fordham University Church, a 2003 Lumen Award by the New York Section of the IES, and a 2003 International Illumination Design Award by the IESNA for his work on Rewarding Lives for American Express in New York City. His work has been profiled in *Lighting Design + Application*, *Lighting & Sound America*, *Architectural SSL*, and *Design Bureau* magazines.

Mr. Livingston has taught theatrical and architectural lighting design in New York City since 1993. He currently teaches architectural lighting design at Parsons the New School for Design and Pratt Institute. He has also taught theatre lighting design at New York University and architectural lighting design at Fashion Institute of Technology.

He is a member of the IES Color Committee, and is co-author of their Color and Illumination Design Guide. He holds a BFA in Theatre Arts from University of Miami and an MFA in Theatre Lighting Design from New York University, and is a member of Illuminating Engineering Society, International Association of Lighting Designers, and United Scenic Artists Local 829.

CHAPTER 1

The Lighting Design Profession

"Architecture is the correct and magnificent play of forms brought together in light."

Le Corbusier

Without light there is no vision. Without light we cannot see the work of the architect, interior designer, and others who have contributed to creating a beautiful building. Add enough light to enable vision and we can see the shapes of the architecture and the colors of the materials, although perhaps not see them well. Add thoughtfully designed light, however, and it reveals the beauty of the architecture's forms and rhythms, and the subtle colors and textures of the materials. Light embraces and unifies the other elements of the space. Light directs our attention to important features and allows us to see our work with comfort and ease. It is the finishing touch on the overall experience that the owner and designers have sought to create. This is the work of a professional lighting designer.

The lighting designer Richard Kelly expressed this when he said, "Visual beauty is perceived by an interplay of . . . light. . . . It is therefore of first importance to plan lighting whether creating a new structure, altering an old or making existing conditions tolerable. By the judicious and artful control of [light] you can make an imagined water-color rendering become the real thing, become your idea of the beauty of architecture or decoration . . . light [can] make it easier to see, make surroundings safe and reassuring and stimulate the spirit. . . . To play with light is like playing with magic and is best done with a trained eye to recognize real and relative values, with experience and knowledge of physical techniques."[1]

Every building needs light, although not every building's design team will include a lighting designer. Some estimates suggest that less than 10 percent of construction or renovation design teams include a professional lighting designer. The reasons range from the owner's lack of understanding of what a lighting designer adds to a project to the architect's desire to keep fees low with the belief that other team members can take care of the lighting just as well as a lighting designer. The "others" who may provide some or

[1] Excerpt from "Lighting's Role in Architecture," *Architectural Forum*, February 1955. pp 152–153.

all of the lighting design include the architect, interior designer, electrical engineer, electrical contractor, and lighting salesperson. While they each have something to contribute, lighting design is not their primary field, making it is more likely that they will not have the basic and continuing education of a professional lighting designer, that they will not be current with new technologies, and that they will not be skilled in the broadest range of lighting techniques.

These other professionals act as lighting designers because the practice of lighting is so young. The first independent lighting design firm opened in 1935. Compared to the centuries-old professions of architecture and interior design, specialists in light are new. However, as awareness of the importance of lighting increases, and as building codes place more requirements and restrictions on lighting, the need for knowledgeable, professional lighting designers is great and growing.

In this book we will be discussing lighting design as a distinct profession. We will look at the ways in which the lighting designer collaborates with the other design team members, develops the lighting requirements for a project, and applies tools and techniques to achieve a successful lighting design.

The Lighting Designer's Scope of Practice

A lighting designer is someone with the specialized education, knowledge, and experience to apply the art and science of lighting design to the places people occupy. The broad scope of the practice for lighting designers is generally agreed upon, although the details vary by project, organization, and contract requirements. Lighting designers, of course, must possess a great deal of knowledge and skill related to light and lighting, but they are expected to know so much more because their work must fulfill so many functions:

■ *visual task*
A vision related activity, such as reading a book.

Provide light that is appropriate for *visual tasks* by:

- Identifying visual tasks that are to be performed
- Determining light levels that are typically required for the visual tasks
- Considering factors that suggest the light levels be higher or lower than typical, such as occupant's age, then selecting the project's target light level

Design light that supports the room's aesthetics or environment by:

- Providing light of the appropriate brightness and color
- Defining zones, boundaries, links, and/or separation among spaces
- Using lighting techniques to expand or contract the perceived size of a room, indicate activity levels, and influence overall impressions

Create visual interest within the space by:

- Revealing objects, materials, and surfaces selectively and appropriately

- Using variations in *distribution* to emphasize important room elements/areas and deemphasize unimportant ones
- Applying decorative lighting techniques and decorative fixtures to create additional visual variety

■ *distribution*
The way light is spread over an area or throughout a space.

Conserve energy, environmental resources, and the client's money by:

- Integrating *daylighting* into the lighting design where appropriate
- Choosing energy efficient light sources and optically efficient fixtures
- Selecting fixtures and lamps that offer the best value by weighing cost, quality, and performance
- Including controls as part of the lighting design for an added layer of energy savings

■ *daylighting*
The use of daylight as a significant source of light in a building.

Comply with building codes and energy usage regulations by:

- Understanding the applicable building code(s) and designing within their boundaries
- Collaborating with the design team to select the best energy conservation strategy to meet or exceed the limitations of the applicable energy code
- Choosing and locating fixtures to comply with the Americans With Disabilities Act (ADA) and other relevant codes

A designer's contract with an architect, interior designer, or owner may have additional project-specific requirements, such as achieving target brightness levels for special applications. Likewise, a designer may limit the scope of work by excluding certain spaces (often spaces with low design requirements, such as stock rooms, loading docks, and electrical and mechanical rooms) or limiting attendance at meetings.

There are several professional organizations that have their own, slightly different, definitions for the role and responsibility of the professional lighting designer. For example, the International Association of Lighting Designers (IALD) cites the following tasks:

- Meet the illumination needs of the people who use the space
- Select cost-effective and energy-efficient products most appropriate for the project
- Create an innovative lighting solution that achieves the perfect balance of function and aesthetics
- Solve the unique lighting challenges of a wide range of interior and exterior environments
- Strengthen and enhance any space through creative, yet functional, lighting plans

Clearly, a lighting designer does so much more than just "light" spaces. The lighting designer is an equal member of the design team who uses his or her specialized knowledge to provide a design in light that meets the project's requirements while supporting and enhancing the work of the other design professionals.

Professional Lighting Design Credentials

Unlike architecture and engineering, lighting design is not a licensed profession. This is both good and bad. On one hand, it allows designers with a broad range of backgrounds, education, and experiences to enter the profession. On the other hand, it means that anyone can call themselves a lighting designer, regardless of their experience or education. In the past, most lighting designers began their career with an education and work history in one of three other professions—architecture, electrical engineering, or theatre lighting design. A fourth, and the newest, path is to enter the profession after completing an MA or MFA in architectural lighting design.

How do you establish yourself as a talented and knowledgeable lighting designer to potential employers or clients? The first way is by showing your work. Nothing says more about your skills and talents than the designs you've already created. Another way of demonstrating that you are serious about your profession is by holding one or more professional credentials. One form of a professional credential is membership in a lighting-related organization or society. For example, the IALD, mentioned earlier, is dedicated to the concerns of independent, professional lighting designers. The Illuminating Engineering Society (IES) is an organization with membership drawn from the entire range of professionals involved in lighting that includes designers, electrical engineers, lamp and fixture engineers, educators, and researchers.

Another type of professional credential is earned by passing a test of lighting knowledge. The National Council on Qualifications for the Lighting Professions (NCQLP) administers the most important of these, the Lighting Certified (LC) exam. Through a peer-review process, the NCQLP established the education, experience, and examination requirements for baseline certification for anyone involved in the field of lighting, including lighting designers, electrical engineers, architects, sales representatives, and lamp or fixture engineers. The exam, which tests for minimum knowledge and application of that knowledge, is regularly reviewed and updated. The exam content as of 2013 was in these areas:

- Survey/audit of existing buildings and lighting installations
- Design phase
- Financial and energy analysis
- Bid and negotiation phase
- Construction phase
- Operations and maintenance of lighting systems

LC professionals are required to recertify every three years to insure their knowledge of lighting applications and technology is current. Part of what makes the LC credential significant is that the U.S. Government's General Service Administration, the government's landlord, requires that the lighting design for all federal buildings be performed or supervised by a designer who holds the LC credential.

More recently, in 2010, the IALD established a task force to determine the scope of practice and eligibility requirements for a lighting design credential that is more stringent and represents a higher level of knowledge than the LC credential. In 2012 the task force announced the results of a worldwide survey that established seven "domains of practice" for architectural lighting designers:

Goals and outcomes—the design of lighting solutions that satisfy the project requirements and the design intent so the solution performs as predicted

Collaboration—the interaction with other disciplines by serving as an integral member of the team so that lighting relates to its context and adds value to the project

Ingenuity—the contribution of ideas that demonstrate innovation, creativity, originality, imagination, or resourcefulness to foster the goals of the project

Synthesis—the integration of the technical and aesthetic elements of lighting with space and form to shape and enhance the overall experience

Science—the demonstration of how light interacts with people, materials, and building systems by applying the principles of light to meet the relevant technical criteria

Stewardship—the response to known and potential social and environmental impact by designing solutions that avoid or minimize harm, discomfort, and waste

Human experience—the design of lighting solutions that positively affect people

The IALD has decided on a portfolio review format for their credential, but (as of mid-2014) has not announced a timeline for implementation. Readers should consult the IALD Web site, listed at the end of this chapter, for additional and current information.

Finally, the body of knowledge that lighting designers are expected to possess is constantly increasing and changing. As a result, continuing education is an important part of the lighting profession. Keeping up with lamp technologies and changes to building codes is the biggest issue, but sustainability, lighting applications and techniques, vision and psychology, controls, daylighting, and light's affect on human health are all areas that require continuing education as well.

Online Resources

Illuminating Engineering Society, www.ies.org

International Association of Lighting Designers, www.iald.org

IALD Credentialing Task Force Mini-Site, www.iald.org/about/IALDCertificationNews.asp

National Council on Qualifications for the Lighting Professions, www.ncqlp.org

Designing with Light Resources

Wiley's companion site to *Designing with Light*, www.wiley.com/go/designingwithlight

Author's companion site to *Designing with Light*, www.designinglight.com

References

"About Lighting Design," International Association of Lighting Designers, accessed December 1, 2012, www.iald.org/design/index.asp.

"Candidate Handbook NCQLP Lighting Certification 2013," National Council on Qualifications for the Lighting Professions, Austin, 2013.

DiLaura, David et al., *The Lighting Handbook, Tenth Edition,* New York: Illuminating Engineering Society, 2011.

"IALD Credentialing Task Force Update," International Association of Lighting Designers, accessed December 1, 2012, www.iald.org/about/IALDCertificationOrgUpdate.asp.

"IALD Credentialing Task Force Update: Webinar on IALD's Action to Date to Develop an International Certification for Architectural Lighting Designers," by David Becker and Judy Hale Ph.D., June 30, 2013.

"NCQLP Scope of Practice and Services," National Council on Qualifications for the Lighting Professions, accessed December 1, 2012, www.ncqlp.org/about.

CHAPTER 2

Designing with Light

"Design must be functional and functionality must be translated into visual aesthetics, without any reliance on gimmicks that have to be explained."

Ferdinand A. Porsche

What Is Lighting Design?

What is a lighting design? How do we conceive of, develop, and execute a design? What kind of framework underpins our design ideas? What criteria do we need to consider, and are those criteria the same for all designs, or do they change with different applications? These are the questions that get us talking about lighting design.

Let's begin with a few introductory thoughts on design. First, design is as much a *process* of intellect and intuition as it is the *product* delivered at the end of that process. Second, design is exploratory and iterative. Some iterations lead to dead ends or undesirable outcomes. Others lead to refining the design and moving toward a beautiful solution to a problem.

Next, there is not a one-size-fits-all lighting design process. Some designs require careful attention to technical aspects of the lighting system, some designs have very strict illumination or energy consumption criteria, and other designs are exclusively about creating an evocative mood, atmosphere, or environment. Designers should understand a variety of design methods, and apply the most appropriate method or approach to each project.

Finally, the goal of every design is to create, in collaboration with the rest of the design team, an environment that is appropriate to the use and the users, and that meets the owners' requirements of cost, project timeline, efficiency, etc.

To achieve a design's goals, architectural lighting designers must have a thorough understanding of both the art of design and the technology used to create and control light. Some aspects of the design process can be organized into checklists, making them fairly easy to address. Other aspects require the lighting designer to understand architecture, interior design, and/or electrical engineering to integrate the lighting with the work of the rest of the team. The biggest challenge a designer faces is to connect a variety of elements into a comprehensive whole: to see beyond what is to what can be or to connect abstract ideas to real world conditions and, in the process, add layers of intention or meaning to a design. In doing so, we transition from being illumination engineers, to lighting designers, to artists working with light.

There are many paths that a design might take. Each new project begins with exploring and understanding the requirements and expectations for that project, and then adopting an appropriate approach or strategy to develop and execute the design.

Beginning the Design

The first step in any design process is to gather relevant information so we can understand the requirements of the design. General questions will lead to more specific questions until we have a thorough knowledge of those aspects of the design that are required, those that are expected, and those that are desirable but optional. The following sets of questions are typical.

Questions for the owner and/or users:

- "What are your general expectations for the lighting design?" If there are general expectations, and there may not be, this is a good open-ended question to start the conversation.
- "What overall mood/image/feeling(s) do you want the space(s) to have?"
- "What are the activities that occur in each of the spaces?" This information is necessary to begin to establish illuminance (brightness) requirements for each space. This is covered in detail in Chapter 13.
- "Are you asking the design team to achieve any sustainability goals, such as a Leadership in Energy and Environmental Design (LEED) certification?" LEED and other sustainability programs are optional, and have more stringent requirements than building codes. Sustainability is covered in Chapter 15.
- "Do you have any existing facilities that we can tour? What aspects of the lighting do you like or want to retain? What aspects do you dislike, and why?"
- "What is the budget for the project?"
- "What is the timeline for the project?"

Questions for the architect and/or interior designer:

- "What are the applicable building, electrical, and energy conservation codes?" Codes set requirements and restrictions for our designs, and compliance is not optional. Codes are covered in detail in Chapter 14.
- "What is the site like? Do we have the flexibility to adjust the orientation of the building to take advantage of daylight?" In urban areas especially, there may be little or no flexibility.
- "What is the color palette? What is the materials palette?" These will influence the choice of warmth/coolness of the light and the methods used to illuminate some surfaces.

- "Which spaces are dedicated to an activity? Which spaces are flexible?" This will inform us about the need for flexibility in the lighting system.
- "What are your goals or desires for the overall mood/image/feeling of the space(s)?"

   Questions for the electrical engineer:

- "Are there power limitations that are more stringent than the energy conservation code?" This question is especially relevant for renovations.
- "What voltage do you plan on providing for the lighting system?" Higher voltage is more efficient. 277V is a common voltage for the lighting system in larger, nonresidential buildings.

   It is helpful to summarize the answers to these questions and keep them in one location for future reference. A project summary form is available for download at this book's Web site.

   With answers in hand we can begin to think about how to achieve the requirements and goals for illumination levels, aesthetic values, energy consumption, appropriate lamp and fixture types, control systems, and more. As we develop the design, additional, more specific, questions will present themselves. Questions, answers, ideas, and solutions (even dead-end solutions or those that later are found to be inappropriate) are all a natural part of the design process.

   Let's begin looking at lighting design by examining some ways of thinking about light itself, then move on to thinking about lighting fixtures, architecture, and space. We'll see that many of these ideas overlap and intermingle in a completed design.

Thinking about Light

Design Elements of Light

A lighting designer selects lighting fixtures and lamps, and determines luminaire placement and quantity in order to control the light in each space to achieve the desired results. One framework we can use to consider our own work, or study the work of another, is to evaluate the controllable elements of light. Of course, we can't control what we don't know or understand, so the first question is, "What are the controllable aspects of light?"

   Such a list might include brightness, color, direction, the technology used to produce the light, beam spread, illumination angle, beam edge softness/hardness, location and depth of shadows, and many others. To make this list manageable, we can reduce it to four design elements of light: intensity, color, distribution, and movement.

   Intensity, or brightness of light in a space, is the most obvious controllable element. The desired intensity is determined by the designer, achieved by fixture quantity and fixture brightness, verified through calculations, and possibly adjusted on-site using a control system if one is part of the project.

■ *intensity*
The amount of light from a source or on a surface.

The brightness of a space affects our expectations about activity levels and overall experience. High illumination levels usually signal high levels of activity, public spaces, and lower product costs (such as in open office plans, fast food, and discount retailers). Lower illumination levels are subjectively associated with reduced levels of activity, higher levels of service, exclusivity, and higher product costs (such as in private offices, expensive restaurants, and exclusive stores).

As we've all experienced, brightness can also draw our interest and focus our attention. Theatre lighting designers use a followspot to draw our attention to the main character on the stage and hold it there. Brightness draws our attention in an architectural setting, too. For example, research has demonstrated that when given a choice of turning left or right at a "T" intersection, the brighter path is chosen 70 percent of the time or more. While light cannot replace signage, barriers, or architecture in controlling movement, we can use light levels to influence movement and the path that people take through a space.

Color is another important element of light. Color considerations include the warmth or coolness of the light, how well it allows us to perceive the colors of objects, and whether to use white light or colored light to achieve a project's goals. Color is discussed in detail in Chapter 8.

Distribution refers to the way that light is used to fill a space. Is the light even from wall to wall, or are there areas of either higher or lower illumination, and, if so, why? Distribution is examined in Chapter 6.

Movement is probably the least obvious element of light and refers to a change of any of the other three elements over time. At a music concert the movement of the followspots and moving lights is obvious. In an architectural environment, movement is experienced in more subtle ways: changes in intensity, color, and distribution caused by changes in the daylight entering through windows; changes in intensity and distribution as a control system makes automatic adjustments; changes in intensity, color, and distribution as one walks from one part of a room or building to another. A thoughtful lighting design has considered all of these and minimizes or prevents unpleasant or inappropriate movement.

Richard Kelly's Three Forms of Lightplay

Of course, there are many other ways of considering the use of light as a design medium. The best known is a method developed and practiced by Richard Kelly.

Richard Kelly (Figure 2.1) was one of the great pioneers in the profession of architectural lighting and is often referred to as the "father" of architectural lighting design. He opened his professional practice in New York City in 1935, and over the next four decades worked on over 300 projects with most of the major architects of the mid-twentieth century, including Philip Johnson, Ludwig Mies van der Rohe, Louis I Kahn, I. M. Pei, and Eero Saarinen.

His study of architecture and theatrical lighting design, along with his professional experience, led Kelly to identify three forms of lightplay that became the basis of his

■ *color*
The property possessed by an object of producing different sensations on the eye as a result of the way the object reflects or emits light.

■ *distribution*
The way light is spread over an area or throughout a space.

■ *movement*
A change in the intensity, color and/or distribution of light over time.

design approach: focal glow, ambient luminescence, and play of brilliants (Figures 2.2, 2.3, and 2.4). Over the years these distribution patterns and their descriptions have permeated the architectural lighting design profession. Today, they are universally understood and employed by many lighting designers. Here are Kelly's own words describing his ideas:

> *"Focal glow is the campfire of all time, the glowing embers around which stories are told, or the football rally bonfire. It is the light burning at the window or the welcoming gleam of the open door. Focal glow is the limelight of aphorism, and the followspot on the modern stage or the aircraft beacon. It is Klieglight on a theatre façade or flashlight on a stair. Focal glow is the sunburst through the clouds and the shaft of sunshine that warms the far end of the valley. It is the movie screen in the theatre, the pool of light at your favorite reading chair, your airplane seat light. Focal glow is the end of the rainbow. The attraction of focal glow commands attention and creates interest. It fixes the gaze, concentrates the mind and tells people what to look at. It sells merchandise. Focal glow separates the important from the unimportant. It establishes precedence, can induce movement, and direct and control traffic. Focal glow can help people see.*
>
> *"Ambient Luminescence is a snowy morning in the open country. It is twilight haze on a mountaintop, or a cloudy day on the ocean. It is underwater in the sunshine, or in a white tent at high noon. Ambient*

Figure 2.1 Richard Kelly (1910–1977). *Courtesy of Estate of Richard Kelly.*

(a)

(b)

Figure 2.2 Focal Glow.
2.2a Courtesy of Ed McCarthy, 2.2b Courtesy of Studio T+L, LLC.

(a)   (b)

Figure 2.3 Ambient Luminescence.
2.3a Courtesy of Paul Bartlett, 2.3b Courtesy of R2Architects.

luminescence is the full cyclorama of the open theatre and a brilliantly lighted room without visible lights. It is vaporous light and all we can sense of indirect lighting. Ambient luminescence minimizes the importance of all things and all people. It fills people with a sense of freedom of space and can suggest infinity. It is usually reassuring and restful. The background of ambient luminescence is created at night by fixtures that throw light to walls, curtains, screens, ceilings, and over floors for indirect reflection from these surfaces. A background of ambient luminescence is created by using light colored walls, curtains and ceilings as part of the lighting fixtures. Even light carpet has reflecting surfaces to light.

"The Play of Brilliants is the aurora borealis. It is a cache of diamonds in an open cave or the Versailles hall of mirrors with its thousands of candle

(a)   (b)

Figure 2.4 Play of Brilliants.
2.4a Courtesy of Paul Bartlett, 2.4b Courtesy of Ed McCarthy.

flames—a ballroom of crystal chandeliers. Play of brilliants is Times Square at night. It is night automobiles at a busy clover-leaf or a city at night from the air. It is sunlight on a tumbling brook, sparking fountains against a hedgerow or a water fight at high noon. Play of brilliants is the heaven full of stars. It is summer lightning or a swarm of lightning bugs—the phosphorus waters in the churning wake of a motor boat. It is birch trees interlaced by a car's headlights. Play of brilliants is the magic of the Christmas tree, Fourth of July skyrockets, and torchlight parades. It is the fantasy excitement of carnival lights, and restrained gaiety of Japanese lanterns at a fete. These brilliants are the jewels worn by your home. Play of brilliants excites the optic nerve, in turn stimulates the body and spirit and charms the senses. It creates a feeling of aliveness, alerts the mind and awakens curiosity, and sharpens the wit. Play of brilliants quickens the appetite and heightens all sensation. It can be distracting or it can be entertaining."[1]

Ambient, Task, and Accent Light

A variation on Richard Kelly's approach emphasizes ambient or general lighting, task lighting, and accent lighting. *Ambient lighting* blankets a space and provides the base or minimum level of illumination. Ambient light may be an important factor in establishing an impression or creating a mood.

■ *ambient lighting*
The general light in a space.

Task lighting provides additional light in areas where the visual tasks require it. For example, the desktop of an office cubical would require a high level of illumination for task lighting, while the circulation area around the cubical would require a lower level of ambient illumination. We'll cover the specifics of illumination levels in Chapter 13.

■ *task lighting*
Illumination provided to a specific area, such as a desktop, for the tasks performed there.

Accent light provides visual interest in a space by highlighting architecture or calling attention to important items, such as featured merchandise in a store, or decorative items, such as artwork. Accent light can also provide information or guide people through a space.

■ *accent light*
A directional light used to emphasize an object or draw attention.

Light, Shadow, Variety, and Contrast

Our concern with the performance of visual tasks, such as reading, causes us to focus our attention on the amount of light we provide. It can often seem as if more is better, and shadows and darkness should be eliminated. However, studies have shown that the lighting arrangement judged the least pleasant is one that consists exclusively of evenly distributed light from overhead. We seek out visual variety, and the lighting design that provides none creates a lackluster environment.

There are many ways the lighting designer can add variety to make a space more engaging. We can add contrast by allowing areas such as circulation paths to be brighter or dimmer than

[1] Statement to Mrs. Edward Emerson, editor of *The Bulletin* after a talk at Garden Club of America Forum in New York City — November 15, 1962.

their surroundings. Grazing walls with light to reveal texture creates highlights and shadows that can be very interesting, and may provide a localized increase in brightness. Decorative fixtures can add new materials, shapes, and colors to a space (and should be coordinated with the architect and/or interior designer). These techniques, and others, add variety and contrast to a space, making it more interesting and appealing than it would be without them.

Thinking about Luminaires

Light fixtures, or luminaires, are visible to the occupants of a space and therefore become a part of the interior design. Another way of approaching a lighting design is by considering the visual impact of luminaires as an element of the interior design. A luminaire's size, shape, and material should be in harmony with the architecture and interior design. If we treat luminaires as graphic design elements, we can think of them as points, lines, and planes.

Point Source

A point source is a small, concentrated source of light (Figure 2.5). Examples of point sources are the sun (on a clear day) and track lights focused on a display. Because it is relatively small, a point source's reflection on a reflective surface is also small. This enhances sparkle in materials such as jewelry, glass, and metallic thread. Point sources also cast shadows with crisp edges.

Figure 2.5 Point Light Sources.
Courtesy of Ella Bromblin.

Figure 2.6 Linear Light Sources.
Courtesy of R2Architects.

Line Source

Line, or linear, sources can be a single source or a series of multiple sources that are tightly spaced (Figure 2.6). Linear sources are considerably greater in length than in cross section. Examples include linear fluorescent lamps, a row of incandescent lamps or light emitting diodes (LEDs), a cove, or an architectural detail creating a slot of light.

Plane Source

A plane source is a vertical or horizontal source of diffuse light (Figure 2.7). A plane source is usually large relative to the objects being illuminated. This reduces, softens, or even eliminates shadows. Examples include a cloudy sky, a backlit ceiling of translucent material, and indirect light reflected from a matte surface with high reflectance.

Thinking about Architecture

The spaces we light are, of course, bound by the walls, floor, and ceiling. Those surfaces, and others such as columns and steps, may be illuminated or they may be luminous (glowing) as part of the lighting and interior designs. For example, the verticality of columns can be emphasized by accent lighting them from above or below. Some common techniques for illuminating architecture are shown in Figure 2.8. We'll discuss drawing some of the details in Chapter 11.

Figure 2.7 Planar Light Sources.
Courtesy of R2Architects.

Ceilings can be illuminated from coves (Figure 2.8a), or they can be made of translucent materials and become luminous (Figure 2.8b).

Walls can be grazed with light (Figure 2.8c), washed with light (Figure 2.8d), or partially illuminated with soffits (Figure 2.8d). Niches or recesses in walls can be illuminated.

Thinking about Everything—Layers of Light

■ *layering*
Using multiple overlapping lighting techniques.

The most interesting and successful designs usually make use of more than one lighting technique. This is called "*layering*" light (Figure 2.9). The techniques discussed thus far are often freely mixed in the creation of a design. For example, the theatre shown in Figure 2.9a has been provided with light so that the audience can read their programs, but has several additional layers of light drawing attention to the architecture and the proscenium. The layers of light in the photo are:

- Downlight throughout the seating area
- Decorative wall sconces
- Accent uplighting on the decorative ceiling panels
- Accent lighting on the proscenium arch

(a)

(b)

(c)

(d)

Figure 2.8 Lighting Architecture.
2.8a–c Courtesy of R2Architects.

- Colored light illuminating the curtain
- Accent light on the decorative panel over the proscenium arch

    Layering is used in a different way to create the ambience shown in Figure 2.9b.

Communicating Design Ideas

It can be challenging to convey design ideas to our colleagues and clients without using technical language. We have to, though, for two reasons. First, most of our colleagues and clients don't understand the technical language of the lighting profession. Second,

(a)

(b)

Figure 2.9 Layering Light.
2.9a Courtesy of Studio T+L, LLC, 2.9b Courtesy of Mayo Foundation for Medical Education, and Schuler Shook.

architecture is a visually oriented field. People want to hear how the lighting will look or feel but, more importantly, they often want to see it.

Language

The first skill that every lighting designer needs is the ability to describe light in clear, nontechnical terms. Light is ephemeral. It is difficult to envision. Many people simply are not aware of lighting unless it is wonderful or terrible. In order to convey design intentions to colleagues and clients, we need a rich vocabulary that can paint pictures in the minds of the people we're talking to. Don't be afraid to use grand language to describe light.

Here's an example from Shakespeare's *Romeo and Juliet*. Rather than say, "It's morning, and I have to collect some herbs before it gets too late," Friar Lawrence paints a picture for the audience:

> The grey-ey'd morn smiles on the frowning night,
> Chequering the eastern clouds with streaks of light;
> And flecked darkness like a drunkard reels
> From forth day's path and Titan's fiery wheels:
> Now, ere the sun advance his burning eye
> The day to cheer, and night's dank dew to dry,
> I must up-fill this osier cage of ours
> With baleful weeds, and precious-juiced flowers.

Another beautiful, though more visceral, description of light in the world is in A.R. Ammons' *The City Limits*:

> When you consider the radiance, that it does not withhold
> itself but pours its abundance without selection into every
> nook and cranny not overhung or hidden; when you consider
> that birds' bones make no awful noise against the light but
> lie low in the light as in a high testimony; when you consider
> the radiance, that it will look into the guiltiest
> swervings of the weaving heart and bear itself upon them,
> not flinching into disguise or darkening; when you consider
> the abundance of such resource as illuminates the glow-blue
> bodies and gold-skeined wings of flies swarming the dumped
> guts of a natural slaughter or the coil of shit and in no
> way winces from its storms of generosity; when you consider
> that air or vacuum, snow or shale, squid or wolf, rose or lichen,
> each is accepted into as much light as it will take, then
> the heart moves roomier, the man stands and looks about, the
> leaf does not increase itself above the grass, and the dark
> work of the deepest cells is of a tune with May bushes
> and fear lit by the breadth of such calmly turns to praise.

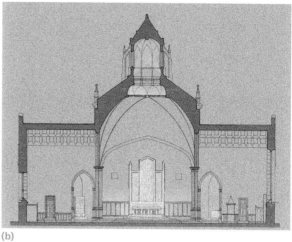

(a)   (b)

Figure 2.10 Hand Drawn Light Sketches: Note That the Different Colors in These Studies Were Used to Indicate Different Lighting Techniques.
Courtesy of Studio T+L, LLC.

So, reread Richard Kelly's descriptions of focal glow, ambient luminescence, and play of brilliants, read poetry and prose, and always be on the lookout for ways to describe light to someone so that they'll see it in their mind as clearly as you do in yours.

Sketches

Sketching is another critical skill for any designer (Figure 2.10). It allows us to explore a design quickly and inexpensively, and is often an early step in developing design ideas. Sketching is the fastest way to literally see for ourselves the light and color we're considering for an architectural space. We can experiment with a wide range of lighting ideas and color combinations in a short time and, based on the results, determine which ideas deserve additional exploration and refinement.

Computer Generated or Modified Images

Computer generated images, either modifications to existing photos in software such as Photoshop (Figure 2.11a and 2.11b) or models generated from programs such as AutoCAD or SketchUp (Figure 2.12), are a great way to refine the placement, brightness, and color of light, and can give clients a clear picture of the proposed design.

Mock-Ups

Often, the best way to evaluate a light fixture, lighting technique, or color is to create a mock-up. Mock-ups can range from simple assemblies of foam core and masking tape to test soffit or cove dimensions, to full-scale rooms built to evaluate a design before widespread implementation. Every designer's office should have an ample supply of lamps,

(a)

(b)

Figure 2.11 Original (a) Photo of a Park Scene and (b) the Same Photo After Editing to Show the Proposed Lighting Design.
2.11a Courtesy of Caroline Culler, 2.11b Courtesy of Studio T+L, LLC.

Figure 2.12 Computer Generated Image of Proposed Interior.
Courtesy of R2Architects.

sockets, fixtures, and model making materials so that ideas can be explored and tested. When specific fixtures are required, lighting designers can contact their sales representatives, who are generally able to provide sample fixtures for testing and evaluation. The role of the sales representative is discussed in Chapter 9.

Approaches to the Lighting Design Process

Starting a design is like facing a blank page or a white canvas. The author or artist knows what she wants to accomplish, but may be unclear on how to begin or how to move from start to finish. Frequently we begin with a design concept, although a concept is not always what a project calls for. The word "concept" refers to an abstract idea that is used as a guide in the design process. Developing and working toward the implementation of an abstract concept is not necessary or appropriate for every project. Sometimes a simpler, more direct approach is better. The designer can take one of three initial approaches to a lighting design: pragmatic, aesthetic, or conceptual.

Pragmatic Designs

Pragmatic designs focus on identifying and solving the lighting requirements and challenges for the project. As each item on the list is solved, it is checked against the others to ensure that the design holds together as a single approach, rather than looking like a mismatched set of solutions. To ensure visual continuity between spaces while solving the design issues, designers often limit the number of luminaire types and patterns for similar spaces and applications.

For example, in a pragmatic approach to lighting a library, the designer might identify the following requirements:

- Light the vertical spines of books on the shelves
- Light the horizontal reading tables and checkout desks
- Provide ambient light in the lobby and reading areas
- Highlight displays, bulletin boards, and artwork
- Limit energy consumption to that allowed by the applicable energy code
- Include occupancy sensors and other controls as required by the applicable energy code

Pragmatic Design Criteria

There are several basic goals that almost every lighting design must achieve in order to provide lighting that is appropriate to the use and users:

- Task illumination—Provide a light level appropriate to the tasks being performed and the age of the users of the space. Illuminance levels are discussed in Chapter 13.
- Ambient illumination—In addition to task lighting, the designer should provide ambient light throughout the space. This brightens the overall space, creates a more pleasant environment, fills in shadows, and reduces task/ambient contrast, which may otherwise cause eye strain.
- Visual comfort—Minimize direct glare by selecting well-shielded luminaires and by limiting the brightness of decorative fixtures such as wall sconces.
- Pleasantness—Select color, brightness, and distribution that are in harmony with the interior design and the use of the space. Create variety and interest by accenting artwork or interesting architectural features.
- Code compliance—Limit energy consumption and employ lighting controls as required by the applicable energy code. Install sconces and pendants at or above minimum heights as specified by ADA or building codes. Specify only luminaires and installations that meet the requirements of applicable electrical and building codes.

CASE STUDY   Pragmatic Lighting Design for a Multimedia Conference Room

Project: A 40-person, multimedia conference room with additional uses
Architect: Lee H. Skolnick Architecture + Design Partnership
Lighting Design: Studio T+L, LLC

Lighting Requirements:

- The primary lighting requirement is to provide quality lighting for video cameras that is also acceptable to the room occupants.
- The secondary requirement is to illuminate the map sculpture at the center of the room.
- Tertiary lighting goals are flexibility to accommodate multiple alternate uses, clean and unobtrusive aesthetics, and energy efficiency.

continues

Project Limitations and Challenges:

- The lighting designer is brought to this project late in the process, and the space is already designed. This includes the floor plan (Figure 2.13), the ceiling plan (Figure 2.14), sections (Figure 2.15), and the materials and finishes.
- Power available for lighting is limited.

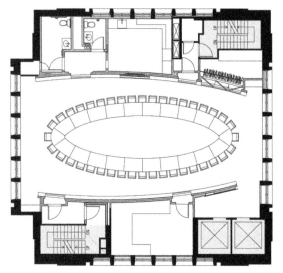

Figure 2.13 Ground Plan: Crosshatched Areas Were Not Included in the Project.
Courtesy of Big Show Construction Management.

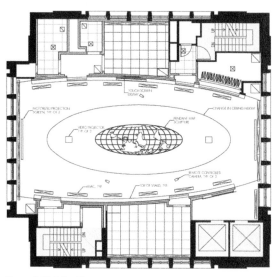

Figure 2.14 Ceiling Plan.
Courtesy of Big Show Construction Management.

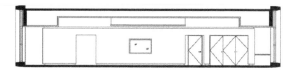

Figure 2.15 Section.
Courtesy of Big Show Construction Management.

- The curved walls are not vertical. The tops are closer to the center of the rooms than the bottom, so that the walls tip downward.
- All luminaires must be recessed. TV studio, portable, and temporary luminaires are not to be used in this room.

Collecting Relevant Information

1. Meet with the architect and client to review the activities planned for the room, the requirements of the lighting system, the project calendar, and the project budget.
2. Meet with the audiovisual (AV) designer to obtain camera specifications. For a quality image the camera requires that people and objects in the room are illuminated to a minimum of 15 foot-candles (fc).
3. Meet with the electrical engineer. We determine that this small renovation does not have to meet the current energy code, but that a limited amount of power is available on this floor. The lighting system must consume no more than 8,000W. Occupancy sensors are required in the bathrooms and in the storage room.

Developing and Implementing the Design

1. To balance foreground and background brightnesses for the camera, all luminaires in the main room must be dimmable.

continues

2. To create ambient light around the table the lighting designer wants to install a fluorescent cove. The architect has drawn a "top hat" ceiling without a cove to hold and hide the luminaires. The architect agrees to add a cove and asks for dimensions.

3. The lighting designer selects a fluorescent cove luminaire with a dimmable ballast and forward throw optics to illuminate the ceiling. This will also bounce light off of the ceiling to backlight the glass map sculpture. After selecting the luminaire, a sketch of the cove with required dimensions is made and sent to the architect.

4. To illuminate the walls, recessed wall wash luminaires with a small aperture are desired. The designer selects a lensed MR16 luminaire. To limit the electrical load, the designer selects a 37W lamp with an infrared (IR) coating that provides slightly more light than a standard 50W lamp.

5. To provide direct light on the faces of attendees when the video cameras are in use, the designer adds recessed adjustable luminaires in the high ceiling. To simplify maintenance, these luminaires will use the same lamp as in the wall wash fixtures.

6. To provide illumination in doorways and alcoves so that they are visible to the camera, the designer selects a simple recessed linear fluorescent luminaire.

7. The room is modeled in lighting calculation software to confirm that the camera's illumination requirements will be met.

8. Minor adjustments are made based on the calculation results.

9. All fixtures are connected to a control system, accessible from two locations in the room and from the video control room. The system is preprogrammed with four settings for the primary uses of the room: (1) meetings; (2) video meetings; (3) panel discussions; (4) receptions.

10. Completed design documentation is delivered to the architect for inclusion in the project construction documents. See Figure 11.1 for an example.

11. The designer makes four site visits during construction. Two are to inspect the progress of the work. Two are to work with the architect, client, and AV designer to set light levels for the recorded scenes. See Figure 2.16 for the final lighting design.

Figure 2.16 Final Lighting Design.
Courtesy of Raeford Dwyer.

Aesthetic Designs

Aesthetic designs focus on the mood, feeling, or environment that the lighting design is called upon to create or support, while also meeting the project's pragmatic requirements. An aesthetic approach usually uses a list of adjectives as guides. For example, a client may ask that the lighting in their restaurant be "warm," "comforting," and "romantic." The decisions made during the design process are in support of the desired aesthetic.

CASE STUDY | Aesthetic Relighting a Church Interior

Project: Relight an 8,500 SF Catholic church
Original Architect: Unknown
Lighting Design: Studio T+L, LLC

Lighting Requirements

- The primary goals are increased illumination in the pews and sanctuary, and installation of a new dimming and control system.
- The design must retain the "warm, intimate" feel of the church.
- The design must enhance the overall aesthetics and architecture.
- The design must shift the visual focus forward to the sanctuary.

Project Limitations

- There is no additional power available for lighting. Any lighting load that is added must be balanced by a reduction elsewhere.
- Interior finishes are not part of the project. The lighting must work with the existing colors and finishes.

See Figures 2.17, 2.18, and 2.19, respectively, for the ground plan, the ceiling plan, and the section. The sanctuary and nave of the existing building before renovation are shown in Figures 2.20 and 2.21.

Collecting Relevant Information

1. Meet with representatives of the church to discuss the activities that occur, the problems with the current lighting and dimming systems, requirements of the new lighting and dimming systems, the project calendar, and the project budget.

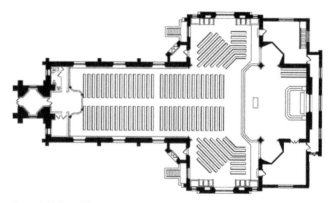

Figure 2.17 Ground Plan.
Courtesy of Matthews Moya Architects.

 continues

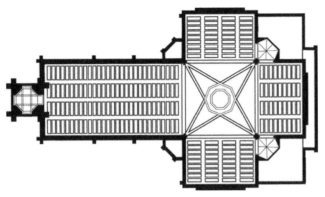

Figure 2.18 Ceiling Plan.
Courtesy of Matthews Moya Architects.

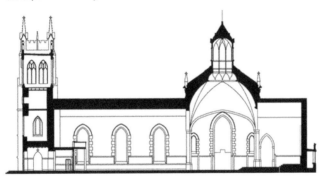

Figure 2.19 Section.
Courtesy of Matthews Moya Architects.

2. Review existing drawings of the building and the lighting system.
3. Take light level readings throughout the pews (average 4 *fc* horizontal See Chapter 13) and sanctuary (average 10 fc vertical).
4. Photograph the existing conditions (Figures 2.20 and 2.21) and take notes on observations and initial design ideas.

■ *fc*
fc–abbreviation for
footcandle.

Developing and Implementing the Design

1. The church is on the campus of a university, so the congregation is almost exclusively young adults ages 18–25. It is determined that horizontal illuminance of 10 fc in the pews and vertical illuminance of 20 fc in the sanctuary are appropriate.
2. The existing pendant luminaires are beautiful, and the team would like to keep them. The designer inspects the luminaires and determines that new lamp arrays can increase the overall ambient light, increase the uplight on the painted ceiling, and increase the downlight in the pews.
3. The crown molding even with the base of the windows is large enough to hide new luminaires. The designer begins to sketch options for lighting the carved panels in the wainscot and grazing light up along the walls, as illustrated in Figure 2.10. Other ideas include fixtures to illuminate the stained glass windows from outside of the church, and paler glass panels in some of the pendants to allow more light to exit the fixtures.
4. The client prefers demonstrations over light sketches and asks that all presentations of lighting options be done through on-site tests. Multiple demonstrations mean that the design phase is going to take more time than estimated. Fortunately, the client doesn't have a deadline for the renovation; their desire is to have it done correctly.
5. A group of four pendants are relamped to evaluate the new lamp arrays. The new lamps deliver more light and consume less power. The client likes the results and the new lamp arrays are approved.

(continues)

Figure 2.20 View toward Sanctuary before Lighting Renovation.
Courtesy of Studio T+L, LLC/Paul Bartlett.

Figure 2.21 View of Nave before Lighting Renovation.
Courtesy of Studio T+L, LLC/Paul Bartlett.

continues

6. At a second day of demonstrations the client approves uplighting the walls from within the crown molding. They are undecided about illuminating the carved wainscot panels. Lighting the stained glass windows from outside is evaluated and rejected by the team. Samples of colored glass to replace some glass in the pendants are evaluated and rejected.

7. At a third demonstration the team looks at alternate luminaires to illuminate the wainscot panels, and the client decides against the idea. The team evaluates LED luminaires to illuminate the sanctuary. Since the mounting location is 45' high, LEDs, with their long service life, would be a great improvement over the existing incandescent fixtures, saving on both electricity and maintenance. However, 60' is a very long throw distance for an LED luminaire. Three different luminaires are tested. After observing and measuring the illumination delivered, the team agrees that one of the luminaires is bright enough. The LED luminaires to illuminate the sanctuary are selected and approved.

8. At a fourth demonstration the team evaluates luminaires to highlight statuary in the transepts. By focusing a luminaire across the transept and evaluating the result, the client approves the idea and the luminaires.

9. With most of the design elements approved, the discussion turns to the requirements for the control system. How many control locations? Two. How many saved settings? Many. Are there any settings that should occur automatically? Yes, on at 6 a.m. and off at midnight. A meeting is held with various users (choir, student groups, music groups, clergy) to discuss their specific lighting requirements and settings.

10. The lighting plan and details are drawn, and computer calculations are performed. Light levels at full intensity greatly exceed the target illuminances. This assures the designer that luminaires can be dimmed to balance the brightness throughout the church while still providing the required light levels.

11. The control system power and data risers and control interface devices are drawn. All documents are reviewed with the client. After approval, the completed design documents are delivered to the university for contractor bidding.

12. The designer makes eight site visits to inspect the progress of the installation, focus the adjustable luminaires in the sanctuary and the transepts, and set light levels in the control system. See Figures 2.22 and 2.23 for the final lighting design. This design received the IES's Illumination Award of Merit.

Figure 2.22 View toward Sanctuary after Lighting Renovation.
Courtesy of Studio T+L, LLC/Paul Bartlett.

continues

Figure 2.23 View toward Nave after Lighting Renovation.
Courtesy of Studio T+L, LLC/Paul Bartlett.

Conceptual Designs

Conceptual designs use a simile or metaphor to create a visual or mental image that illustrates the design goal. The concept should be open and flexible enough to allow for changes as the design develops. The concept is not a prescription for the design, but rather a guide that is referred to frequently during the design process. For example: At night the building should glow like light leaving a lantern. This tells the designer that the facade of the building will receive little or no light, and that light will be visible through windows instead. The concept statement is loose enough to allow many solutions to the design challenge. In fact, it does not offer a solution. Instead, it guides by providing an image and an end goal. Aesthetic and pragmatic considerations are part of the conceptual approach.

CASE STUDY   Conceptual Lighting Design for a Historic Facade

Project: Create a new facade lighting design for an historic building in New York City (Figure 2.24).
Original Architect: D. H. Burnham & Co.
Lighting Design: Studio T+L, LLC

(continues)

Figure 2.24 Existing Building during Daytime.
Courtesy of Studio T+L, LLC.

Lighting Requirements

- The owner has asked for a contemporary lighting design that is still respectful of the historic building.
- The design must be as distinctive as the structure.
- Light levels on the facade must be high enough to overcome ambient light at night, especially at the lower floors.

Project Limitations

- New York City Landmarks Preservation Commission requires that fixtures added to the facade of historic buildings be of a simple design, small size, and neutral finish so as not to detract from architectural features of the building.
- There are limited mounting locations for lighting fixtures.

Developing the Concept

This project is a blank canvas. The first task is to determine what light could or should do for this unique, well-known building. A conventional "wedding cake" design would illuminate the horizontal layers of the building by placing lights on the ledges created by the moldings (Figure 2.25).

But, a conventional design isn't what the owner is looking for. So . . . what is this building, and how can light express that?

- It's a triangle.
- It's a wedge.
- It's a knife.
- Its shape, an arrowhead in plan view, points north.
- Arrows and arrowheads point at things, but they can also indicate movement.

continues

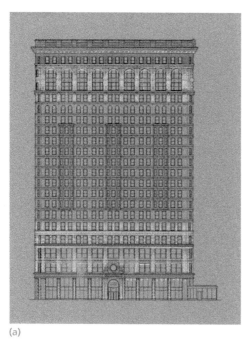

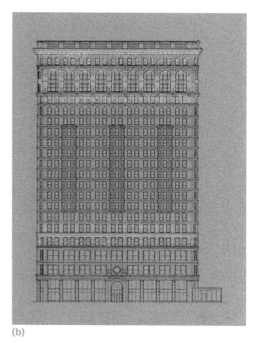

(a)   (b)

Figure 2.25 Sketches Exploring Typical Facade Lighting.
Courtesy of Studio T+L, LLC.

Movement . . . that's an interesting idea for a stationary object like a building. Conceptually, then, this is not a building, it's something else. . . . It's something that moves. . . . It's a <u>ship</u>! A ship sailing through the streets of Manhattan! That's the lighting concept: The building is a ship cruising through an urban sea. Use light to define and emphasize the prow, waterline, decks, and figurehead, and to imply forward motion.

- The narrow edge of the building is the prow. The top floors are the deck. The roof balustrade is the bridge. The statue on the roof is the figurehead. The bottom floors are the waterline. Each of these is illuminated separately.
- Use horizontal color gradients to imply movement (Figure 2.26). Use pale colors at the forward edge of the building, the prow, and deeper colors at the trailing end of the building, the stern.

This concept is presented to the owner's representative and approved.

Collecting Relevant Information

1. Collect and examine drawings of the existing building.
2. Determine which ledges are likely to be deep enough to hide and support luminaires. Confirm this with a site visit.
3. Calculate the heights and throw distances for various portions of the facade.
4. Begin researching LED exterior, multicolored wall grazing luminaires. Also begin researching projectors that will illuminate the prow from the street level "hut," which projects from the building. The longest throw distance is nearly 200'.
5. Begin to consider control system requirements: time of day events, different lighting programs for holidays, ability to control thousands of parameters, Internet connection to make changes remotely, backup of data, and others.

continues

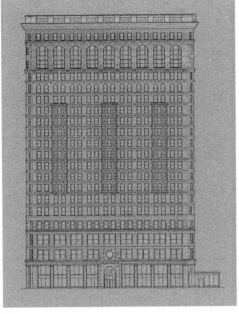
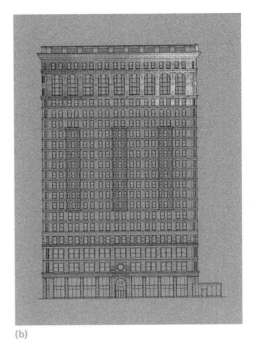

(a)   (b)

Figure 2.26 Color and Light Gradient Studies.
Courtesy of Studio T+L, LLC.

Developing and Implementing the Design

1. Visit manufacturer's showrooms and offices to evaluate luminaires and control systems that are under consideration for the project.
2. The IES recommended illuminance level is 20 fc vertical. Make hand and computer calculations to determine which luminaires under consideration can achieve that light level.
3. The designer meets with the owner's construction manager (CM) and electrical contractor (EC) to discuss the project's challenges. First, the ledges are sloped and 100 years of weathering have left them uneven. The team will need to develop a mounting bracket that levels the luminaires. Second, the design requires that data from the control system (probably located in the hut) be brought through the building to the luminaires. Is there an available path? If not, is there a wireless solution? Third, is there enough power on each floor, or do we need to bring new power from the basement to each floor? How much power is available? The lighting designer and CM will work on the design of a leveling bracket. The EC will investigate the power issues and data paths and report back.
4. The CM hires a model maker to develop a 3-D model of the building, and then create several renderings of the illuminated building at night. The owner's representative approves of the renderings.
5. The renderings are presented to the owner, who approves the lighting concept and requests a budget.
6. The designer draws preliminary lighting plans, and power and data risers so that the EC can budget his portion of the work.
7. The team meets to discuss installation methods and a schedule for focusing and setting light levels.
8. The CM and EC prepare a budget and submit it to the owner's representative. The budget is more than the owner is ready to spend. Rather than cut back on the design, the owner decides to put the project on hold.

Additional Considerations

Up to this point we've emphasized the design side of lighting—determining the qualities and layers of light for a space or project. Of course, there are other considerations that will affect design goals, lamp and fixture selection, and a variety of other decisions. One of those considerations is budget. Every project has a budget, of which a certain amount is allocated to lighting. A designer may find that the perfect luminaires for the project are too expensive and that less expensive luminaires must be considered in order to stay within the budget. Or, the design may have to forgo a custom designed and built luminaire in favor of one that already exists. There are mitigating factors that may allow a designer to exceed the initial budget. For example, LED fixtures generally cost more than incandescent or compact fluorescent fixtures but will require less maintenance and consume less electricity, so they are less expensive to operate. The savings in the building's operating cost may persuade the owner to increase the lighting budget.

Energy consumption is another major consideration. The federal government requires all states to have a commercial building energy code at least as stringent as ASHRAE/IES 90.1-2010. Once a project's lighting power allowance is calculated, the lighting designer has to balance the lamp wattage, fixture efficiency, and fixture spacing to remain within the allowance. Energy codes are covered in more detail in Chapter 14.

Yet another obstacle may be the manufacture and delivery schedule for the preferred lighting equipment. A manufacturer who offers fixtures with many variations may not fabricate fixtures until an order is received. If so, there may be a delay of six to eight weeks (or more) between placing an order and delivery. On most new construction projects this isn't a problem because it takes much longer than that to erect the building. However, some projects, especially renovations, can have shorter schedules that compel the designer to specify luminaires from manufacturers who can ship in just a few weeks, or even a few days. As discussed in Chapter 9, designers can request manufacture and shipping time frames from their sales representative.

Other issues include the available recessing depth in walls or ceilings, limitations on the capabilities of certain technologies, and accessibility for maintenance.

Online Resources

Advanced Lighting Guide—Design Considerations (subscription required), www.algonline.org

Advanced Lighting Guide—Application Directory (subscription required), www.algonline.org

Designing with Light Resources

Wiley's companion site to *Designing with Light,* www.wiley.com/go/designingwithlight

Author's companion site to *Designing with Light,* www.designinglight.com

References

DiLaura, David, et al., *The Lighting Handbook, Tenth Edition*, New York: Illuminating Engineering Society, 2011.

Egan, M. David, *Concepts in Architectural Lighting*, New York: McGraw-Hill, 1983.

Flynn, John E., et al., "Interim Study of Procedures for Investigating the Effect of Light on Impression and Behavior," *Journal of the IES*, October 1973, 87–94.

"Lighting's Role in Architecture," *Architectural Forum Magazine*, February 1955, 152–159.

Steffy, Gary, *Architectural Lighting Design, Third Edition*, Hoboken: John Wiley & Sons, 2008.

Taylor, Lyle H., and Eugene W. Socov, "The Movement of People Toward Lights," *Journal of the IES*, April 1974, 237–241.

CHAPTER 3

What Is Light?

"One may conceive light to spread successively, by spherical waves."

Christiaan Huygens

"Radiant light consists in Undulations of the Luminiferous Ether."

Thomas Young

"For the rest of my life I want to reflect on what light is."

Albert Einstein

"It is impossible to travel faster than light, and certainly not desirable, as one's hat keeps blowing off."

Woody Allen

As lighting designers, our first goal is to understand the medium we will be working with, both scientifically and artistically. What is light? The answer depends on whom you ask. The average person on the street, a scientist, an architect, a designer, and an artist will all give different answers. In their own way, each one of them is right.

Light Is Illumination

To the average person light is . . . light. It's what we need to see. It's what we get when we flip the switch. Most people don't pay much attention to light. We can have it literally at the touch of a button. We can adjust it as needed. We can easily have the light we want, from dim candlelight for a relaxing dinner to fluorescent light for brightly illuminated stores. Light is so readily available and so effortless to manipulate that we don't think much about the light surrounding us unless there is a problem with it or it is beautiful. We notice bad lighting when it's too dim to read, or when we can't identify the color of our car in a parking lot. We notice beautiful lighting during a sunset or at a stage show or in a beautiful room. Beyond that, though, the average person takes light and vision for granted.

As lighting designers, we must be more aware of light than the average person. A lighting designer notices the color, intensity, distribution, and movement of light at all times and asks, "Is this good lighting? Why or why not?" and "How would I do this better?"

Although most people don't notice light, all people are affected by it. The work of the lighting designer is subtle but, as we shall see, it is significant. That is why we study lighting design.

Let's start with some history. For centuries, philosophers and scientists sought to understand light, some just by thinking about it and some by conducting experiments. What is light? How does it travel through space? How does light enable sight? In some respects, as you'll see, we're still asking these questions.

Light Is Rays of Vision

Around 300 B.C. Euclid (Figure 3.1), the father of geometry, published a work on light, vision, and optics called *Optics and Catoptics*. In it he said that light traveled in straight lines, and he discussed reflection. He also believed that our eyes emitted rays that enabled vision (known as the emission theory of vision). Euclid was such a well-respected authority that his theory was still accepted 400 years later when Ptolemy (c. 85 A.D.–165 A.D.), wrote *A Work on Optics* that expanded on Euclid's original hypotheses.

Light Is Material

In 1020 A.D. the Arabic scientist Ibn Al-Haytham (Figure 3.2) wrote his *Book of Optics* that was to be highly influential for the next six centuries. In it, he rejected the emission theory of vision

Figure 3.1 Euclid (c. 325 B.C.–265 B.C.); Sculpture by Nino Pisano (Italian, active ca. 1343–1368). *Wikimedia Commons, PD-User: Jastrow, accessed on Sept. 13, 2013.*

Figure 3.2 Ibn Al-Haytham. *Wikimedia commons, PD-User: Wronkiew, accessed on Sept. 13, 2013.*

on the argument that if it were true, we should be able to see at night, and that looking at the sun wouldn't be difficult or painful. He separated light from vision and asserted that light was a material produced by luminous bodies such as fire and the sun. Light that bounced off of objects and entered the eye (the intromission theory) produced vision.

Al-Haytham appears to have had little interest in identifying the substance of light. He was instead interested in understanding the behavior of light and vision. He developed a series of experiments to understand such phenomenon as reflection, refraction, and vision.

Light Is Waves

In the late 1670's, Christiaan Huygens (Figure 3.3), a Dutch mathematician and physicist, began work on a theory of light as waves. This theory was finally published in 1690 in his *Treatise on Light*. Today, we still use waves as one way of describing light.

The *electromagnetic spectrum* is a wide range of energies, from radio waves at one end to gamma rays at the other end. The energy of the spectrum is conventionally described as waves (Figure 3.4). We define light as the portion of the electromagnetic spectrum that is perceived by our eyes.

The distance from crest to crest (or trough to trough) of a wave is called the *wavelength*. The wavelengths of radio waves can be kilometers long, while gamma rays are fractions of a billionth of a meter. Electromagnetic waves exist in a continuous range of frequencies and energies. *Light*, with wavelengths from 380 to 770 nm (nanometer or billionth of a meter), makes up less than 1 percent of the electromagnetic spectrum. The other portions of the spectrum, such as microwaves, radio waves, and gamma rays, enter our eyes but have no effect.

All wavelengths travel at the same speed, so more short waves pass any point each second than do long waves. More waves per second passing a point is described as a higher frequency. Fewer waves per second is a lower frequency. The amount of energy in a wave is proportional to its frequency. Shorter wavelengths have a higher frequency and also have more energy, while longer wavelengths have a lower frequency and less energy. In light, red has the longest wavelength and the lowest frequency and energy. Violet has the shortest wavelength and the highest frequency and energy.

Light Is Particles

Though it became widely accepted as the scientific explanation of light, the wave theory didn't explain every aspect of the behavior of light. Most importantly, waves can only travel through a medium, such as water or air. It was known that light traveled from the sun to

Figure 3.3 Christiaan Huygens (1629–1695); Painting by Caspar Netscher, 1671.
Wikimedia Commons, PD-User: Jan Arkesteijn, accessed on Sept. 13, 2013.

■ *electromagnetic spectrum*
The continuous range of electric and magnetic radiation.

■ *wavelength*
The distance from crest to crest of a wave.

■ *light*
The portion of the electromagnetic spectrum, ranging from about 380 to 770 nanometers, that is capable of exciting the retina and producing visual sensation.

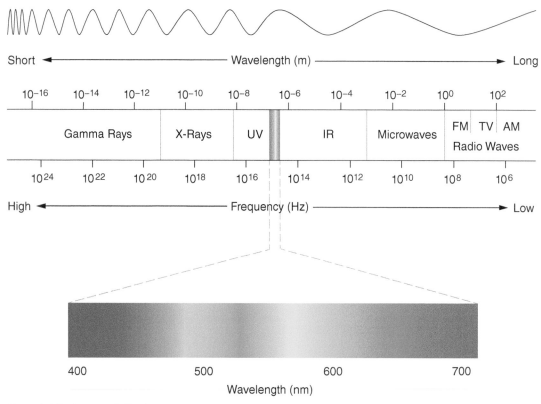

Figure 3.4 Electromagnetic Spectrum.

Figure 3.5 Sir Isaac Newton (1642–1727); Engraving by James McArdell, 1760.
Courtesy of Prints and Photographs Division, Library of Congress, LC-USZ62-10191.

the earth, but through what medium? The wave theory held that light traveled through "ether," an undetectable substance whose only purpose seemed to be a medium to transmit waves of light.

The physicist Sir Isaac Newton (Figure 3.5) proposed an alternative theory of light as corpuscles (particles), which was fully explained in his *Optiks* in 1704. In addition to solving the problem of a medium of transmission (particles don't need one), particles also explained the perfectly straight reflection of light. Waves, depending on where they are in their cycle, would not consistently reflect along the same straight line. Because of this, and Newton's reputation, the particle theory of light held sway throughout the 1700s.

Light Is Waves, Again

In 1801 the wave theory received a boost when Thomas Young (Figure 3.6) used his now famous double slit experiment to demonstrate that light behaves as a wave. In the experiment Young focused monochromatic light on a barrier with two slits (carefully placed at just the right distance apart). If light behaved as a particle, the result should have been two lines of light on the screen behind the barrier. However, what Young saw was not two bands of light corresponding to the two slits but an interference pattern (Figure 3.7). This marked the beginning of the end of the particle theory of light.

In 1873 James Clerk Maxwell (Figure 3.8) proposed a new wave theory in his *A Treatise on Electricity and Magnetism* that is still used today. He demonstrated that the waves of earlier physicists were simultaneously fields of electricity and of magnetism undulating at right angles to one another and that the direction of travel was perpendicular to both (Figure 3.9).

Light Is Waves and Particles, aka Quanta

How can light behave as both waves *and* particles? The answer came about in 1900 when Max Planck (Figure 3.10) theorized that all energy, including light, existed as discrete packets of energy called "quanta." This theory solved some of the persistent problems with the wave theory, but seemed to suggest light as particles, an idea that had been discredited by Young a century earlier. However, Planck wasn't suggesting the particles of classical physics but something entirely new—that light was composed of units of energy, not units of matter. This idea later developed into the quantum theory that explains actions at the subatomic scale.

A few years later, in 1905, Albert Einstein suggested that the quantum of light, the *photon*, was a massless particle that also had a vibration frequency. Today we understand light as having a particle-wave duality, meaning that light can behave as a wave *or* a particle, depending on how one approaches it.

Figure 3.6 Thomas Young (1773–1829); Portrait by Sir Thomas Lawrence.
Wikimedia Commons, PD-User: Kelson, accessed on Sept. 26, 2013.

■ *photon*
A particle of light.

Light Is Art

It is not just scientists who are interested in light. For the painter, photographer, sculptor, or lighting designer, light is a component of artistic expression or a tool used to achieve that expression. It can be used to direct attention and emphasize elements of a composition, reveal three-dimensional form and texture, set a mood, create an ambience, support an activity, define the boundaries of a space, and so much more.

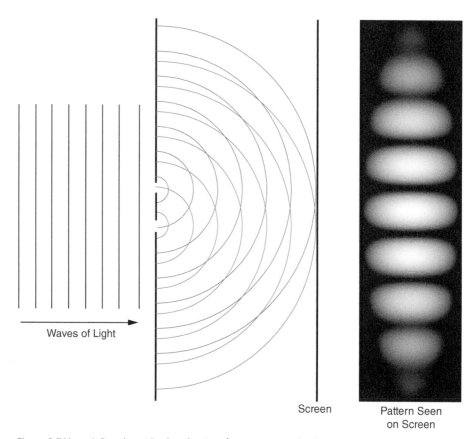

Waves of Light

Screen

Pattern Seen
on Screen

Figure 3.7 Young's Experiment Produced an Interference Pattern Like the One Shown in This Illustration.

In Vermeer's *The Milkmaid* (Figure 3.11), for example we see the effect of diffuse northern light entering the room through a high window. The pale wall is gently washed with light and fades into the background, while the vivid yellow and blue of the woman's dress draw our attention to her. The light, entering from the left, reveals the roundness of her form and the plasticity of her face. Her gaze directs us to her work and to the bread on the table.

The subject matter of this painting, a woman pouring milk, is commonplace and perhaps barely worth noticing. However, the artist's use of color and light captures our attention and compels us to take a second look.

Light is also used in conjunction with other art forms, such as music and theatre, to set a mood or evoke an emotional response (Figure 3.12). At its most abstract and refined, light is its own form of art or sculpture (Figure 3.13).

Light Is a Tool

Light is a phenomenon of the physical world. To scientists, light can be understood as both a wave and a particle. Light is a medium of artistic expression. To artists light is an element of composition and a revealer of three-dimensional form.

To architectural lighting designers, light is the tool that we use to turn our design intent into real world results. We employ our knowledge of the properties and behavior of light, human vision and psychology, light sources and fixtures, art, and design to set the scene for every project. We may wield light with technical expertise, with artistic virtuosity, or both, as we develop our designs from a list of tasks, an aesthetic style, or an abstract concept to a fully realized work.

Figure 3.8 James Clerk Maxwell (1831–1879). *Wikimedia Commons, PD-User: Loveless, accessed on Sept. 26, 2013.*

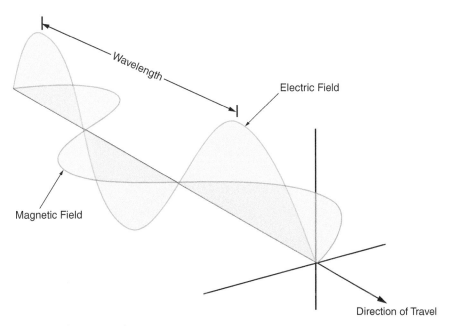

Figure 3.9 Electromagnetic Wave.

Figure 3.10 Max Planck (1858–1947), 1930.
Wikimedia Commons, PD-User: Lobo, accessed on Sept. 26, 2013.

Figure 3.11 Johannes Vermeer, *The Milkmaid* (c. 1660).
Wikimedia Commons, PD-User: DcoetzeeBot, accessed on Sept. 13, 2013.

Figure 3.12 Light Used to Evoke an Emotional Response in Entertainment.
Courtesy of Lenore Doxsee.

Online Resources

HyperPhysics, Web site from the Georgia State University Department of Physics and Astronomy, http://hyperphysics.phy-astr.gsu.edu/hbase/hph.html

Hyperphysics is also available as an app on iTunes.

Designing with Light Resources

Wiley's companion site to *Designing with Light,* www.wiley.com/go/designingwithlight

Author's companion site to Designing with Light, www.designinglight.com

References

Bova, Ben, *The Story of Light*, Naperville, IL: Sourcebook, Inc., 2001.

DiLaura, David, et al., *The Lighting Handbook, Tenth Edition*, New York: Illuminating Engineering Society, 2011.

DiLaura, David, *A History of Light and Lighting*, New York: Illuminating Engineering Society, 2006.

IES Nomenclature Committee, *RP-16-05 Nomenclature and Definitions for Illuminating Engineering*, New York: Illuminating Engineering Society, 2005.

Figure 3.13 Light as Sculpture (Avenue Champs-Elysées, Paris, France).
Photo by Didier Boy de la Tour, © ACT Lighting Design 2011.

CHAPTER 4

How We See

"The best thing that we're put here for's to see"

Robert Frost, from "The Star-Splitter"

Sight is the most important of our five senses. How can we say this? Consider the following:

- Sight provides us with the most information of all our senses, and is the most relied upon sense. In fact, a 2013 study of classical music competitions found that the most reliable predictor of the winner was the visible passion displayed during performance, not the music performance itself.
- Sight gives us twice as much information about our surroundings than does hearing, which is our second most relied upon sense.
- Around the world, in every culture, fear of darkness is one of the three most common fears.

Vision is extremely important, so it makes sense that we know about the process that allows us to see. Certain aspects of vision will become important later when we discuss the way that light affects *visual acuity*, perception of contrast and distance, and human health.

■ *visual acuity*
The ability to see fine or small details.

The Path of Light

Let's begin by examining the path light takes to allow us to see (Figure 4.1). We begin with primary light sources. Primary light sources generate light or introduce light into the environment we are observing. Primary light sources may be naturally occurring such as light from the sun, sky, or a full moon, or they may be man-made such as fluorescent, incandescent, or LED light bulbs.

Primary light sources are the major contributors of light to a given environment. At night a single candle may be the main light source in a room. During the daytime, daylight or sunlight coming through the window become the primary light sources, and the candle's contribution becomes insignificant. It ceases to be a primary light source.

Of course, light doesn't travel from a primary light source directly to our eyes. Light reflects off of every object in our environment. Natural features such as trees and mountains, architectural features such as walls and ceilings, and objects within a space such as furniture and people all reflect light and as such are considered secondary light sources.

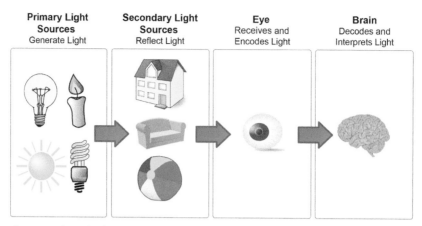

Figure 4.1 The Path of Light.

After bouncing off of one or more objects, light enters our eyes. Light strikes our retina, which converts the energy of visible light into electrical signals that are sent, via the optic nerve, to the brain. There the information is received and decoded. It's really in the brain where vision occurs; visual information is interpreted and analyzed, which gives rise to our understanding of the space around us.

The Eye

■ **cornea**
The clear covering over the iris and pupil.

Let's take a look at the path of light through the eye (Figure 4.2). Light first passes through the *cornea*, where it is refracted (bent) and most of the focusing occurs as light is directed through the pupil at the center of the iris.

■ **pupil**
The opening of the iris that allows light into the eye.

The iris is a muscle that opens and closes based on the available light, regulating the amount of light entering the eye through its center, the *pupil*. The area of the pupil has a range of over 5:1. In a dark room the pupil can open to almost .3" in diameter (8 mm). In bright light the pupil can close down to a diameter of only .13" (3.5 mm).

■ **retina**
A membrane lining the eye, opposite the pupil, which contains photo-sensitive cells that provide vision.

When light passes through the pupil, it enters the lens, a flexible disk with muscles attached to the perimeter. Focus on objects is fine-tuned by the lens. The muscles surrounding the lens constrict, compressing the lens and making it thicker so we can see nearby objects, or relax, allowing the lens to assume its thinner, natural shape when we view objects that are farther away. These changes to the lens keep light from objects, both near and far, properly focused on the retina, the back wall of the eye where photoreceptors (light-sensitive cells) reside.

■ **rods**
Photoreceptors that provide black and white vision.

In the *retina* there are several types of photoreceptors that contribute to vision (Figure 4.3). *Rods* are active at low light levels and provide us with black and white vision. *Cones* are active at higher light levels and provide us with color vision. A new type of photoreceptor, the ganglion cell, was discovered in 2002. Ganglion cells aren't related to vision. They send information to the part of the brain that regulates our circadian rhythms (See Chapter 16).

■ **cones**
Photoreceptors that provide color vision.

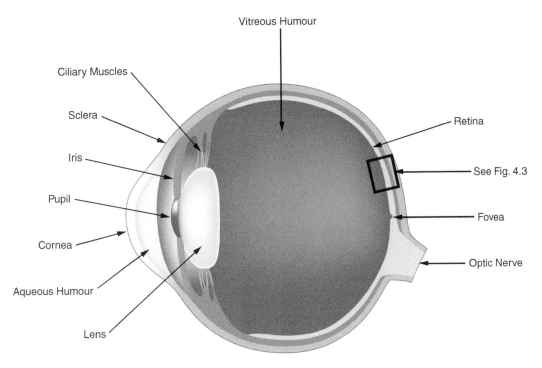

Figure 4.2 Parts of
© Alila Medical Media, Used under license from Shutterstock.com.

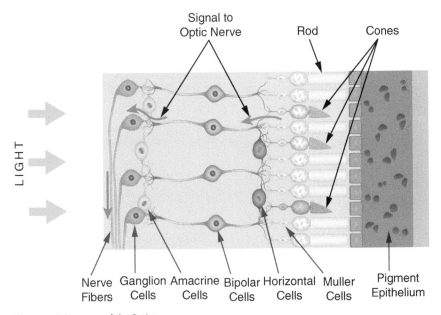

Figure 4.3 Structure of the Retina.
© Alila Medical Media, Used under license from Shutterstock.com.

Rods and cones are not evenly distributed across the retina. The eye has approximately 6.4 million cones, which require more light than rods do in order to be active, and are concentrated closer to the center of the retina. Three types of cones give us our color vision.

Rods, about 125 million of them, provide only black and white vision, and are more plentiful toward the perimeter of the retina. Rods are significantly more sensitive to light than are cones. In dim or dark environments there is insufficient light to stimulate cones, so we lose our color vision; but rods remain active, providing us with black and white vision.

When rods and cones absorb light, the energy of the light breaks down pigments, which release chemicals that cause adjacent nerves to send electrical pulses, via the optic nerve, to the brain. It is in the brain that information from the eye is decoded and interpreted, and where we experience vision.

The eye is a remarkable device that is constantly performing many separate operations to give us clear sight. Two of the important actions of the eye are accommodation and adaptation.

■ *accommodation*
The eye's ability to change focus from one distance to another.

■ *fovea*
The area at the center of the retina where we have detailed vision.

■ *adaptation*
The eye's ability to adjust to different illumination levels.

Accommodation

Accommodation is the eye's ability to refocus. It seems that everything we look at, both near and far, is in focus because the muscles surrounding the lens make very rapid adjustments in response to where we are looking. They do this to keep light focused on the retina, especially at the center of the retina on an area called the fovea.

As we've noted, rods and cones are not evenly distributed across the retina. The *fovea* is an area about 1.5 mm in diameter that is located directly behind the lens. It is where cones are most densely packed, and where our detailed, color vision occurs. Because the fovea is so small compared to the whole retina, we have a very narrow cone (about 2°) of clear and detailed vision when compared to our full field of vision.

To experience foveal vision for yourself, try this: Look at the X in the middle of the following row of letters and use your peripheral vision to see how many letters on either side of the X can be seen clearly. You will probably find that only three or four of the letters are clear.

E F P T O Z L P E D **X** D E P L Z O T P F E

There are a number of defects to the eye that can interfere with vision.

Astigmatism is a misshapen cornea that causes blurred vision. Astigmatism can be corrected with glasses or contact lens.

Cataract is a clouding of the lens. Cataract is corrected with surgery.

Color blindness is caused by a lack of one of the cones, or an inability of the cones to transmit signals to the brain. Color blindness is a recessive trait linked to men, who are twenty times more likely than women to have it.

Glaucoma is excess pressure of the aqueous humour that causes poor night vision and blind spots, and can lead to blindness.

Hyperopia is farsightedness. The eye does not bend or refract light properly to focus it onto the retina. With hyperopia, distant objects are clear, but near objects are blurred. Hyperopia can be corrected with glasses or contact lenses.

Myopia is nearsightedness. The eye does not bend or refract light properly to focus it onto the retina. With myopia, near objects are clear, but distant objects are blurred. Myopia can be corrected with glasses or contact lens.

Presbyopia is age-related farsightedness. It is a loss of elasticity of the lens and usually begins in the mid-40s. Presbyopia can be corrected with glasses or contact lenses.

Adaptation

Adaptation is the eye's ability to adjust to changes in brightness. The iris works to maintain optimal illumination on the retina by closing in bright conditions and opening in dark conditions. The rods and cones in the retina also undergo adjustments, but at a much slower rate. Complete adaptation can take several minutes.

Dark adaptation (a shift to seeing mainly with rods) is rapid for the first few seconds, then slows down and can take an hour to complete. In the process the eye gains sensitivity and loses acuity (detail vision) because cones in the fovea are not in use. Light adaptation (a shift to seeing mainly with cones) is completed within a few minutes.

In addition to adapting their sensitivity to light, our eyes' response to light changes based on the amount of light available. The full range of brightness that we can see is separated into three categories: photopic, mesopic, and scotopic.

We see with *photopic vision* in the range from a dark overcast day to the brightest, sunniest day. Photopic vision is dominated by the cone photoreceptors. This means that color is perceived and fine details are discerned at the fovea. Nearly all of our work involves providing illumination at photopic levels.

At lower light levels, from the most illuminated roadways to the light of a quarter moon, we see with *mesopic vision*. Mesopic vision uses both rods and cones, with rods assuming a larger role and cones a smaller role as illuminance decreases. As the cone photoreceptors stop working, color perception is lost, as is detail vision of the fovea, which is dominated by cones.

Scotopic conditions exist under a night sky with no moon. *Scotopic vision* relies only on rods. It has no sense of color, and detail vision is minimal. At night, one does not see an image that falls on the fovea because it contains only cones.

■ *photopic vision*
Vision resulting from the cone cells of the retina. Also called daytime vision.

■ *mesopic vision*
Vision utilizing both rods and cones at low light levels.

■ *scotopic vision*
Vision at very low light levels that relies only on rods.

How We See Color

Color vision starts when light is absorbed by three variations of the cone photoreceptors. Since we have three receptors for color, our color vision is described as trichromatic. The trichromatic theory of vision (sometimes called the Young-Helmholtz trichromatic theory) was first proposed by Thomas Young (Figure 3.6) in 1802, and later demonstrated by Hermann von Helmholtz (Figure 4.4) in 1852. It took another hundred years for the cells responsible for trichromatic vision to be confirmed, which happened in 1956!

Our cones are frequently referred to as red, green, and blue cones to identify the color of light that stimulates each type of cone. This is not quite accurate. Our cones are sensitive to a broader range of wavelengths than just those three individual colors, and together they give us sensitivity to the entire visible spectrum. Cones are better described as short wavelength (S), medium wavelength (M) and long wavelength (L) cones. Today's understanding of rod and cone sensitivity is shown in Figure 4.5.

When we add the S, M, and L sensitivity curves together, we get a curve called $V(\lambda)$ (Figure 4.6). This curve shows us that our

Figure 4.4 Hermann von Helmholtz (1821–1894); Engraving by Thomas Johnson (c. 1895). *Courtesy of Prints and Photographs Division, Library of Congress, LC-USZ62-42291.*

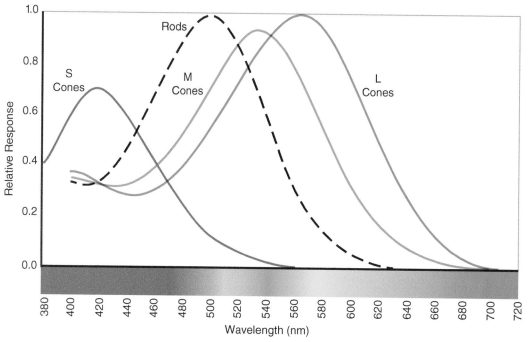

Figure 4.5 Rod and Cone Sensitivity Curves.

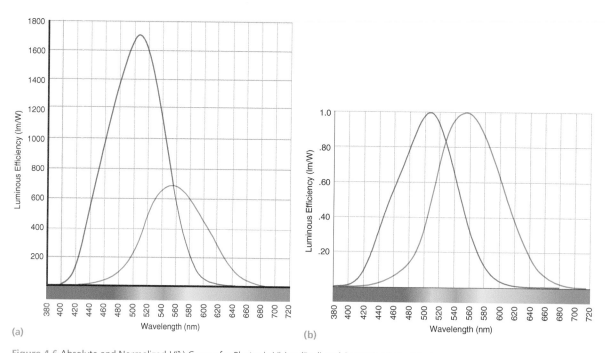

(a)

(b)

Figure 4.6 Absolute and Normalized $V(\lambda)$ Curves for Photopic Vision (Red) and Scotopic Vision (Blue).

eyes are not equally sensitive to all colors of light. During photopic vision (that is, cone vision under normal lighting conditions), our sensitivity peaks at approximately 555 nm (green-yellow) and decreases toward both the red and blue ends of the spectrum. We want to measure light the same way our eye sees light, so V(λ) is incorporated into the other units of measurement for light, and into the sensitivity and calibration of devices such as light meters.

During scotopic vision our peak sensitivity shifts to approximately 507 nm. This shift is known as the Purkinje effect or the Purkinje shift and is named after the Czech anatomist and physiologist Johannes Evangelista Purkyne (Figure 4.7), who discovered it.

Visual Performance

There are several factors that affect how well we are able to perform a visual task. They are discussed in this chapter on vision, but it would be just as appropriate to place them in the chapter on design because they must be considered when determining the amount of light provided for the users of a space. Those factors are:

Figure 4.7 Johannes Evangelista Purkyne (1787–1869); Photo by Rudolf Hoffman, 1856. *Courtesy of Prints and Photographs Division, Library of Congress, LC-USZ62-133404.*

- Size
- Viewing time
- Brightness
- Contrast

Size and Viewing Time

The importance of size and viewing time are obvious from your own experience. Large objects are easier to see than small objects. You will see more detail in something that you observe for one minute than you will in something that you observe for one second.

As simple as these two elements are, they must be kept in mind because they are significant factors in one's ability to perform a task. Visual tasks of small size, such as a tailor threading a needle, require more light than do tasks of similar difficulty but of larger size, such as putting a coin into a vending machine. High speed tasks with short viewing times, such as a bank teller counting bills, require more light than tasks of equal difficulty but longer viewing time, such as a poker player looking at a hand of cards.

Brightness

Our eyes are more versatile than any film or camera yet devised. They are sensitive to light over a range of more than one trillion to one (1,000,000,000,000:1). We cannot make use of that entire range at one time, though. Our average brightness sensitivity is 1,000:1. In light that is brighter than the range we're adapted to, we may experience blinding glare. In light that is below that range we're adapted to, we see only darkness.

Since we can adapt to see within such a huge range, but not all of it at once, we find that brightness is relative, not absolute. If our eyes are adapted to candlelight, a 100W light bulb may be blindingly bright. If our eyes are adapted to a sunny day, though, that same light bulb will seem dim. This phenomenon is called *apparent brightness*. Since brightness is relative, or apparent, it is often more useful to speak about it in ratios rather than in absolute terms.

■ *apparent brightness*
The perceived brightness of a light source or illuminated object.

Contrast

Contrast is the relationship between the object being viewed and the simultaneously visible surroundings (Figure 4.8). A greater difference in illumination and/or reflection results in higher contrast. When we talk about contrast, we usually measure differences as a ratio. A surface that is 80 percent reflective (that is, reflects 80 percent of the light that falls on it) compared to one that is 40 percent reflective has a 2:1 contrast ratio.

■ *contrast*
The relationship between the brightness or color of an object and its surroundings.

The same holds true for illumination. If the foreground is illuminated to a level of 20 fc and the background illuminated to a level of 10 fc, we have a 10-fc difference and a 2:1 ratio. If we raise the foreground lighting to 100 fc and the background to 50 fc, we will still experience a 2:1 ratio, although we will be aware that it is brighter. Now raise the background to 90 fc, and the contrast almost vanishes. The 10-fc difference that had been so pronounced is now insignificant. Absolute contrast can be measured scientifically with light meters. Perceived contrast is a function of the visual system.

This can create optical illusions like the one shown in Figure 4.9. The gradient of the background is so strong, and the contrast at the left and right ends of the gray bar is so high, that it creates the illusion that the center gray bar is a gradient, too. Remove the

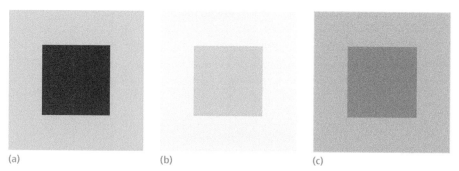

(a)   (b)   (c)

Figure 4.8 Absolute and Relative Contrast: Figure (a) Has a Foreground of 90 Percent Gray and a Background of 30 Percent Gray, Resulting in a 3:1 Ratio. Figure (b) Has a Foreground of 30 Percent Gray and a Background of 10 Percent Gray, Also Resulting in a 3:1 Ratio. Figure (c) Has a Foreground of 60 Percent Gray and a Background of 30 Percent Gray.; the Separation by Percentage (30 Percent) Is the Same as Figure (b), but the Contrast Ratio Is 2:1, the Lowest of the Three Images.

background gradient and we discover that the bar is a solid gray—there is no gradient!

Our perception of color is also relative, as the images in Figure 4.10 and 4.11 demonstrate. Background color affects our perception of foreground color. If you look at the circles on the left and right sides of Figure 4.10, it seems as though they are different colors. However, if we isolate the circles (Figure 4.11), we find that they are actually the same color, and that the surrounding colors have affected our color perception making them appear to be different. See Chapter 8 for more information about color and color perception.

Figure 4.9 Brightness Perception Is Relative, Not Absolute. The Gray Bar in the Center Is a Solid Tone, Not a Gradient.

Online Resources

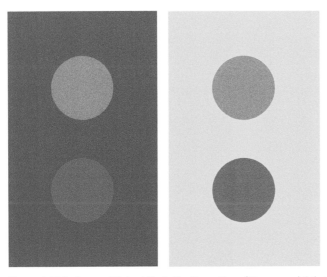

Figure 4.10 Background Color Affects Our Perception of Foreground Color.

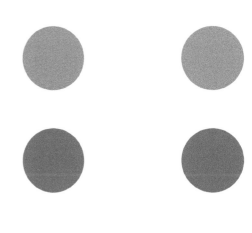

Figure 4.11 Remove the Background Color and We See That the Foreground Colors Are the Same.

HyperPhysics, Web site from the Georgia State University Department of Physics and Astronomy, http://hyperphysics.phy-astr.gsu.edu/hbase/hph.html

Hyperphysics is also available as an app on iTunes.

Designing with Light Resources

Wiley's companion site to *Designing with Light,* www.wiley.com/go/designingwithlight

Author's companion site to *Designing with Light,* www.designinglight.com

References

DiLaura, David, et al., *The Lighting Handbook, Tenth Edition*, New York: Illuminating Engineering Society, 2011.

Rea, Mark S., *Value Metrics for Better Lighting*, Bellingham, WA: Society of Photo-Optical Instrumentation Engineers (SPIE), 2013.

Rookes, Paul, and Jane Willson, *Perception: Theory, Development and Organisation*, Philadelphia: Taylor & Francis, Inc., 2000.

Tsay, Chia-Jung, "Sight Over Sound in the Judgment of Music Performance," *Proceedings of the National Academy of Sciences of the United States of America 110,* no. 136 (14580–14585), www.pnas.org/cgi/doi/10.1073/pnas.1221454110.

"Webvision," University of Utah School of Medicine, accessed February 13, 2012, http://webvision.med.utah.edu.

CHAPTER 5

Light, Vision, and Psychology

"Always the laws of light are the same, but the modes and degrees of seeing vary."

Henry David Thoreau (1817–1862)

Light enables vision, thus providing a significant means of connecting with our world. It makes sense that we respond to what we see based on the way that light reveals the world to us. Therefore, it's important for us to understand that there is a difference between simply seeing the space around us and our response to, or understanding of, that space.

Let's begin by defining a few terms. Vision is "the faculty or state of being able to see." A lighting designer is always concerned with vision. Vision permits object identification and allows one to navigate a path through a space. However, lighting designers must do more than simply provide enough light to enable vision. We must provide illumination that is appropriate to the visual tasks people will perform in the spaces we design, that supports the goals of the architecture and interior design, and that creates an appropriate ambiance. Determining and achieving task specific light levels is relatively easy. Illumination requirements are fairly well understood, and there are a wide range of light sources and fixtures that will satisfy those needs.

Throughout this book I talk about creating an environment. An environment is the area surrounding an individual that engages multiple senses, offers information, and requires active perception. Environments may contain or convey symbolic meaning and/or messages. Environments have ambiance or atmosphere (other words I'll use frequently). Architects and interior designers create the space, but the way in which we reveal that space with light goes a long way toward creating the environment.

Perception

Perception is a way of regarding, understanding, or interpreting something: a mental impression. There are two components to perception that the lighting designer can know about a space and the people who visit that space. First, we can know a typical person's experience with a given building type. Second, we know that experience gives rise to a set of expectations. If we've seen a number of office spaces, we expect the next office space to be sufficiently similar to those we've already seen, and, therefore, we can identify a new one. We don't have to be told the purpose of each new space we see. If we've had dinner at a number of romantic French restaurants, we expect the next one to be similar enough to the others that we can identify it as such.

Psychologists call these templates affecting our expectations and interpretations "*schema.*" Schemas are mental structures that organize our knowledge and assumptions about something, and are used for interpreting and processing information. They are based on past experiences and one's knowledge of the target of one's perception. Schemas help us to make sense of the vast amount of sensory information, decide which information is important and which isn't, and interpret and understand information that is ambiguous.

So, if we understand the typical schema, or set of expectations, of a space or building type, we can choose, as designers or artists, to fulfill those expectations or not. If we choose to challenge those expectations, we can do so in a way that is interesting, attention getting, and exciting.

It is important to remember that there are many schemas relating to the built environment, and that a schema allows for a good deal of variation. A designer should consider his or her own schemas as they relate to a design project, and confirm their accuracy and appropriateness early in the design process. If the designer's schemas are inconsistent with the project's goals, the design will be misguided. The designer must also consider the schemas of the visitors to the space being designed. For example, a modestly priced restaurant near a college campus will attract a clientele whose expectations differ from those at an expensive restaurant near the city's opera house. Even if the cuisine is the same, the designer's understanding of the different expectations held by the two sets of clientele can, and should, lead to two different designs.

■ *schema*
A mental framework or concept that helps us interpret and organize new information.

Impressions

We want to do more than simply meet people's expectations. The lighting designer also seeks to guide or influence the viewer's responses to a space. We refer to this as affecting a viewer's impression or subjective impression. An impression is an idea, feeling, or opinion, especially one formed without conscious thought. Changing the lighting of a space changes our impression by affecting the way we perceive, interpret, and respond to that space. Controlling brightness contrast and color contrast, among other things, sends signals to the viewers that guide their response.

A great artistic example is in the many paintings of Rouen Cathedral by Claude Monet (visit www.learn.columbia.edu/monet/swf/). In over two dozen paintings he captured not just the architecture, but the light—its color, direction, clarity, brightness, the contrast between the highlights and the shadows, and the contrast between the foreground and the background of the sky. Each painting has a different feel to it and elicits a different response in the viewer.

Lighting, Architecture, and Impressions

In the 1970s John Flynn and his colleagues at Kent State University conducted a series of experiments on room lighting and the occupants' response. They knew that in evaluating our visual environment we search for meaningful information. Could lighting provide cues or signals to the occupants of a space? Could lighting aid in, or alter, a user's understanding of, or response to, a space? Specifically, could patterns of lighting produce consistent responses or impressions in the occupants of a room?

The experiments used a conference room with six different lighting arrangements each of which produced a range of responses. The categories of subjective impressions, and the range of each category, are listed in Table 5.1.

Table 5.1 Subjective Impressions and Their Ranges

Subjective Impression	Positive End of Range	Negative End of Range
General evaluation	Pleasant, satisfying, interesting	Unpleasant, frustrating, monotonous
Perceptual clarity	Clear, bright, distinct	Hazy, dim, vague
Spatial complexity	Simple, uncluttered	Complex, cluttered
Spaciousness	Large, long, spacious	Small, short, cramped
Formality	Rounded, informal	Angular, formal

The six lighting arrangements, and the subjective impressions created by each arrangement, are as follows.

Arrangement 1: Overhead downlighting on the conference room table (Figure 5.1) at a low intensity (10 fc on table) produced perceptual clarity impressions of hazy and dim;

Figure 5.1 Arrangement 1—Low Intensity Downlighting.

Figure 5.2 Arrangement 2—Low Intensity Perimeter Lighting.

spatial complexity impressions of simple and uncluttered; and spaciousness impressions of small and cramped.

Arrangement 2: Lighting all perimeter walls (Figure 5.2) at a low intensity (10 fc on table) produced evaluative impressions of pleasantness; spatial complexity impressions of simple and uncluttered; and spaciousness impressions of large and spacious.

Arrangement 3: Overhead diffuse lighting (Figure 5.3) at a low intensity (10 fc on table) produced evaluative impressions of unpleasantness and monotony; perceptual clarity impressions of dimness and dullness; and spatial complexity impressions of simple and uncluttered.

Figure 5.3 Arrangement 3—Low Intensity Indirect Lighting.

Figure 5.4 Arrangement 4—Low Intensity Downlighting and Wall Grazing.

Arrangement 4: Combining the first arrangement with lighting the end walls of the room (Figure 5.4) at a low intensity (10 fc on table) produced evaluative impressions of pleasantness and being interesting; spaciousness impressions of being long; and the judgment that it was the least formal of the six lighting arrangements.

Arrangement 5: Overhead diffuse lighting (Figure 5.5) at a high intensity (100 fc on table) produced evaluative impressions that were strongly unpleasant and monotonous; perceptual clarity impressions that were strongly clear and bright; spaciousness impressions of being large and spacious; and the judgment that it was the most formal of the six lighting arrangements.

Figure 5.5 Arrangement 5—High Intensity Indirect Lighting.

Figure 5.6 Arrangement 6—Moderate Intensity Downlight, Indirect Light, and Wall Grazing Light.

Arrangement 6: A combination of arrangements 1, 2, and 3 (Figure 5.6) at a medium intensity (30 fc on table) produced evaluative impressions that were strongly pleasant, satisfying, and interesting; perceptual clarity impressions that were strongly clear and bright; and spaciousness impressions of being large and spacious.

General diffuse lighting (arrangements 3 and 5) by itself had the lowest general evaluation rating and was judged as being too monotonous. High levels of general diffuse lighting (arrangement 5), however, did increase the level of perceptual clarity and spaciousness.

When arrangements 1 and 3 were compared, 1 consistently produced a more positive evaluative impression. Illuminating the walls consistently increased impressions of pleasantness and spaciousness, and improved perceptual clarity.

By manipulating aspects of light that all designers use, such as bright/dim, even/uneven, and perimeter/center, Flynn showed that the experience of a lighted space is a shared one, and that room occupants tend to have similar responses to certain lighting patterns. This is because lighting affects the presentation of information in the visual field, which in turn affects the way that information is weighted and evaluated. Thus, lighting can be an effective means of communicating ideas or reinforcing the impressions desired by the designers.

The work of Flynn and others gives us several ways of reinforcing desired impressions that we can use in our designs. Visual clarity is reinforced by higher light levels on horizontal surfaces (i.e., work plane and ceiling), light in the center of the room, some wall illuminance, and cooler white light (Figure 5.7).

Spaciousness is reinforced by uniform perimeter lighting, especially on the walls (Figure 5.8).

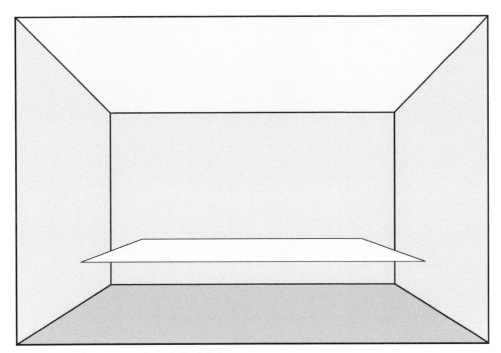

Figure 5.7 Reinforcing Impressions of Visual Clarity.

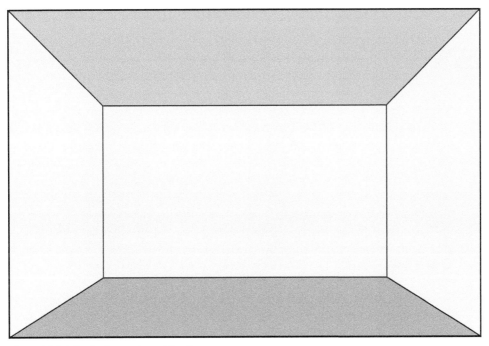

Figure 5.8 Reinforcing Impressions of Spaciousness.

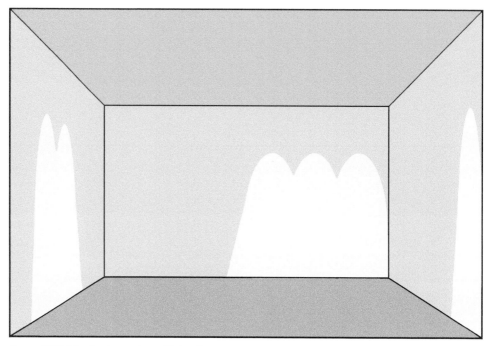

Figure 5.9 Reinforcing Impressions of Relaxation.

Relaxation is reinforced by nonuniform perimeter lighting, especially on walls, lower light levels, and warm sources of light (Figure 5.9).

Privacy is reinforced by nonuniform distribution of light, lower light levels in the area of the occupant, and higher light levels in the zones surrounding the occupant (Figure 5.10).

Other research has shown that an illuminated or luminous ceiling gives the impression that the ceiling is higher than one that is not illuminated. Higher ceilings also create the impression that a room is more spacious, even though the square footage is the same (Figure 5.11).

For a more in-depth exploration of the psychological impressions affected by space and light, you may want to consider taking a course in environmental psychology. This field is the study of human behavior and well-being in relation to the environment, whether it is a home, office, or neighborhood. It explores the way people interact with their surroundings, and uses theory and research to develop practical applications in architecture and design.

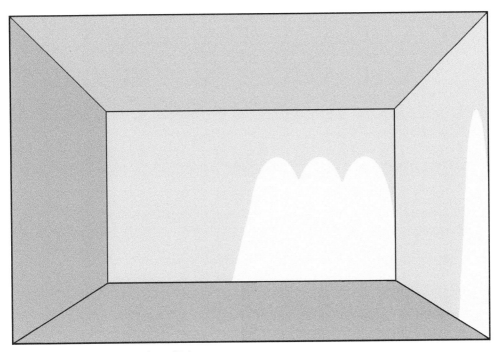

Figure 5.10 Reinforcing Impressions of Privacy.

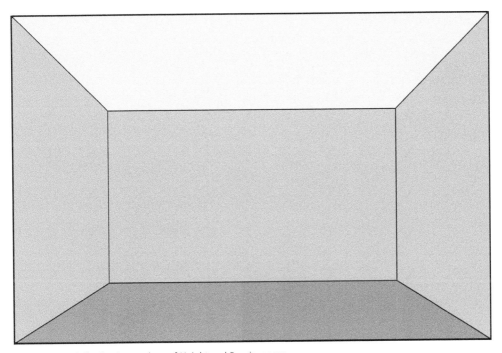

Figure 5.11 Reinforcing Impressions of Height and Spaciousness.

Online Resources

Environmental Psychology Lecture Series on iTunes,

http://itunes.apple.com/us/course/environmental-psychology/id529650093

Seeing Myself See: The Ecology of Mind, Neuroscientist R. Beau Lotto lecture at the Royal Society for the Encouragement of Arts, Manufacture and Commerce, http://fora .tv/2009/06/24/Seeing_Myself_See_The_Ecology_of_Mind

 ## Designing with Light Resources

Wiley's companion site to *Designing with Light*, www.wiley.com/go/designingwithlight

Author's companion site to *Designing with Light*, www.designinglight.com

References

Egan, M. David, *Concepts in Architectural Lighting*, New York: McGraw-Hill, 1983.

Flynn, John, et. al., "Interim Study of Procedures for Investigating the Effect of Light on Impression and Behavior," *Journal of Illuminating Engineering Society*, October (1973): 87–94.

Rookes, Paul, and Jane Willson, *Perception: Theory, Development and Organisation*, Philadelphia: Taylor & Francis, Inc., 2000.

Stokols, Daniel, "Environmental Psychology PPD151 / PSYBEH171S / PUBHLTH151," Spring 2012, iTunes and University of California at Irvine, online class lecture video series.

CHAPTER 6

Distribution of Light

"The days then rapidly grew thick into all darkness with only small spaces of light (that is autumn) and then remained solidly all darkness with only small patches of light (that is winter), and then the darkness slowly thinned out (that is spring), but the light was never as overwhelming in its way as the darkness was overwhelmingly dark in its way (that is summer). So, too, was the night dark except for when the moon was full and the day bright with light, except for when clouds blocked out the sun."

Jamaica Kincaid

As discussed in Chapter 2, we want to understand the design elements of light so that we understand how to control them. Distribution of light from the *luminaire* is a result of the combination of the light fixture's components and the *lamp*. Brightness and contrast in our design are the result of the distribution of light from the luminaire and light's interaction with the room's surfaces.

■ *luminaire*
A complete lighting unit.
Also called a light fixture.

■ *lamp*
Light bulb.

Interaction of Light and Materials

One aspect affecting the distribution of light is the way surfaces interact with light. What we perceive as brightness is not just the amount of light in a room. Room brightness is a combination of the intensity of the light and the reflecting, diffusing, transmitting, and absorbing properties of the surfaces in the room. As lighting designers, we need to understand how the choices made by the architect or interior designer will affect our lighting, and how our lighting will affect their choices.

Reflection

There are three general types of reflection, which depend on the qualities of the reflective surface. First, *specular* surfaces are very smooth and reflective and their reflection is mirror-like. (Figure 6.1). The *angle of incidence* is equal and opposite to the angle of exitance or reflection. Materials that produce a specular reflection include glass, polished stone, and polished metal.

Semi-specular surfaces partially scatter the reflected light (Figure 6.2). As with specular surfaces, the angle of incidence is equal to the angle of reflection, but the reflection is

■ *specular*
Describes a mirrored or polished surface.

■ *angle of incidence*
The angle between a ray of light striking a surface and a line perpendicular to that surface.

■ *semi-specular*
Describes a reflective material that is partially mirror-like.

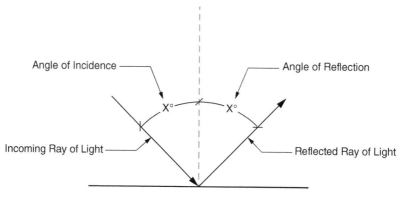

Figure 6.1 Specular Reflection.

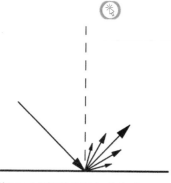

Figure 6.2 Semi-Specular Reflection.

Figure 6.3 Matte or Diffuse Reflection.

■ **matte**
Describes a surface that reflects light, but scatters it in all directions.

not perfect and some of the light is partially spread and diffused. Some image may be seen in the material, but the image is hazy, not crisp. Materials that produce a semi-specular reflection include brushed metal, wood with a satin finish, and fabric with a sheen.

Matte surfaces diffuse light so that it is reflected in all directions (Figure 6.3). Materials that produce a matte or diffuse reflection include flat paint, bond paper, unfinished or sanded wood, and unpolished stone.

No material is a perfect reflector. When light strikes any surface some of it is absorbed. The amount of light absorbed depends on the material's surface and color. Table 6.1 shows the reflectance ranges for some common materials.

Table 6.1 Reflectance of Common Materials

Reflectance Type	Material	Reflectance
Specular	Mirrored and optical coated glass	.80–.99
	Metalized and optical coated plastic	.75–.97
	Processed anodized and coated aluminum	.75–.95
	Stainless steel	.60–.65
Semi-Specular	Processed aluminum	.70–.80
	Porcelain enamel	.65–.90
	White glass	.75–.80
	Brushed aluminum	.55–.60
Diffuse	Matte white paint	.75–.90
	Limestone	.35–.65
	Acoustic ceiling tiles	.72–.90

From Table 1.2 in *Lighting Handbook, Tenth Edition.*

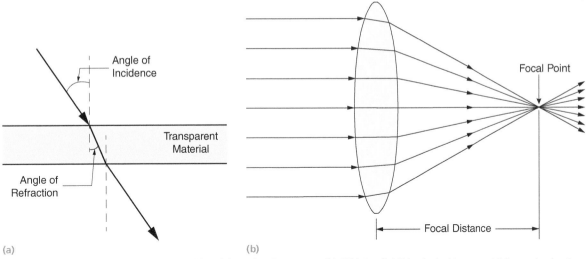

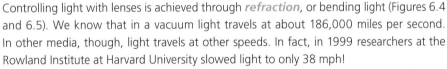

(a)   (b)

Figure 6.4 Refraction of Light through Glass (a) and through a Convex Lens (b): With Parallel Sides the Incidence and Exitance Angles Are the Same for a Glass Plate, Resulting in Little or No Change to the Direction of Light; When the Sides Are Not parallel (as in the Lens), the Direction of Light Changes.

Refraction

Controlling light with lenses is achieved through *refraction*, or bending light (Figures 6.4 and 6.5). We know that in a vacuum light travels at about 186,000 miles per second. In other media, though, light travels at other speeds. In fact, in 1999 researchers at the Rowland Institute at Harvard University slowed light to only 38 mph!

When light passes from a medium where it is faster to a medium where it is slower, the light is bent toward the line perpendicular to the boundary between the two. The reverse is also true. Light bends away from perpendicular when passing from a medium where it is faster to one where it is slower. Determining the degree to which light is bent begins with the angle of incidence. Light that is perpendicular to a surface isn't bent. Larger angles of incidence (measured from perpendicular) correspond to larger angles of refraction. The angle of incidence and the *index of refraction* for both materials are used in a mathematical formula called Snell's Law to calculate the angle of refraction.

Note that some light will be reflected off of the specular surface of a lens. To prevent this, some lenses have an antireflective coating applied to their surface.

Diffusion

Unlike a lens, which uses refraction to precisely concentrate or spread light, *diffusers* use refraction to scatter light (Figure 6.6). As light passes through a diffusing material, it is refracted, but not in a way that gives the light a specific direction or pattern.

■ **refraction**
The bending of light as it passes between materials.

■ **index of refraction**
The index of refraction is the speed of light in a vacuum divided by the speed of light in the medium.

■ **diffusers**
A translucent piece of plastic or glass that scatters light passing through it.

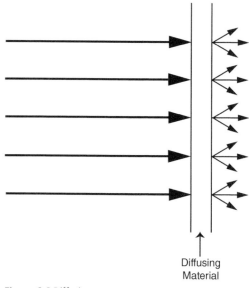

Diffusing
Material

Figure 6.5 Refraction. The Angle of Light Changes as It Passes through Different Materials Creating the Illusion That the Pencil is Not Straight.

Figure 6.6 Diffusion.

■ *transmission*
The passage of light through a material.

Diffusers are often used to hide or obscure the lamps in a fixture, as with a shade on a table lamp. Diffusers can also be used to soften shadows by turning a point or linear light source into a planar light source, as discussed later in this chapter in Shadows and Luminaires.

Transmission

■ *transmittance*
The percentage of light that passes through a material.

Transmission refers to the passage of light through a material. *Transmittance* is expressed as a percentage of the light passing through the material. Materials can be described as having the following types of transmission.

■ *transparent*
Describes a material with no diffusion of the light passing through it.

Transparent: Virtually all light passes through. Objects can be clearly seen through the material. Example—Clear glass.

■ *translucent*
Describes a material that diffuses light passing through.

Translucent: Light passes through, but the material scatters some of the light, blurring the object seen through the material. Examples are frosted plastic or etched glass.

Opaque: No light passes through. Examples are wood and metal.

■ *opaque*
Describes a material which blocks the passage of light.

Table 6.2 shows common materials and their transmittance ranges.

Table 6.2 Transmittance of Common Materials

Material	Transmittance
Clear glass	.80–.99
Etched or sandblasted glass	.75–.85
White glass	.15–.40
Clear prismatic plastic lens	.70–.95

Surface Reflection and Absorption

Almost every surface in a room reflects light, thus becoming a secondary light source. With most materials, that reflection is diffuse. Light bouncing off of a room's surfaces is called *inter-reflection*. Inter-reflection fills in shadows, reduces contrast, and produces a more uniform brightness.

Light-colored and high reflectance finishes reflect more of the incident light (light landing on them), increasing inter-reflection (Figure 6.7). This produces spaces with lighter shadows and lower contrast, which contributes to the impression of a bright space.

Dark-colored, low reflectance materials absorb much of the incident light (they are inefficient secondary light sources). This produces spaces with little inter-reflection, darker shadows, and higher contrast, which contributes to the impression of a dark space (Figure 6.8).

■ *inter-reflection*
Describes rays of light bouncing off of multiple surfaces within a room.

Figure 6.7 Inter-Reflection in Light Colored Spaces Minimizes Shadow and Contrast.
© Goncharuk Maksim, Used under license from Shutterstock.com.

Figure 6.8 Little Inter-Reflection in Dark Spaces Deepens Shadows and Heightens Contrast.
© *photobank.ch, Used under license from Shutterstock.com.*

Shadows and Luminaires

Room surface reflectance isn't the only factor affecting shadows. The physical size of the light source has an effect on the sharpness of the shadow's edge. As shown in Figure 6.9, light emitted by a small source radiates outward from a point. When an object blocks some of that light source and casts a shadow, there is a sharp delineation between the area in light and the area in shadow—the shadow edge is crisp and clear.

Figure 6.10 shows light emitted by a large source. The light behaves as though it is radiating outward from many points. When an object blocks that light source and casts a shadow, some direct light from the source is blocked, but some of it passes by the object at a range

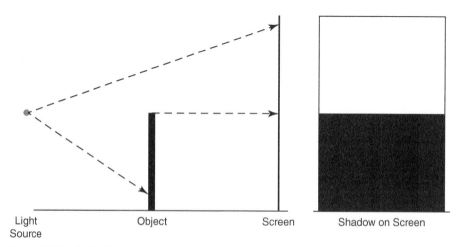

Light   Object   Screen   Shadow on Screen
Source

Figure 6.9 Small Light Sources Produce Sharp Shadows.

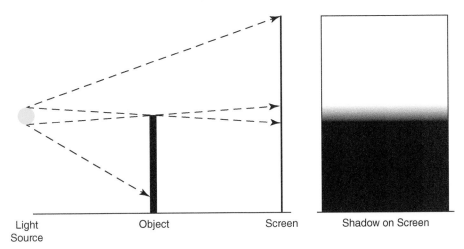

Light Source   **Object**   **Screen**   **Shadow on Screen**

Figure 6.10 Larger Light Sources Produce Softer Shadows.

of angles. The result is an area of full illumination, an area of a gradient from full light to shadow, and an area of shadow. The shadow edge is softened, as shown in Figure 6.11.

Distance is another factor affecting the edge of a shadow. As an object moves closer to a surface, its shadow becomes sharper. As an object moves away from a surface, its shadow becomes softer.

Glare

Glare is bright light that interferes with vision, either by creating discomfort or by overwhelming the visual system. There are three types of glare. The first is *reflected glare* or veiling reflections, which occur when the viewer sees a light source or brightly illuminated

■ **glare**
The effect of brightness within the visual field sufficiently high to cause annoyance, discomfort, or loss of visual performance.

■ **reflected glare**
The reflection from a specular or semi-specular surface that obscures the object being observed.

(a)   (b)

Figure 6.11 Small Light Sources Produce Sharp Shadows (a). Larger Light Sources Produce Softer Shadows (b).

Figure 6.12 Veiling Reflection in a Shop Window.

object reflected from a specular surface such as a magazine or shop window (Figure 6.12). Since we tend to focus on the brighter image, we see the reflection and have difficulty focusing on the objects behind it.

Reflected glare can be especially problematic in retail and museums. In both cases the object of our interest is on the other side of a pane of glass. If lit incorrectly, we will see the refection of the lamp or luminaire on the specular surface of the glass. Avoiding this problem is not difficult. When lighting specular surfaces, such as glass and marble (Figure 6.13), follow these four steps:

1. Determine the location of the viewer.
2. Determine the viewing angle.
3. Determine the mirror angle.
4. Place lights in the concealment zone.

■ *direct glare*
Glare produced by a direct view of a light source or its reflection.

The second type of glare is ***direct glare***, where a viewer sees a light source, or a strong reflection of the light source, directly (Figure 6.14). The light source is brighter than the surrounding visual field. It is annoying and may be uncomfortable if the light source is bright enough. Examples of direct glare are a direct view of a bare lamp, seeing a lamp reflected in the specular surface of a light fixture or work surface, or having a direct view of the sun through a window. To control glare, luminaire manufacturers

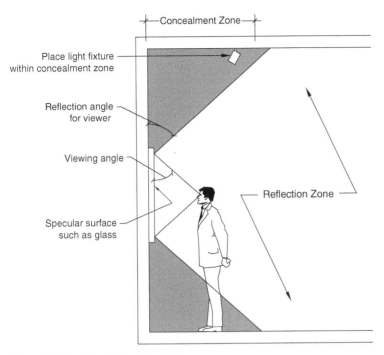

Concealment Zone

Place light fixture
within concealment zone

Reflection angle
for viewer

Viewing angle

Specular surface
such as glass

Reflection Zone

Figure 6.13 Avoiding Veiling Reflections.

design their products to limit the angle at which the lamp is in direct view, called the
cut-off angle or *shielding angle*.

■ *cut-off angle*
*The angle from a fixture's
vertical axis at which a
shielding device cuts off
direct view of a lamp.*

■ *shielding angle*
*The angle from the ceiling
plane to the line of sight
where the lamp in a
luminaire becomes visible.*

Figure 6.14 Direct Glare on a Glass Desktop.

The third type of glare is disability glare, which is caused by the direct view of a light source that is significantly brighter than the surrounding field. Everyone has experienced this type of glare at night when confronted with the headlights of an oncoming car. The intense light makes it difficult or impossible to see anything else, and can be dangerous and painful. No lighting designer should be so careless as to create disability glare.

Types of Distribution

There are many ways to classify luminaires. One way is by the percentage of light that is directed upward and downward. The Commission Internationale de l'Eclairage (International Commission on Illumination, or CIE) method is the most common method for indoor lighting fixtures. The CIE categories of distribution are direct, semi-direct, direct/indirect, semi-indirect, and diffuse.

A luminaire with a *direct distribution* (Figure 6.15) sends all of its light directly into the occupied area of the room, typically down toward the work plane. A direct distribution luminaire may be recessed, surface mounted, or pendant mounted. See Chapter 9 for more information about mounting conditions.

Semi-direct distribution luminaires direct 60 percent or more of the light downward, toward the occupied area and work surfaces, and 40 percent or less upward to be reflected off of the ceiling (Figure 6.16).

■ *direct distribution*
Describes light leaving a fixture and entering the illuminated space without first bouncing off of any architectural elements such as the ceiling or walls.

■ *semi-direct*
A light distribution pattern in which 60 percent or more of the light is directed downward and 40 percent or less is directed upward.

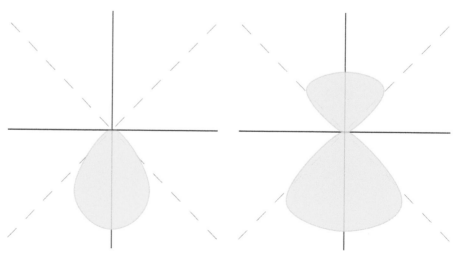

Figure 6.15 Direct Distribution.   Figure 6.16 Semi-Direct Distribution.

Direct/indirect distribution describes luminaires that direct 40–60 percent of the light downward and 40–60 percent of the light upward (Figure 6.17).

Semi-indirect luminaires direct 40 percent or less of the light downward and 60 percent or more upward. (Figure 6.18).

■ *direct/indirect*
A light distribution pattern or luminaire in which 40–60 percent of the light is directed downward and upward.

■ *semi-indirect*
A light distribution pattern in which 40 percent or less of the light is directed downward and 60 percent or more is directed upward.

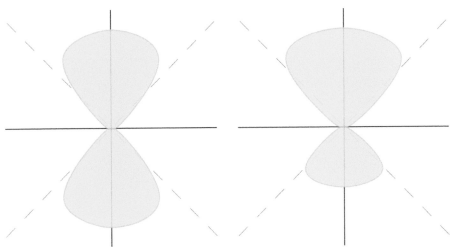

Figure 6.17 Direct/Indirect Distribution.

Figure 6.18 Semi-Indirect Distribution.

Luminaires designed for *indirect* distribution send all of their light upward to be bounced off of the ceiling (Figure 6.19).

Diffuse distribution describes luminaires that send light in all directions (Figure 6.20).

■ *indirect*
A light distribution pattern in which all of the light is directed upward to bounce off of the ceiling.

■ *diffuse*
A light distribution pattern in which light is dispersed in all directions.

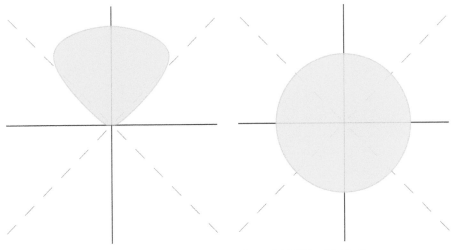

Figure 6.19 Indirect Distribution.

Figure 6.20 Diffuse Distribution.

Online Resources

Advanced Lighting Guide—Luminaires and Distribution (Subscription required), www
.algonline.org

Designing with Light Resources

Wiley's companion site to *Designing with Light,* www.wiley.com/go/designingwithlight

Author's companion site to *Designing with Light*, www.designinglight.com

References

DiLaura, David, et al., *The Lighting Handbook, Tenth Edition*, New York: Illuminating
Engineering Society, 2011.

Egan, M. David, *Concepts in Architectural Lighting*, New York: McGraw-Hill, 1983.

IES Nomenclature Committee, *RP-16-05 Nomenclature and Definitions for Illuminating
Engineering*, New York: Illuminating Engineering Society, 2005.

"Refraction of Light," HyperPhysics. Georgia State University, Department of Physics and
Astronomy, accessed March 5, 2012.

CHAPTER 7

Lamps

"We now know a thousand ways not to build a light bulb."

Thomas Edison, on his many failed attempts to produce a viable incandescent lamp

A lighting designer needs to control light in order to achieve his or her design goals. One of the first steps in achieving control is identifying the qualities of light that are desired, and then selecting the proper lamp to provide them. There are many lamp shapes and technologies available, and the designer's understanding of this fundamental component of a lighting system is essential.

■ *incandescent*
Emitting light as a result of being heated.

Incandescent Lamps

Experimentation with *incandescent* light sources began in the early 1800s and continued throughout the century. Although there isn't a specific date of invention, two people are usually given credit. The first is Sir Joseph Swan, a British physicist, who began work on the problem in 1850, and by 1880 had achieved enough success to install his lamps in theatres and private homes.

The second individual is Thomas Edison (Figure 7.1). He began work on the incandescent lamp in 1878, and by 1879 had already filed patents on his work. Edison's first incandescent lamps used filaments made of carbon, but by 1910 the carbon was replaced by tungsten. The incandescent lamp we know today is only incrementally changed from lamps made in the early twentieth century.

An incandescent lamp creates light by passing an electric current through the filament, which is made of tungsten, a material with a high resistance to electricity. The resistance to the flow of electricity causes the filament to become heated. If the resistance is high enough, the filament will become so hot that it gives off light or becomes incandescent.

Figure 7.1 Thomas Edison (1847–1931), c. 1878.
Courtesy of Prints and Photographs Division, Library of Congress, LC-USZ62-78764.

Glass bulb or envelope

Fill gas

Filament

Lead/support wires

Base

Figure 7.2 Parts of an Incandescent Lamp.
Courtesy of Philips Lighting Company.

The components of an incandescent lamp are relatively simple (Figure 7.2). The base provides a means of support for the lamp and is where the electrical connection is made. Support wires suspend the filament in the proper location within the glass bulb. The bulb, or envelope, has had the air pumped out of it (thus removing oxygen and preventing the filament from igniting), and the air is replaced with inert gases such as argon and nitrogen.

Incandescent lamps have the lowest *efficacy* of any electric light source. Efficacy is often confused with *efficiency*, which describes the effectiveness of a device with the same form of energy in and out. The efficacy of light sources is measured in lumens per watt (lm/W). A *lumen* is a unit of light produced. A watt is a unit of power consumed. Candles have an efficacy of about .3 lm/W. Incandescent lamps have an efficacy of 8–15 lm/W. This translates into less than 3 percent of the energy consumed by an incandescent lamp becoming light. The rest of the energy is turned into heat.

Today, as clients ask for greener buildings, and as energy conservation codes (see Chapter 14) limit the amount of power that the lighting system can use, the standard incandescent lamp, with its very low efficacy, is reaching obsolescence, especially in commercial buildings. On one hand, we should applaud the shift to more energy efficient sources of light that preserve the environment and save building owners' money. On the other hand, many designers mourn the loss of an inexpensive, easily controllable light source with excellent *color rendering* properties. Fortunately, many of the qualities of

■ **efficacy**
Describes to the effectiveness of a device that has different forms of energy in and out.

■ **efficiency**
Refers to the effectiveness of a device that has the same form of energy in and out.

■ **lumen**
Lumen is a lamp's total light output in all directions.

■ **color rendering**
Refers to the way colors appear when viewed under a given light source.

standard incandescent lamps are also available in an improved incandescent lamp—the halogen lamp.

Halogen Lamps

In the early 1960s, an improvement on the incandescent lamp, the *halogen lamp*, was introduced (Figure 7.3). It differed from the older incandescent lamps in two ways that improved the efficacy and extended the life. First, the bulb is made of quartz instead of glass. Second, the atmosphere inside the bulb is a halogen gas.

These two changes give rise to several differences with the older incandescent lamps. The light produced by a halogen lamp is described as whiter or bluer than that of an incandescent. Halogen lamps have a lifetime more than twice as long as a comparable incandescent. Finally, the halogen lamp is approximately twice as efficient as the old incandescent. Table 7.1 shows how these light sources compare.

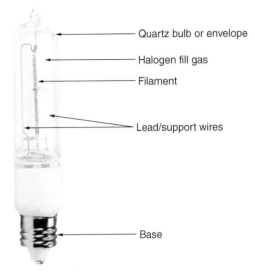

Quartz bulb or envelope

Halogen fill gas

Filament

Lead/support wires

Base

Figure 7.3 Halogen Lamp Parts.
Courtesy of Philips Lighting Company.

■ *halogen lamp*
An incandescent lamp with a lamp envelope made of quartz and a fill gas of one or more halogens.

Table 7.1 Light Source Efficacy and Average Life

Lamp Technology	Efficacy	Average Life
Candle	.3 lm/W	—
Incandescent	8–15 lm/W	750–1,500 hrs.
Halogen	10–35 lm/W	3,000–5,000 hrs.

The longer life of a halogen lamp comes from the halogen cycle. In a standard incandescent lamp, atoms of tungsten evaporate off of the filament during use and deposit on the inside of the glass envelope, in much the same way that steam evaporates off of your morning shower and condenses on the mirror. In a halogen lamp the evaporated tungsten combines with the halogen gas, before it has a chance to deposit on the quartz bulb. As the tungsten-halogen molecules float in the gas, they eventually come into contact with the filament again. The halogen separates from the tungsten and the tungsten is redeposited onto the filament.

You may have heard of halogen lamps, quartz lamps, quartz halogen lamps, and tungsten halogen lamps. These names are merely a marketing strategy to differentiate one manufacturer's product from another. The names do not reflect any difference in the materials or technology of the lamp.

Low Voltage Lamps and Transformers

Some incandescent and halogen lamps are designed to operate at a reduced voltage and are called *low voltage lamps*. (See Chapter 12 for information on electricity). *Transformers* are the devices that reduce or increase voltage, and are usually integrated into the light fixture, since their life is much longer than that of a lamp. Line voltage electricity is delivered to the transformer, which reduces the voltage before sending it to the lamp socket. Low voltage lamps typically operate at 12V, although some lighting systems use 24V.

Transformers are generally sized by the wattage (or load) that they can support. For example, a transformer inside a fixture that holds a single lamp may be sized for a 50W or 75W load, while a larger transformer powering a low voltage track system may be sized for a 250W or 500W load.

There are two technologies used in transformers. The older technology is electromagnetic transformers, which are also called magnetic or core-and-coil transformers (Figure 7.A). In a magnetic transformer the input wiring and output wiring are both wrapped around an iron-

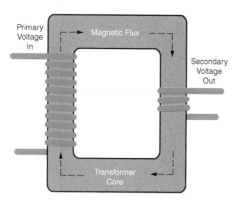

Figure 7.A Magnetic Transformer.

containing core. When electricity passes through the input wiring, it induces a magnetic field in the core, which then induces an electric field in the secondary wiring. The ratio of turns or windings between the primary and secondary sides determines the decrease or increase in the voltage.

Electronic transformers perform the same function, but more efficiently, using transistors instead of an iron core.

There are two important considerations for safety and proper operation when dimming low voltage luminaires. The first is to confirm that the transformer is designed for dimming applications. The second is to match the transformer type (magnetic or electronic) and the dimmer type. See Chapter 12 for information on the various types of dimmers.

Fluorescent Lamps

Fluorescent lamps use an entirely different technology than do incandescent lamps. Rather than creating heat to produce light, they create ultraviolet light to stimulate phosphors, which in turn produce visible light (Figure 7.4). The process is called fluorescence.

Fluorescent lamps begin with a sealed tube of glass with an electrode at each end. That tube is filled with one of several gases (typically argon, krypton, neon, or xenon, often two of these together) and mercury. When an electric arc is established between the two electrodes, the electricity flowing through the mercury causes it to emit *ultraviolet* (UV) light. If you've ever been to a tanning salon, the purple lamps in the tanning bed are essentially fluorescent lamps without the internal phosphor coating.

UV light, though, isn't what we're after. To transform UV to visible light the inside of the fluorescent lamp is coated with phosphors, which are minerals that emit visible light when they are subjected to UV light. Three phosphors are used: one producing a range of colors centered on blue light, one centered on green light, and one centered on orange-red light. The relative proportions of the phosphors can be adjusted to produce warm, neutral, or cool light. There are about a dozen important phosphors, and each manufacturer has a unique phosphor recipe. As a result, you may notice color differences between the lamps of two manufacturers, even though they have the same color designations. This, and other color-related issues, will be covered in Chapter 8.

The electricity in a home or office can't create and sustain the arc through the fluorescent tube without assistance. All fluorescent lamps require a *ballast* (see proceeding sidebar titled *ballasts*), which is a device that increases the pressure of the electricity, and establishes and maintains the electric arc inside the tube. The ballast is installed in the light fixture since its life is longer than that of fluorescent lamps. The one exception is for fluorescent lamps that are intended as incandescent or halogen lamp replacements (called self-ballasted lamps).

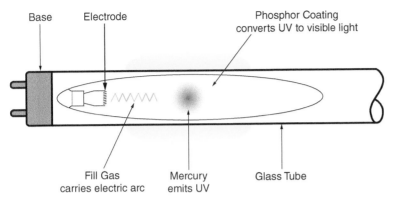

Base   Electrode   Phosphor Coating
                           converts UV to visible light

Fill Gas   Mercury   Glass Tube
carries electric arc   emits UV

Figure 7.4 Operation of a Fluorescent Lamp.

Fixtures that are designed to use incandescent lamps, such as a residential table lamp, do not have ballasts built into them, so the ballast is built into the base of the retrofit fluorescent lamp.

Unlike simple screw base incandescent lamps, it is usually not possible to change the wattage of the lamp in a fluorescent luminaire because most ballasts are designed to operate a unique lamp or set of lamps. Specialty ballasts can dim fluorescent lamps, operate lamps in very cold conditions, or save energy by under-driving the lamp.

Most designers and manufacturers separate fluorescent lamps into two groups: linear and compact. Linear fluorescents include straight tubes, usually ranging from 2' to 8' in length; large U-shaped tubes; and circular tubes (Figure 7.5). *Compact fluorescents* (CFLs) include small U-shaped and "swirl" lamps (Figure 7.6).

Although they use a two-step process (create UV, then convert the UV to visible light), both linear fluorescent and compact fluorescent lamps are much more effective at converting electricity to light than either type of incandescent lamp. Fluorescent lamps also have a much longer life than incandescent lamps (see Table 7.2). These two facts explain why we use fluorescent lamps in so many applications. A longer life and more light for less electricity results in reduced maintenance requirements and lower energy bills for the building's owner and less disruption for the building's occupants.

■ *low voltage lamps*
A lamp that operates at lower than 120V, typically 12V, and requires the use of a transformer.

■ *transformers*
A device that increases or decreases electrical pressure.

■ *fluorescent lamps*
A light source consisting of a glass tube lined with phosphors and filled with argon, krypton, or other inert gas along with mercury.

■ *ultraviolet*
Energy that is shorter in wavelength and higher in frequency than visible violet light (literally beyond the violet light).

■ *ballast*
A device required to operate fluorescent and HID lamps; it provides the necessary starting voltage and regulates the current during operation.

■ *compact fluorescents*
A small fluorescent lamp that is often used as an alternative to incandescent lighting.

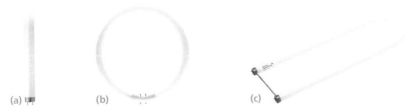

(a)   (b)   (c)

Figure 7.5 (a) Linear, (b) Circular, and (c) U-Shaped Fluorescent Lamps.
Courtesy of Philips Lighting Company.

(a) (b)

Figure 7.6 (a) U-Shaped Pin Base and (b) Swirl Self-Ballasted Compact Fluorescent Lamps.
Courtesy of Philips Lighting Company.

Table 7.2 Light Source Efficacy and Average Life

Lamp Technology	Efficacy	Average Life
Candle	.3 lm/W	—
Incandescent	8–15 lm/W	750–1,500 hrs.
Halogen	10–35 lm/W	3,000–5,000 hrs.
Self-Ballasted CFL	35–65 lm/W	6,000–8,000 hrs.
Pin-Based CFL	50–80 lm/W	10,000–20,000 hrs.
Linear Fluorescent	70–100 lm/W	15,000–45,000 hrs.

■ **high intensity discharge**
An electric discharge lamp in which an electric arc through a gas-filled chamber produces light without intermediate steps.

■ **arc tube**
The tube that contains the arc stream in an HID lamp.

■ **metal halide**
A type of HID lamp which produces light by passing an electric arc through of metal halide and mercury vapors.

High Intensity Discharge

Like fluorescent lamps, *high intensity discharge* (HID) lamps use a ballast to create an arc in a gas-filled chamber, called the *arc tube*. The contents of the arc tube, however, produce visible light without the need for phosphors, although phosphors may be used. There are several families of HID lamps including mercury vapor, sodium vapor, metal halide, and ceramic metal halide. HID lamps are very efficient, making them the ideal choice for many applications. Only *metal halide* (MH) and ceramic metal halide (CMH) lamps have color characteristics that are appropriate for indoor commercial use in spaces like atria, malls, and supermarkets, and outdoor applications such as stadiums.

The arc tube of a metal halide lamp is made of quartz, while that of a ceramic metal halide is made of ceramic. Electrodes are installed at both ends of the tube. Both types of lamps use argon, xenon, and/or neon gas to fill the tube along with any of a dozen metallic elements. The arc passes through the fill gas and causes the metals to become gaseous also, and the gases and metals both emit various wavelengths of light. In some cases phosphors may also be used to improve efficacy and color rendering by converting the lamp's UV output to visible light.

HIDs can be single- or double-ended tubular lamps (Figure 7.7). They are often enclosed in an outer bulb to protect the lamp and to filter out excess UV. The single-ended lamp can also be set inside an AR-, MR-, or PAR-shaped reflector, just as with halogen lamps.

HID lamps can be dimmed, but their response is not like that of incandescent or fluorescent lamps. They respond much more slowly than other light sources, and the dimming range is usually limited to 100–50 percent. Many HID lamps that are heated from use and then turned off must cool down before the arc can be reignited. The amount of time required is called the restrike time. Lamps that do not require a cooling period are described as *hot restrike* or hot restart. The efficacy and average life of metal halide lamps are shown in Table 7.3.

Ballasts

All fluorescent and high intensity discharge lamps require a ballast to operate. Ballasts initially provide the proper voltage to establish the arc between the lamp's electrodes. Once the arc is established, they regulate the current flowing through the lamp to maintain the light output. There are three types of *electronic ballasts*.

Rapid start electronic ballasts start the lamp in less than 1 second by heating the lamp electrodes before and during lamp operation. This heating consumes about 2W per lamp.

Instant start electronic ballasts start the lamp(s) "instantly," meaning in less than 0.1 seconds, by providing a very high starting voltage (about 600V for 4' T8 lamps). The high starting voltage means that instant start ballasts do not need to preheat the electrodes. Instant start ballasts are best suited for applications with a limited number of switch cycles (off/on) per day.

Programmed start electronic ballasts start lamps in 1 to 1.5 seconds, and are intended for applications with frequent switching, such as with luminaires connected to an occupancy sensor. Programmed start ballasts heat the lamp electrodes, but do so in a much more tightly controlled way to preserve the electrodes and extend the life of the lamp.

Most fluorescent lamps can be paired with a dimming ballast. As with transformers, dimming ballasts must be matched to the dimmer or electronic control system to operate properly.

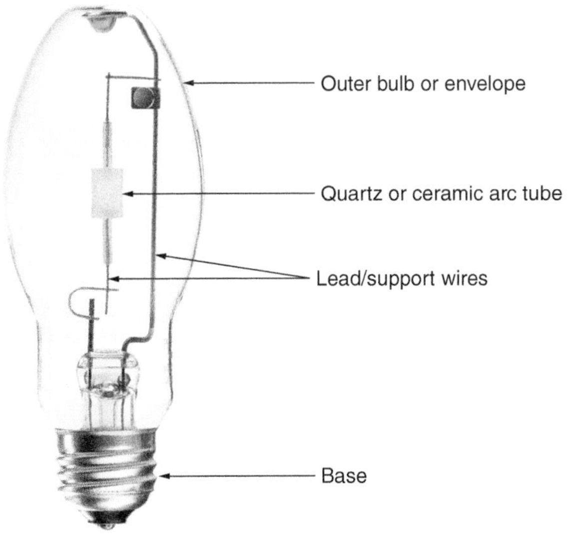

Figure 7.7 Metal Halide Lamp with Protective Outer Enclosure.
Courtesy of Philips Lighting Company.

- Outer bulb or envelope
- Quartz or ceramic arc tube
- Lead/support wires
- Base

■ *hot restrike*
Restoring the arc in an HID light source after it has been turned off.

■ *electronic ballasts*
Ballasts that use semiconductors to increase the frequency of electricity for fluorescent and HID lamp operation.

■ *rapid start electronic ballasts*
Ballasts that preheat the lamp cathodes to start the lamp.

■ *Instant start electronic ballasts*
Ballasts that ignite the lamp instantly with a very high starting voltage.

■ **programmed start
electronic ballasts**
*Ballast with a controlled
start procedure designed to
withstand frequent switching.*

Table 7.3 Light Source Efficacy and Average Life

Lamp Technology	Efficacy	Average Life
Candle	.3 lm/W	—
Incandescent	8–15 lm/W	750–1,500 hrs.
Halogen	10–35 lm/W	3,000–5,000 hrs.
Screw-Based CFL	35–65 lm/W	6,000–8,000 hrs.
Pin-Based CFL	50–80 lm/W	10,000–20,000 hrs.
Linear Fluorescent	70–100 lm/W	15,000–45,000 hrs.
Quartz Metal Halide	70–120 lm/W	10,000–20,000 hrs.
Ceramic Metal Halide	80–125 lm/W	10,000–30,000 hrs.

Light Emitting Diode

■ **light emitting diode**
*A solid state lighting device
that emits a directional beam
of light.*

The *light emitting diode* (LED) differs from the previously discussed light sources in several significant ways. First, LEDs are solid, with no gas or vacuum chambers (so they are also referred to as solid state lighting). Second, an LED naturally produces directional light. Third, each LED produces only a narrow band of the visible spectrum, which is why they are sometimes referred to as "narrow band emitters."

LEDs are comprised of two layers of materials sandwiched together (Figure 7.8). The first material is generically referred to as "P" type because it has a dearth of electrons and thus has a positive charge. The second, or "N" type material, has an excess of electrons and is negatively charged. Where the materials touch, electrons cross the juncture and create a depletion zone spanning both sides of the juncture.

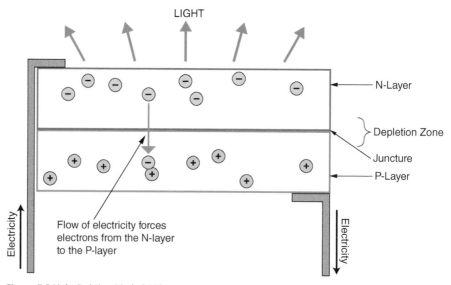

Figure 7.8 Light Emitting Diode (LED).

When direct current is applied to the N side, the electrical pressure forces electrons across to the juncture to the P side. You can think of this as balls crossing a line to fill holes on the other side. As the holes are filled, energy is emitted. With the proper P and N materials, the energy is emitted as visible light (infrared and ultraviolet LEDs also exist).

Manufacturers strive for consistency in their products, but the process of creating LEDs makes this difficult. The result is that there will always be variations in any batch of LEDs and between batches.

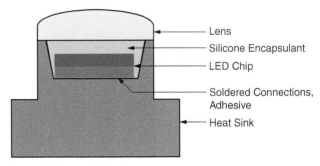

Figure 7.9 Typical LED Package.

Manufacturers test each LED for color characteristics and electrical requirements, and then sort them in a process referred to as "*binning*." If the luminaire manufacturer has very strict requirements for the LEDs they find acceptable they will have access to fewer LEDs from each production run and will therefore pay a higher price. If a luminaire manufacturer has loose requirements for the LEDs they will be able to use more of a production run and pay a lower price.

We never see LEDs by themselves. What we see are LED packages (Figure 7.9). The P and N materials are mounted on a base (which may be silicon, sapphire, ceramic, or others). LEDs are very susceptible to heat, so the base is mounted on a *heat sink*, usually made of aluminum, to draw the heat away from the juncture. A lens covers the LED to protect it and to distribute the light.

LEDs require a *driver* (also called a power supply) to operate. The driver is similar to a transformer in that it reduces the incoming voltage to voltage appropriate for the LED package. The driver also regulates the current and may convert the alternating current to direct current. If the LED luminaire is intended to dim, the driver may also include dimming electronics.

As mentioned earlier, the materials used in LEDs produce only a narrow portion of the visible spectrum. There are two methods of converting this colored light into white light. The first method is to use LEDs that produce short wavelength light (blue or UV) and phosphors like those used in fluorescent lamps. The short wavelength light excites the phosphors, which then emit visible light. The result is a range of white light similar to that available from fluorescent lamps. The phosphor method can be applied in two ways: integral phosphors or remote phosphors.

Integral phosphor white LEDs have phosphors on the LED under the lens. Remote phosphors are integrated into a lamp or luminaire (Figure 7.10). With a remote phosphor luminaire the phosphors are bonded to glass or plastic that enclose one or more LEDs.

The second method of creating white light with LEDs is to mix the light of several colored LEDS to create white (called additive mixing). This is typically done with red, green, and blue LEDs that are either assembled into an array, with mixing occurring in the space between the light source and the illuminated surface, or by focusing the

■ *binning*
The sorting of LEDs by their color characteristics and electrical requirements.

■ *heat sink*
A metal component, usually aluminum, used to draw heat away from an LED and dissipate it.

■ *driver*
The electronic device regulating electricity to LEDs.

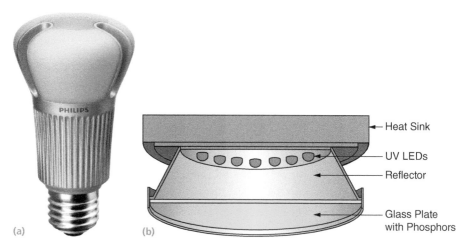

Figure 7.10 (a) Remote Phosphor Lamp and (b) Luminaire.
7.10a Courtesy of Philips Lighting Company.

LEDs into an optical chamber so that the mixing occurs before light leaves the LED luminaire.

The lamps we've discussed up to now (incandescent, fluorescent, HID) eventually fail. They completely stop producing light. The calculation of their lamp life is the length of time when one-half of a sample set has failed. LEDs themselves rarely fail completely. As they age, their light output diminishes. At some point we would say that the light output is below the minimum required for the application, so the light source must be replaced, even though light is still being produced. See the sidebar for additional information on measuring LED light output and life.

LEDs are a rapidly evolving technology, with major advances often happening several times per year. Most designers keep up-to-date on advances by following developments in industry magazines (see Appendix II), Web sites, and trade shows. You can also find updated information, links, and a blog on the authors' Web site at www.designinglight .com.

Other Lamp Technologies

Induction or Induction Discharge

Induction lamps are similar to fluorescent lamps, except that they do not have electrodes, which are the primary cause of fluorescent lamp failure. Instead of an electric arc passing through the gas-filled tube, induction lamps use an electromagnetic (EM) field to excite the fill gas and mercury (Figure 7.11). Like fluorescent lamps, the mercury produces UV light, which excites phosphors on the lamp envelope to create visible light.

Because there are no electrodes that can fail, induction lamps have a rated life of up to 100,000 hours, which makes them a good choice for hard to reach locations where the long life is the key advantage over other lamp technologies. Induction lamps are also relatively immune to effects from low temperatures, making them a good choice for use in areas subject to cold.

Cold Cathode

Cold cathode lamps are similar to fluorescent lamps. A glass tube is filled with gases, and an electric current passes through the gas to produce light. The two differences separating fluorescent and cold cathode are the lamp size/shape, and the range of colors.

Cold cathode lamps are generally made by hand and therefore can be fabricated in almost any shape and length. They are especially useful in cove lighting because they do not create socket shadows and can be made to follow the outline of curved coves. Cold cathode lamps are available in a wide range of color temperatures and colors. They have a long life, with some manufacturers claiming up to 100,000 hours. In many applications cold cathode lamps are being replaced by LEDs.

Arriving Technologies

Organic Light Emitting Diodes

Another type of *solid state lighting* (SSL), *organic light emitting diodes* (OLEDs) are similar to LEDs in that they have positive and negative layers. Light is emitted when electrons are forced from the negative layer to the positive layer. OLEDs differ from all other light sources in that they are planar in nature, not point or linear sources. OLEDs are made by placing a series of films between two conductors and encapsulating those layers for protection. When electricity is applied, the layers emit light (Figure 7.12).

The most exciting aspect of OLEDs is that the layers can be applied to a flexible surface, or substrate. In the monitor industry, this may lead to folding or roll-up displays. In the lighting industry it may mean that we will be able to apply a sheet of luminous material to any surface—the ceiling, a column, a curved wall—to deliver a soft wash of light.

As of this writing, OLEDs are suitable for use as sources of architectural illumination, but still have some drawbacks. OLEDs are less efficacious and more expensive than LEDs.

Measuring LED Life and Output

Measuring lamp life and light output of LEDs is different than it is for other light sources. This can cause confusion for designers and may result in inaccurate information from manufacturers. There are several new and evolving standards that are intended to address some of the issues. To date, the IES has taken the lead in developing the standards and encouraging manufacturers to adopt and comply with them.

The first of these standards is LM-79-08 Approved Method: Photometric Measurements of Solid State Lighting Products. (Note that LM stands for Lumen Maintenance, and the -08 indicates that the current standard was approved in 2008.) Published by the IES, LM-79 describes the procedures for testing and reporting reproducible measurements of total light output, color temperature, color rendering index, electrical power characteristics, and efficacy (in lumens/watt).

LM-79 requires testing of a complete lighting fixture. It does not apply to LED products that require external components, such as a power supply, or to bare LED packages. It also does not apply to fixtures designed for LEDs but sold without an LED light source.

LM-79 does not measure light distribution or the distribution pattern, only the total light output. As a result, it does not provide us with complete photometric performance of the fixture tested.

The second standard is LM-80-08 Approved Method: Measuring Lumen Maintenance of LED Light Sources. LM-80 does not cover luminaires, only the LED package. LM-80 does not define the end of life for an LED package. It is a method for determining the light output degradation. LM-80 outlines the testing conditions and the measurement methods that are to be used to measure, track, and report the lumen maintenance of an LED package over the course of 6,000 hours. LM-80 does not provide a means of estimating life expectancy or light output beyond 6,000 hours.

TM-21-11 Projecting Long Term Lumen Maintenance of LED Light Sources is the third standard that applies, and picks up where LM-80 leaves off. (TM stands for Technical Memorandum.) It recommends a method for projecting the lumen maintenance of LEDs using the data obtained from LM-80 testing. TM-21 is used to derive L70, which is the number of hours, or life, before the LED package is emitting 70 percent of the initial lumens. L70 is the number most frequently used by manufacturers as the life, or the useful life, of their LEDs. Some designers have criticized 70 percent as too little light output, since other common sources have lumen maintenance of 95 percent (incandescent) to 80 percent (fluorescents). The criticism has caused some manufacturers to also provide lamp life projections for L80 (80 percent of initial lumens).

■ *solid state lighting*
Refers to LED and OLED light sources.

■ *organic light emitting diodes*
A light emitting diode in which the light emitting layer is an organic compound between two electrodes.

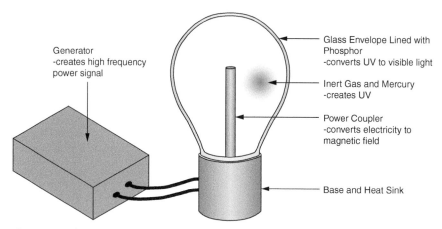

Generator
-creates high frequency power signal

Glass Envelope Lined with Phosphor
-converts UV to visible light

Inert Gas and Mercury
-creates UV

Power Coupler
-converts electricity to magnetic field

Base and Heat Sink

Figure 7.11 Induction Lamp.

They are also harder to manufacture, especially in large sizes. However, efficacy is rising, prices are falling, and researchers and manufacturers seem confident that they will overcome the challenges. Some fixture manufacturers are already producing luminaires with OLEDs, mostly as decorative pendant and sconce fixtures. It remains to be seen if the lighting industry will see widespread adoption of OLEDS, or if they will be a niche product.

OLEDs are another rapidly evolving technology. Most designers keep up-to-date on advances by following developments in industry magazines (see Appendix II), Web sites, and trade shows. You can also find updated information, links, and a blog on the authors' Web site at www.designinglight.com.

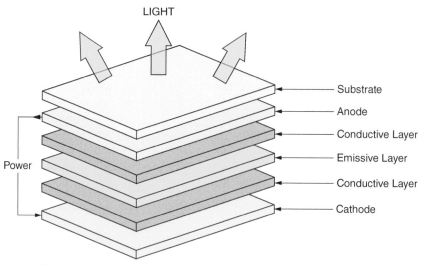

LIGHT

Substrate

Anode

Conductive Layer

Emissive Layer

Conductive Layer

Cathode

Power

Figure 7.12 Section of OLED.

Light Emitting Plasma

Another exciting new technology is *light emitting plasma*, which operates on principals similar to induction lighting. In light emitting plasma, a small quartz capsule is filled with gases and metals similar to those of a metal halide lamp. The capsule is placed in a cavity on the surface of a ceramic resonator (often called a "puck" because of its size and shape) connected to a radio frequency (RF) amplifier (Figure 7.13). The RF in the puck creates an energy wave in the capsule, ionizing the gas and evaporating the metal to create a bright white light source.

Figure 7.13 Plasma "Puck."
Courtesy of Luxim Corporation.

As with MH lamps, changing the materials within the quartz capsule changes the color qualities of the light that is produced. By adjusting the RF, light emitting plasma can be dimmed down to about 20 percent.

A few manufacturers have begun producing light emitting plasma fixtures for street lighting. It remains to be seen whether, and to what extent, this technology will be adopted for other applications.

Plasma is a rapidly evolving technology. Most designers keep up-to-date on advances by following developments in industry magazines (see Appendix II), Web sites, and trade shows. You can also find updated information, links, and a blog on the author's Web site at www.designinglight.com.

■ *light emitting plasma*
A light source in which a halogen gas and metal halides in a quartz capsule are energized to a plasma state by high frequency radio waves.

Lamp Shapes

Until the mid-2000s it was possible to know the technology of just about any lamp based on its shape. Today, manufacturers are fitting multiple technologies into traditional lamp shapes, giving designers and consumers more options than ever, but also separating lamp technology from lamp shape. The most common shape, the A-lamp, for example, is available using incandescent, halogen, compact fluorescent, and LED technologies (Figure 7.14).

It's important that we know about lamp shapes because most fixtures are designed to use only one or at most two of them. The wrong lamp shape will put the center of the light in the wrong location within the reflector, creating unpredictable, but certainly incorrect, brightness and distribution from the luminaire.

Each lamp shape is designated by one, two, or three letters. The lamp shape designation is easy to remember because it is usually the first letter of a word describing the shape.

Omnidirectional Lamps

Omnidirectional lamps emit light in every direction. Control over the distribution, therefore, comes from the light fixture and/or its accessories. The most common omnidirectional lamps are described as follows and shown in Figure 7.15.

(a)   (b)   (c)   (d)

Figure 7.14 A-Shaped (a) Incandescent, (b) Halogen, (c) CFL, and (d) LED Lamps.
Courtesy of Philips Lighting Company.

A (arbitrary) lamps (Figure 7.15a) are typically incandescent or halogen, although man-ufacturers are packaging compact fluorescent and LED lamps in this familiar shape. Wattage can range from 15 to 150W with clear, frosted, white, or colored envelopes. The BT (bulged tubular) lamp (Figure 7.15b) is a variation on the A lamp, and can usually be substituted for one.

B (blunt-tip, or bullet) and CA (candle flame) lamps (Figures 7.15c and 7.15d) are usually low to medium wattage (10–60W), incandescent, decorative lamps used in chande-liers, and wall sconces. Their envelopes may be clear or frosted.

C (cone-shaped) lamps (Figure 7.15e) are usually incandescent. They are commonly used in night-lights and in older style Christmas tree lights.

F (flame) lamps (Figure 7.15f) are decorative incandescent lamps that are available in low to medium wattage (25-60W) with clear, frosted, or amber envelopes.

G (globe) lamps (Figure 7.15g) are medium wattage lamps (25–60W) frequently used as decorative lamps in marquees, decorative fixtures, and around makeup mirrors. Their envelope may be clear, frosted, or white.

P and PS (pear-shaped) lamps (Figure 7.15h) are usually incandescent, high wattage (250W and up) lamps. Their envelopes may be clear or frosted.

T (tube) lamps (Figures 7.15i and 7.15J) are available in incandescent, quartz, fluores-cent, and HID technologies and in a wide range of sizes and wattages. They may have clear, frosted, white, or colored envelopes.

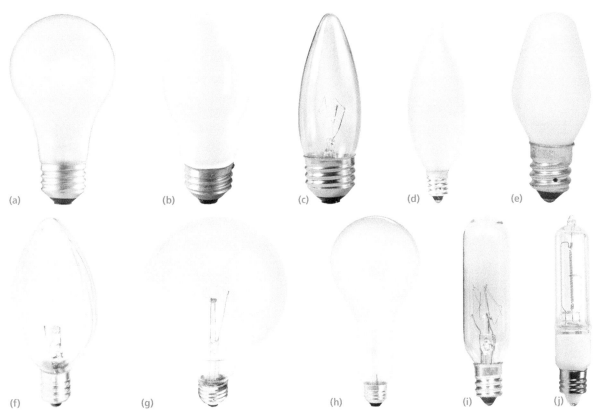

Figure 7.15 Basic Omnidirectional Lamp Shapes (Not to Scale).
Courtesy of Philips Lighting Company.

Directional Lamps

Directional lamps have a built-in reflector, and may have a built-in lens. As a result, the lamp controls most of the distribution, although additional control can be provided by the fixture or its accessories. The most common directional lamps are described as follows and shown in Figure 7.16.

Figure 7.16 Basic Directional Lamp Shapes (Not to Scale).
Courtesy of Philips Lighting Company.

R (reflector) lamps (Figure 7.16a) are used to house most lamp technologies (incandescent, halogen, compact fluorescent, HID). Designed with a very simple reflector, they are usually available in spot or flood beam spreads. The compact fluorescent versions are self-ballasted. The HID versions are not.

PAR (parabolic aluminized reflector) lamps (Figures 7.16b and 7.16c), like R lamps, are used to house most lamp technologies (incandescent, halogen, HID, LED), with halogen being the most common. PAR lamps are available in a very wide range of wattages and beam spreads. To achieve a wide range of beam spreads, the light source (filament or quartz capsule) is placed at the focal point of the parabolic reflector. The parabolic reflector is unique in that all of the light that strikes it is reflected out of the lamp in parallel rays. This makes it relatively easy to design a lens for the face of the lamp that provides excellent beam shaping.

MR (multireflector) lamps (Figure 7.16d) are available with halogen, HID, and LED light sources. They are available in a wide range of wattages and beam spreads. MR lamps are small and are available in MR-8, MR-11, and MR-16 sizes (see the Lamp Sizes section that follows). The many facets of the MR reflector are shaped and oriented to provide the required beam angle. MR lamps are typically low voltage (12V) but are also available for line voltage operation.

AR (aluminum reflector) lamps (Figure 7.16e) are available with halogen or HID light sources. They are unique in two ways. First, the reflector is made of formed aluminum, not glass as with the other directional lamps. Second, the lamp has a cap over it which blocks all light leaving the light source in the direction of the face of the lamp. As a result, all of the light leaving the AR bounces off of the reflector. The reflector's facets, like those of an MR lamp, determine the beam angle.

Lamp Sizes

Each lamp shape is available in several sizes. We have to understand lamp sizing because fixtures are usually designed to accept only one lamp shape of only one size. Lamp size is determined by measuring the lamp at its widest diameter. In the U.S. the unit of measurement is 1/8″, although the denominator is dropped when the size is stated. For example, an MR lamp with a 2″ diameter is measured as 16/8″ and is described at an MR16 (not as an MR16/8). In most of the rest of the world lamp size is measured in millimeters. Figure 7.17 provides a ruler with markings for common lamp sizes.

As you can see from Figures 7.18 through 7.21, all lamp shapes are available in several sizes. The variety of sizes is related to the variety of wattages available.

The most common linear fluorescent lamps are available in T5, T8, and T12 in various lengths (Figure 7.19). However, the T12 lamp is being phased out because it is the least efficient of the three, so designers no longer use them as part of a new lighting design.

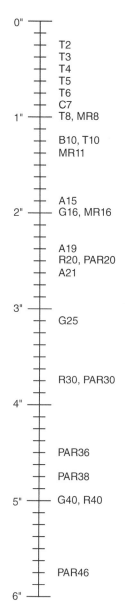

Figure 7.17 Lamp Ruler with Markings for Common Lamps.

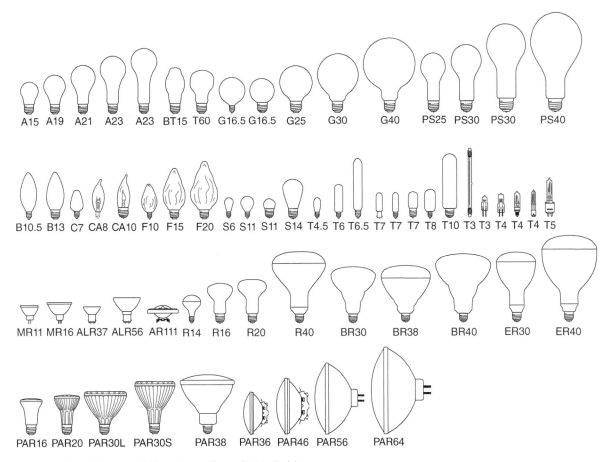

Figure 7.18 Incandescent and Halogen Lamp Shapes (Not to Scale).
Courtesy of Philips Lighting Company.

The shapes of compact fluorescent lamps are similar among manufacturers (Figure 7.20), but the names for those shapes are not. Table 7.4 shows the names that the three largest manufacturers use to describe common CFL shapes. Lamp size (generally meaning length) varies by wattage, with higher wattage lamps longer than lower wattage lamps.

Figure 7.21 illustrates common lamp shapes and sizes for HID lamps.

Table 7.4 Compact Fluorescent Lamp Designations by Manufacturer

Manufacturer	Figure 7.20a	Figure 7.20b	Figure 7.20c	Figure 7.20d
GE	Biax or BX	Double Biax or DBX	Triple Biax or TBX	2D
Philips	PL-S (short)	PL-C (cluster)	PL-T (triple)	PL-Q
Sylvania	Dulux S (single)	Dulux D (double)	Dulux T (triple)	–

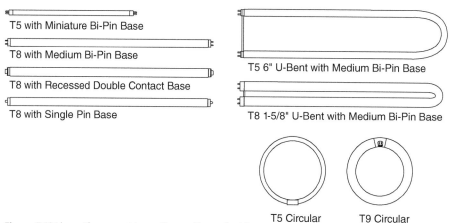

T5 with Miniature Bi-Pin Base

T8 with Medium Bi-Pin Base

T8 with Recessed Double Contact Base

T8 with Single Pin Base

T5 6" U-Bent with Medium Bi-Pin Base

T8 1-5/8" U-Bent with Medium Bi-Pin Base

T5 Circular   T9 Circular

Figure 7.19 Linear Fluorescent Lamp Shapes (Not to Scale).
Courtesy of Philips Lighting Company.

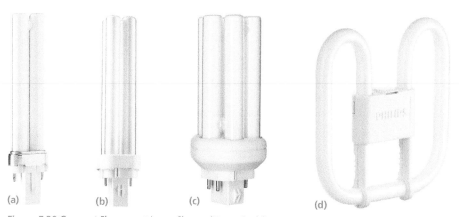

(a)   (b)   (c)   (d)

Figure 7.20 Compact Fluorescent Lamp Shapes (Not to Scale).
Courtesy of Philips Lighting Company.

Lamp Bases

Most fixtures are available with only one type of socket. Many lamp shapes are available with more than one base. So, it's important for us to be able to select a lamp that has the correct lamp shape and size *and* the correct base in order for the lamp to fit into the fixture and perform as expected. Figures 7.22 through 7.25 identify typical lamp bases for each technology.

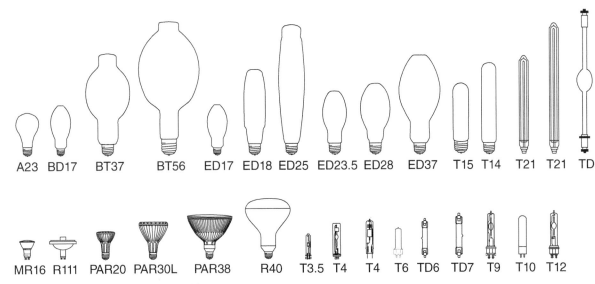

A23 BD17 BT37 BT56 ED17 ED18 ED25 ED23.5 ED28 ED37 T15 T14 T21 T21 TD

MR16 R111 PAR20 PAR30L PAR38 R40 T3.5 T4 T4 T6 TD6 TD7 T9 T10 T12

Figure 7.21 HID Lamp Shapes (Not to Scale).
Courtesy of Philips Lighting Company.

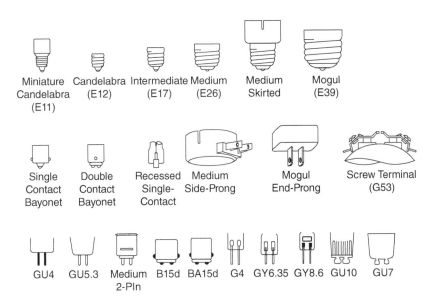

Miniature Candelabra (E11) Candelabra (E12) Intermediate (E17) Medium (E26) Medium Skirted Mogul (E39)

Single Contact Bayonet Double Contact Bayonet Recessed Single-Contact Medium Side-Prong Mogul End-Prong Screw Terminal (G53)

GU4 GU5.3 Medium 2-Pin B15d BA15d G4 GY6.35 GY8.6 GU10 GU7

Figure 7.22 Incandescent and Halogen Bases (Not to Scale).
Courtesy of Philips Lighting Company.

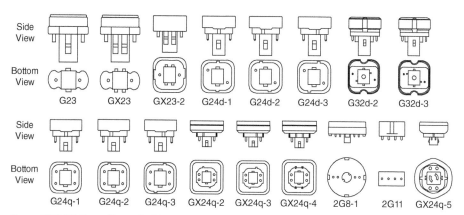

Figure 7.23 CFL Bases (Not to Scale).
Courtesy of Philips Lighting Company.

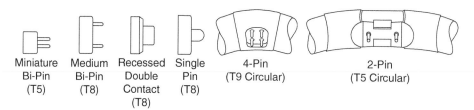

Figure 7.24 Linear Fluorescent Bases.
Courtesy of Philips Lighting Company.

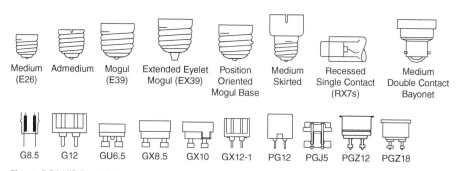

Figure 7.25 HID Lamp Bases.
Courtesy of Philips Lighting Company.

Beam Angle and Field Angle

Directional lamps (AR, MR, PAR, R) produce a cone or beam of light. The center of the beam is also the brightest part of the beam. Regardless of the measured intensity, we can say that the center beam has a relative intensity of 100 percent. As one moves from the center toward the edge of the cone, the intensity decreases and there is a point at which the intensity is 50 percent of the center beam intensity. The angle with its edges at 50 percent of center beam intensity is called the *beam angle* (see Figure 7.26).

The beam angle is the measurement used to describe the cone of light produced by a reflector lamp and is always given by the manufacturer. The designations used to describe the beam angle are shown in Table 7.5.

■ *beam angle*
The angle through the center of the beam where the light level has fallen to 50 percent of the beam's maximum brightness.

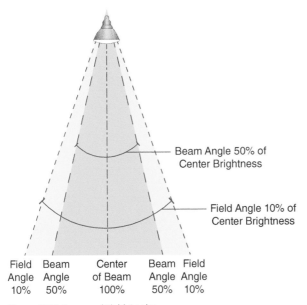

Beam Angle 50% of Center Brightness

Field Angle 10% of Center Brightness

| Field Angle 10% | Beam Angle 50% | Center of Beam 100% | Beam Angle 50% | Field Angle 10% |

Figure 7.26 Beam and Field Angles.

Table 7.5 Beam Angle Designations and Angles

Description	Designation	Approximate Beam Angle (varies by manufacturer)
Very Narrow Spot	VNSP	<10°
Narrow Spot	NSP	5°–15°
Spot	SP	5°–15°
Narrow Flood	NFL	20°–30°
Flood	FL	25°–40°
Medium Flood	MFL	30°–45°
Wide Flood	WFL	40°–50°
Very Wide Flood	VWFL	50°–60°

■ *field angle*
The angle through the center of the beam where the light level has fallen to 10 percent of the beam's maximum brightness.

The beam angle isn't the entire cone of light. As one moves outside of the beam angle, there is a point at which the intensity falls to 10 percent of the center beam intensity. The angle with its edges at 10 percent of center beam intensity is called the *field angle*. The lamp manufacturers do not always provide this information in their catalogs or Web sites.

Of course, there is light beyond the field angle but this is usually disregarded. In most instances the light beyond the field angle blends into the beam and field of adjacent luminaires and is not considered to be significant. There are special circumstances where the field angle, and light beyond the field angle, may be important. For example, imagine a dimly illuminated gallery with art on the walls. If a single lamp illuminates each work of art, we would see the entire cone of light as it hits the wall. In this installation, the quality of the field edge and the light beyond the field could be significant. In this case it would be wise to test the lamps from several manufacturers to observe the beam edge before deciding on the lamp to use.

Describing a Lamp

Incandescent and Halogen Lamps

Within the lighting industry there are basic nomenclature (naming) formats that are used to describe most lamps. The format was established by the National Electrical Manufacturers Association (NEMA). For incandescent and halogen lamps, the format is to list the lamp's wattage followed by the shape and size. This is followed by a slash and then additional information. For example, a 100W A19 that is clear is 100A19/CL.

Wattage	Shape	Size	Additional Information
100	A	19	CL

A 60W G40 that has a white envelope is 60G40/W.

Wattage	Shape	Size	Additional Information
60	G	40	W

To describe or specify any type of directional lamp, the beam spread must be indicated. A 100W PAR38 with a flood beam spread is 100PAR38/FL. Since FL is not very specific, many manufacturers add the actual beam angle to the beam angle description. The PAR described previously with a 35° beam angle would then be 100PAR38/FL35.

Wattage	Shape	Size	Additional Information
100	PAR	38	FL35

Lamp manufacturers may add their own specific information into the format to describe their products and to differentiate them from the competition. For example, a 50W MR16 lamp with a 35–40° beam is described as follows. Note that manufacturer specific additions to the standard format are in red.

GE Lighting	Q50MR16/C/FL40
Philips Lighting	50MR16/FL36
Sylvania	50MR16/FL35/C

When searching a Web site, catalog PDF, or printed catalog, you'll find that a great deal of information is available for each lamp: the lamp base, size, wattage, beam spread, and more. Figure 7.27 is an example of the catalog page where the Philips lamp noted earlier was found.

The lamp catalogs present us with the following additional information:

1. The product number, product code, or PC is the lamp company's internal identification number. We can usually ignore this column.
2. Class filament describes the geometry of the filament. We rarely have a choice of filament designs in any given lamp, so this information is usually not part of our decision making process.
3. MOL stands for maximum overall length. This is the maximum size allowed for this particular lamp according to NEMA standards.
4. MBCP is the middle beam candle power (also CBCP for center beam candle power), which is the light output at the centerline of the beam.
5. Lumens is the total amount of light produced by the lamp.

Halogen Lamps

Mini Reflector, ALR, ALUline PRO III, Twistline, and Linear Lamps

Watts	Bulb	Base	Product Number	Symbols, Footnotes	Ordering Code	Volts	Pkg Qty‡	Description	Class Filament	MOL (In.)	Rated Avg. Life (Hrs.)(93)	Approx. MBCP†	Lumens	Life Years (446)	Energy Cost (445)	Color Temp. (K)
Halogen MR (Formerly Accent Line) (91)													**FTC REQUIREMENTS**			
20	MR16	GU5.3	37802-6		20MR16/SP10 ESX	12	50	Spot 10°	C, C-8	1⅞	3000	3400	240	2.7	$2.41	3100
			37803-4		20MR16/FL36 BAB	12	50	Flood 36°	C, C-8	1⅞	3000	550	240	2.7	$2.41	3100
35	MR16	GU5.3	14056-6		35MR16/FL36	12	50	Flood 36°	C, C-8	1⅞	3000	1000	540	2.7	$4.22	3000
50	MR16	GU5.3	37804-2		50MR16/SP10 EXT	12	50	Spot 10°	C, C-8	1⅞	3000	8800	790	2.7	$6.02	3100
			37807-5		50MR16/NFL24 EXZ	12	50	Narrow Flood 24°	C, C-8	1⅞	3000	2500	800	2.7	$6.02	3100
			37805-9		50MR16/NFL36 EXN	12	50	Flood 36°	C, C-8	1⅞	3000	1600	850	2.7	$6.02	3100
ALUline PRO III																
50	ALU Pro III	G53	13396-6		ALU111MM 50W G53 12V 8D	12	6	Spot 8°	C, C-8	2 31/64	3000	23,000	950	2.7	$6.02	3000
			13397-4		ALU111MM 50W G53 12V 24D	12	6	Flood 24°	C, C-8	2 31/64	3000	4000	950	2.7	$6.02	3000
75	ALU Pro III	G53	13398-2		ALU111MM 75W G53 12V 8D	12	6	Spot 8°	C, C-8	2 31/64	3000	30,000	1575	2.7	$9.03	3000

For the most current product information, go to the e-catalog on **www.philips.com**

Halogen symbols and footnotes located on page 109

Figure 7.27 Typical Printed Catalog Lamp Information.
Courtesy of Philips Lighting Company.

6. Rated life is typically based on tests where the lamps are on for three hours at a time. More frequent switching usually decreases lamp life. Less frequent switching usually increases lamp life.

7. Color temperature describes the relative warmth or coolness of the color of the light. This will be covered in detail in Chapter 8.

Fluorescent Lamps

The designation for linear fluorescent lamps begins with an "F." This is followed by wattage, lamp shape, and lamp size. After the slash is information about the color temperature and color rendering of the lamp (which we'll cover in detail in Chapter 8). The standard format for this information is a three number code. The first number describes the CRI range (8 in the 80s, 9 in the 90s). The next two numbers are the first two numbers of the lamp's color temperature. For example, a 32W T8 linear fluorescent with a CRI of 84 and a color temperature of 3,000K would be described as F32T8/830.

Again, the lamp manufacturers modify the format to identify their products. The lamp described in the previous paragraph is shown next with modifications. Note that the manufacturer's specific additions to the standard format are in red. Figure 7.28 is the catalog page for the Philips lamp.

GE Lighting	F32T8/SPX30/ECO
Philips Lighting	F32T8/TL830/ALTO
Sylvania	FO32T8/830/ECO

Fluorescent Lamps
800 Series T8 Lamps, 700 Series T8 Lamps

Watts	Product Number	Symbols, Footnotes	Ordering Code	Pkg. Qty.	Description	Nom. Length (In.)	Rated Average Life 3 Hr. Start (202)	12 Hr. Start (241)	Approx. Initial Lumens (203, 204)	Design Lumens (208, 239)	CRI
800 Series T8 Fluorescent Lamps											
T8 Medium Bipin Featuring ALTO II Technology											
17	28188-1	$ • †	F17T8/TL835/ALTO	30	TL 835, 3500K	24	24,000	30,000	1350	1280	84
	28189-9	$ • †	F17T8/TL841/ALTO	30	TL 841, 4100K	24	24,000	30,000	1350	1280	82
	28090-9	$ • †	F17T8/TL850/ALTO	30	TL 850, 5000K	24	24,000	30,000	1300	1235	82
25	28190-7	$ • †	F25T8/TL835/ALTO	30	TL 835, 3500K	36	24,000	30,000	2150	2040	85
	28191-5	$ • †	F25T8/TL841/ALTO	30	TL 841, 4100K	36	24,000	30,000	2150	2040	84
	28092-5	$ • †	F25T8/TL850/ALTO	30	TL 850, 5000K	36	24,000	30,000	2150	2040	82
32	28151-9	$ • ® †	F32T8/TL830/ALTO	30	TL 830, 3000K	48	24,000	30,000	2850	2710	85
	28153-5	$ • ® †	F32T8/TL835/ALTO	30	TL 835, 3500K	48	24,000	30,000	2850	2710	84
	28155-0	$ • ® †	F32T8/TL841/ALTO	30	TL 841, 4100K	48	24,000	30,000	2850	2710	82
	27235-1	$ • ® †	F32T8/TL841/ALTO PLZ	1350	TL 841, 4100K	48	24,000	30,000	2850	2710	82
	28156-8	$ • ® †	F32T8/TL850/ALTO	30	TL 850, 5000K	48	24,000	30,000	2850	2710	82
40	36834-0	$ • †	F40T8/TL835/ALTO	25	TL 835, 3500K	60	24,000	30,000	3725	3500	84
	36847-2	$ • †	F40T8/TL841/ALTO	25	TL 841, 4100K	60	24,000	30,000	3725	3500	82

For the most current product information, go to the e-catalog on **www.philips.com**
Fluorescent symbols and footnotes located on page 40

Figure 7.28 Typical Fluorescent Lamp Catalog Page.
Courtesy of Philips Lighting Company.

The additional information specific to linear fluorescent, compact fluorescent, and HID lamps is the following:

1. The light output of all lamps decreases as the lamp is used. The mean lumen values tell us the average output over the life of the lamp.
2. Color rendering index (CRI) describes how well we can distinguish colors when objects are illuminated with this lamp. This will be covered in Chapter 8.

HID Lamps

HID lamps follow a very different nomenclature that is not as easy to read. The sequence of characters is as follows:

Lamp Type Classification Letter Electrical Characteristics Number/Luminaire Characteristic Letter, as in X123/Y.

The first character identifies the lamp type:

B—Self-ballasted mercury lamps

C—Ceramic metal halide lamps

H—Mercury lamps

L—Low-pressure sodium lamps

M—Quartz metal halide lamps

S—High pressure sodium

Other manufacturer specific codes are allowed.

The next three characters describe the lamp's electrical characteristics and have no specific meaning. They is followed by a slash.

The final character identifies the luminaire characteristics:

E—Requires an enclosed luminaire

F—Requires an enclosed luminaire and UV barrier

O—May be used in an open luminaire

S—May be used in open luminaires, but only in certain positions (otherwise requires an enclosed luminaire)

Finally, additional information may be added by the manufacturer.

LED Lamps

White light LEDs are evaluated and specified in the same manner as white fluorescent or HID lamps—by color temperature and color rendition index.

A Note about Luminaires with LEDs

There are always a variety of colored LEDs available to luminaire manufacturers, and the luminaire tested by a designer may not be the luminaire that is later delivered and installed. What does this mean for the designer? What can one do when a color mixing LED fixture tested and specified this year may not have the same LEDs when it's delivered to the job site two years from now? There are two approaches: focus on the color of the LED, or focus on the colors that are to be created in mixing the output of the LEDs.

The first approach requires that the designer identify the color characteristics of the LEDs tested. The information may come from either the luminaire manufacturer or the LED chip manufacturer. That information can be written into a specification that requires the contractor to supply a fixture with the same color characteristics or within a specified tolerance.

The second approach is to identify the colors that the system must be able to create, expressed as *chromaticity* coordinates (a colorimeter used during mock-ups or fixture testing will give the coordinates). As long as those colors fall within the gamut of the delivered luminaire, regardless of the color characteristics of the LEDs, the colors can be produced. Keep in mind, however, that the colors may be *metamers* of the original colors. They will appear to be the same on a white surface, but may not appear the same on colored surfaces. Color issues are covered in detail in Chapter 8.

■ *chromaticity*
Refers to the color of a light source independent of its brightness.

■ *metamers*
Two or more light sources of the same apparent color but having different spectral power distributions.

The LED for illumination industry is young and, as of this publication date, there is no industry standard for specifying colored LEDs. However, there are some common practices. The first is to identify the color by its hue. The second is to identify the color by its peak wavelength. Other information used by manufacturers includes the spectral bandwidth at 50 percent (meaning the bandwidth at 50 percent of the peak intensity) or the wavelengths at 50 percent of peak intensity.

Unfortunately, not only is the information available from LED lamp manufacturers not standardized, but LED lamp and fixture manufacturers may not identify the LED chip manufacturer(s) they use. This gives them the freedom to purchase components from any manufacturer whose LEDs meet the lamp or fixture manufacturer's specifications. Those specifications may change in response to the fixture manufacturer's product development. LED chip development is moving at a rapid pace, and it is common for a particular chip to be in production for only a few years before it is replaced by an improved model that may have different color characteristics. These issues can result in a mismatch between a lamp or luminaire that a designer evaluates and the lamp or luminaire that is delivered to a project.

Selecting a Light Source

Lighting designers must know so much information about the simple light bulb that it can make the process of choosing a light source seem overwhelming. Where does one begin? Start by considering the desirable qualities of the lamps. Think about the light levels, energy efficiency, lamp life, and light quality that the design requires and then search for a light source that has those qualities.

What if you're not sure about the quality of light from a particular lamp? Contact your local sales rep from the lamp manufacturer in question. They can usually send one or two sample lamps at no charge so you can evaluate the lamp for yourself. Any time you are not sure about a lamp, fixture, or detail, it's best to perform a mock-up, as discussed in Chapter 2. Always avoid guessing in favor of knowing.

Light Output

The most obvious question about any lamp is, "How much light does it produce?" In general, we want to select the most efficient light source, but not if it is going to produce too much or too little light, or light of the wrong color or quality. In practice, we need to consider the light output of the lamp and the efficiency of the light fixture as a system. Similar looking fixtures can have widely different efficiencies (meaning they don't all put the same amount of light into the room), resulting in the need for brighter or dimmer lamps to achieve the same illumination levels.

Quality of Light

Each light source has a particular quality of light that can add to, or detract from, the aesthetics of the space being illuminated. The designer must consider the quality of light anew on each project. Issues of color rendition, color temperature, dimming ability, and distribution are considered each time a light source is selected.

Light Control

Efficient and effective optical systems can be built around small light sources such as a halogen, LED, or ceramic metal halide lamps, making them good choices for applications that require excellent control of the light distribution. Applications such as selective illumination of a facade, landscape highlighting, and precise illumination of artworks all require high degrees of control of the beam of light. Designs that depend on broad distribution may rely on lamps such as linear or compact fluorescents.

Energy Efficiency

Efficiency (actually efficacy as discussed at the beginning of this chapter) is always important, but it is more important in some applications than in others. As usage increases, so does cost of ownership and the need to minimize the environmental impact of a light source. For high usage applications such as most commercial projects, select lamps that use less energy such as LEDs, ceramic metal halide, and fluorescent. Low efficacy lamps, such as incandescent and halogen lamps, are a better choice for low brightness and/or short use applications such as residences and restaurants.

Maintenance and Cost of Ownership

The maintenance requirements of a light source and luminaire become important considerations for luminaires that are in use most of the time or are in hard to reach locations. Lamp replacement is the most obvious maintenance issue. Fixtures that are hard to access should use long life lamps to minimize the frequency of replacement. Other maintenance considerations are the life of supporting components such as ballasts and transformers, and the installation environment's impact on the luminaire (incandescent lamps do not do well with vibration, LEDs are sensitive to high temperatures, etc.). The lamp typically represents only 5 percent of the cost of ownership, labor for maintenance 5–10 percent, with the balance of the cost in energy use. All of this information is summarized in Table 7.6.

Table 7.6 Comparison of Light Source Characteristics

Light Source	Output Range	Color Temp.	CRI	Control of Beam	Lamp Life (hrs)	Initial Cost	Cost of Ownership
Incandescent	Low	2,500 to 2,900	100	Excellent	750 to 2,000	$	$$$$
Halogen	Low to Medium	2,800 to 3,200	100	Excellent	2,000 to 5,000	$$	$$$
Compact Fluorescent	Low to High	2,700 to 6,500	Low 80s	Fair	10,000 to 20,000	$$$	$$
Linear Fluorescent	Medium to High	3,000 to 6,500	60 to 90+	Fair	15,000 to 45,000	$$	$$
Metal Halide	Medium to High	2,700 to 5,600	80 to 95+	Good to Excellent	10,000 to 30,000	$$$	$$
LED	Low to High	2,700 to 9,000	60 to mid-90s	Poor to Excellent	20,000 to 50,000	$$$$	$$

Lamp Information for Consumers

Designers whose practice includes residential work can help their clients select the most appropriate lamps by explaining the lighting facts label found on each lamp's packaging. Unfortunately, there are two different lighting facts labels. The U.S. Department of Energy requires manufacturers of LED retrofit lamps (those intended to replace incandescent lamps) to have a label that looks like the one shown in Figure 7.29.

The U.S. Federal Trade Commission requires manufacturers of incandescent, halogen, and compact fluorescent lamps for consumers to have one of the two labels shown in Figure 7.30.

Online Resources

GE Lighting, www.gelighting.com

GE Lighting Online Catalog, http://genet.gelighting.com/LightProducts/Dispatcher? REQUEST=PRODUCTS&PRODUCTLINE=Lamps&CHANNEL=Commercial

Osram Sylvania Lighting, www.sylvania.com

Osram Sylvania online and PDF catalogs, www.sylvania.com/en-us/tools-and-resources/Pages/catalogs.aspx

Philips Lighting, www.usa.lighting.philips.com/

Philips Lighting Online Catalog, www.usa.ecat.lighting.philips.com/l/professional-lamps/39744/cat/

Philips Catalog PDF Download page, www.usa.lighting.philips.com/connect/tools_literature/

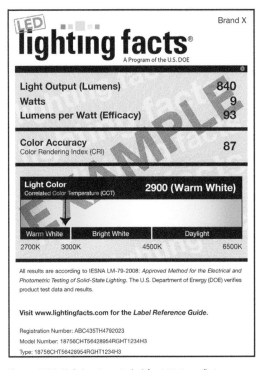

Figure 7.29 Lighting Facts Label for LED Retrofit Lamps.
Courtesy of U.S. Department of Energy.

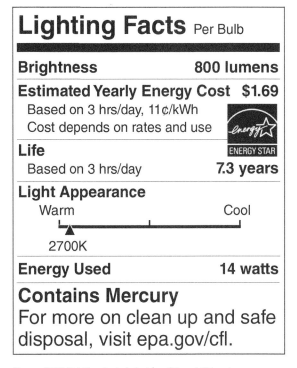

Figure 7.30 Lighting Facts Label for CFL and Other Lamps
Containing Mercury
Courtesy of Philips Lighting Company.

Philips catalog is also available as an app in the iPad and Android stores.

Satco, www.satco.com

Ushio, www.ushio.com

Advanced Lighting Guide www.algonline.com click on Sources & Auxiliaries

American National Standards Institute (ANSI), www.ansi.org

Lighting Facts (for LEDs), www.lightingfacts.com

Lighting Facts (for other lamps), www.energy.gov and search for "Lighting Facts Label"

National Lighting Product Information Program at the Lighting Research Center, www
.lrc.rpi.edu/programs/NLPIP/index.asp

NEMA, www.nema.org

EPA site for consumer information about CFLs such as recycling and cleanup of a bro-
ken lamp, www.epa.gov/cfl

Designing with Light Resources

Wiley's companion site to *Designing with Light*, www.wiley.com/go/designingwithlight

Author's companion site to *Designing with Light*, www.designinglight.com

References

ANSI C78.380-2005 High-Intensity Discharge Lamps, Method of Designation, Roslyn, VA: National Electrical Manufacturers Association, 2005.

Atlas Full Line Catalog 2012–2013, Philips Advance, accessed September 19, 2013, www.usa.lighting.philips.com/pwc_li/us_en/connect/advance/assets/4-01_to_4-11_Atlas2012_.pdf.

Bauman, Thomas, Birgit Rudat, and Daniel Volz, "Manufacturing of OLEDs—Challenges and Solutions," *EE Times Europe* article related to LED Lighting, accessed September 19, 2013, www.ledlighting-eetimes.com/en/manufacturing-of-oleds-challenges-and-solutions.html?cmp_id=71&news_id=222908587.

Bernecker, Craig, Chip Israel, Eric Lind, and Naomi Miller. "Fact Versus Fiction: SSL Technology Master Class." International Association of Lighting Designers, Consolidated Edison, New York City. December 1, 2011.

DiLauria, David, et al., *The Lighting Handbook, Tenth Edition*, New York: Illuminating Engineering Society, 2011.

IES Nomenclature Committee, *RP-16-05 Nomenclature and Definitions for Illuminating Engineering*, New York: Illuminating Engineering Society, 2005.

"Induction Lighting: An Old Lighting Technology Made New Again," U.S. Department of Energy, accessed September 20, 2013, http://energy.gov/energysaver/articles/induction-lighting-old-lighting-technology-made-new-again.

"Portfolio," QL Company, accessed September 20, 2013, www.qlcompany.com/en/portfolio/.

CHAPTER 8

Color in Light

"Soon it got dusk, a grapy dusk, a purple dusk over tangerine groves
and long melon fields; the sun the color of pressed grapes, slashed with
burgundy red, the fields the color of love and Spanish mysteries."

Jack Kerouac, *On the Road*

There are two aspects of color and light that lighting designers need to understand: tints of white light and *spectral colors*. For most of the history of lighting design the majority of architectural lighting designers rarely, if ever, worked with colored light. It was not considered appropriate for most architectural settings, so the use of color was limited to warm, neutral, and cool tints of white light.

> ■ *spectral colors*
> *The individual colors of the visible spectrum.*

Today, that is no longer true. Colored light is accepted in a wide range of building types, either as a visual accent or as a primary light source. Color can be an integral part of the lighting design, and can create atmosphere, add accents, and distinguish a project from others like it. Designers who don't understand color are at a distinct disadvantage because it can, if used appropriately, be a very powerful design tool.

Colors of White Light

Everyone is familiar with the terms "warm" and "cool" white light. Warm light sources include candles, incandescent lamps, and some fluorescent lamps. Cool light sources include some fluorescent lamps and daylight. Warm and cool are useful terms to use with clients because they are broadly understood. However, when discussing light with other lighting professionals, or specifying a color of white light, these generic terms are inadequate. Instead, we refer to a light source's color temperature.

Color Temperature

Color temperature is a way of specifying the warmth or coolness of white light. It is based on the changes that occur in an incandescent source as it is heated. For example, if we have an object such as a piece of iron and begin to heat it we find that the first color of light emitted is a dull red. As the temperature increases, the color of light emitted gradually shifts, becoming orange, then yellow, then white, then a pale blue, and then a deeper blue as the object's temperature continues to rise.

> ■ *color temperature*
> *The temperature of a blackbody radiator having a chromaticity equal to that of the light source, expressed in Kelvin.*

■ **blackbody radiator**
A theoretical object that is a perfect absorber of all energy that strikes it, and that is an ideal emitter of energy. Its SPD is based on its temperature.

■ **spectral power distribution curve**
A graphic plot of a light source's radiant power at each wavelength of light.

At a given temperature, different incandescing materials will emit light of different colors, so in order to discuss colors of incandescence we need a standard point of reference. That standard is a *blackbody radiator*. A blackbody is an object or material that perfectly absorbs all electromagnetic energy that strikes it. It is also a perfect incandescent radiator, in that gives off more power at a given wavelength than any other light source with the same temperature.

If a blackbody is heated, it radiates energy but not equally at all wavelengths. As the temperature increases, and thus the amount of radiated energy increases, the peak wavelength of visible light emitted shifts from red (long wavelength and low energy) to blue (short wavelength and high energy). When this information is shown on a graph, it is called a *spectral power distribution curve* (SPD). An SPD is a plot of a light source's radiant power at each wavelength of light. Figure 8.1 shows the SPD of a blackbody at several temperatures. Note that a blackbody is a theoretical object, not a real one. The spectrum is computed mathematically using an equation that was developed by Max Planck (Figure 3.10).

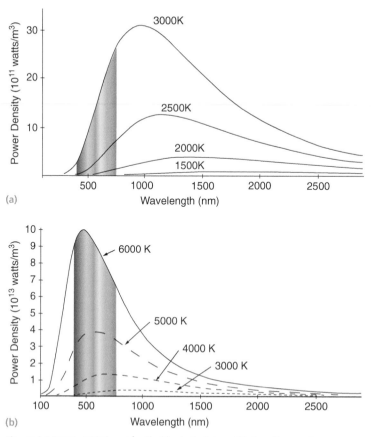

Figure 8.1 Energy Emissions of a Blackbody Radiator at Various Temperatures.

When discussing color temperature the reference standard we use is the color of light emitted by a blackbody radiator. That takes care of the color part, but what about the temperature part? The scale used to measure the blackbody's temperature is the Kelvin scale. It is named after Lord William Thompson, 1st Baron Kelvin (Figure 8.2), a mathematician, physicist, and engineer who was the first person to calculate absolute zero (the coldest temperature possible) as –273°C. The Kelvin scale is similar to the Celsius scale in that each degree of Kelvin measures the same amount of temperature change as a degree Celsius. However, the Kelvin scale's zero point is at absolute zero (–273°C or –459°F) instead of some other reference point as with the Celsius and Fahrenheit scales. Benchmark temperatures in all three scales are shown in Table 8.1.

Now we have a reference standard, a blackbody radiator, which emits a known spectrum and therefore color at each temperature, which we measure in Kelvin. With that information we can now examine the spectrum of other light sources and compare them to our standard. When we do so, we find that a typical 100W incandescent lamp produces a spectrum nearly identical to that of the blackbody when it is heated to 2,850K. Therefore, we say that the color temperature of the incandescent lamp is 2,850K. Some additional color temperatures are given in Figure 8.3.

Figure 8.2 Lord William Thompson, 1st Baron Kelvin (1824–1907); Painting by Sir Hubert von Herkomer. *Wikimedia Commons, PD-User: MaterialScientist, accessed on March 27, 2014.*

There is an online tool that allows you to see the SPD for a blackbody radiator at any temperature at http://phet.colorado.edu/en/simulation/blackbody-spectrum here.

Correlated Color Temperature

Strictly speaking, the concept of color temperature only applies to incandescent light sources because a blackbody radiator is incandescent. However, we can compare the light output of other sources of white light to that of a blackbody to determine the closest color temperature. We then refer to the correlated color temperature (CCT) of that lamp. All non-incandescent light sources—fluorescent, high intensity discharge, LED, OLED, plasma, and induction lamps—are described using CCT.

Table 8.1 Comparison of Temperature Scales

	K	°C	°F
Absolute Zero	0	–273.2	–459.7
Water Freezes	273.2	0	32
Normal Body Temperature	310.2	37	98.6
Water Boils	373.2	100	212

Color References

One of the needs of people concerned with color is a color reference system. Paint manufacturers, for instance, create color cards and swatch books that designers can use to select colors. In 1931 the International Commission on Illumination (or CIE, abbreviated from its French name) created one of the first reference systems that shows all of the colors visible to the human eye. The system is based on the cone sensitivity of a standard observer, and is called the CIE 1931 Color Space, or CIE 1931 (x,y) (Figure 8.A). It is the most well-known way of illustrating the color of a light source. The color, or chromaticity, of a light source is identified using the x,y coordinates. The one drawback to this color space is that it is nonuniform, meaning that the distance between two colors in the color space does not correspond to the perceptual difference between the colors.

Since then there have been several improvements in the CIE color space as our understanding of color perception has improved. In 1960 the CIE introduced a uniform color space, CIE 1960 (u,v), shown in Figure 8.B. This color space is still used to calculate correlated color temperature (CCT).

A decade and a half later the CIE developed CIE 1976 (u',v'), shown in Figure 8.C. This color space is especially useful for describing the perceptibility of color differences. It is also the most visually uniform of the three.

Although CIE 1931 is outdated, it is still the color space used most often when manufacturers illustrate the spectral color or color temperature of their lamps.

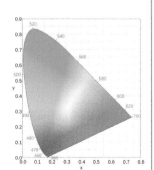

Figure 8.A CIE 1931 (x,y).
Wikimedia Commons, PD-User: Sakurambo, accessed Sept. 26, 2013.

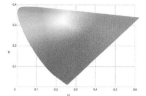

Figure 8.B CIE 1960 (u,v).
Wikimedia Commons, PD-User: Adoniscik, accessed Sept. 26, 2013.

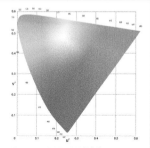

Figure 8.C CIE 1976 (u',v').
Wikimedia Commons, PD-User: Adoniscik, accessed Sept. 26, 2013.

13,700	Average Blue Sky
8,000	Overcast Sky
6,500	Daylight
6,000	Daylight Fluorescent
5,000	Daylight Fluorescent
4,100	Cool White Fluorescent
3,500	Neutral White Fluorescent
3,200	Quartz Lamp
2,850	Incandescent Lamp
1,900	Candle Flame

Figure 8.3 Reference Color Temperatures.

Standard Lamp Color Temperatures

Our visual system is quite flexible and will accept color temperatures from less than 2,500K to over 6,000K as "white light." Within that continuum, the lamp manufacturers produce specific color temperatures of white light, although the exact color temperatures and availability varies by lamp type, wattage, and manufacturer. A general list of the color temperature ranges available to us is shown in Figure 8.4.

Color Rendering

Light allows us to see color. However, not all lamp technologies enable us to see color equally. In fact, some lamps (such as those frequently used in parking lots) distort colors or fail to reveal large portions of the spectrum. This leads us to the problem of color rendering.

2700K is available in a limited range of lower wattage compact fluorescent lamps. Most people are aware of the warmth of this color temperature, but accept it as warm white, not a warm color.

2850K is the color of standard incandescent lamps. Like 2700K compact fluorescent lamps, most people are aware of the warmth of this CT, but accept it as warm white, not a warm color, and find the color to be pleasant.

3000K is the color of lower wattage halogen incandescent lamps, and is available in most compact, linear and circular fluorescent lamps, and a large range of HID and LED lamps.

3200K is the color of higher wattage halogen incandescent lamps.

3500K is available in most compact, linear and circular fluorescent lamps, and a large range of HID and LED lamps.

4000–4100K is available in most compact, linear and circular fluorescent lamps, and a large range of HID and LED lamps.

5000K is available in many compact, linear and circular fluorescent lamps, and a large range of HID and LED lamps.

6000K is available in some compact, linear and circular fluorescent lamps, and a large range of HID and LED lamps.

Over 6000K is available in some LED lamps.

Figure 8.4 Standard Lamp Color Temperatures.

Color rendering is defined by the CIE as "the effect of an illuminant on the color appearance of objects by conscious or subconscious comparison with their color appearance under a reference illuminant."

In other words, color rendering is a measurement of how well a given light source enables us to discriminate between colors viewed under that light source when compared to a standard, or known, light source. A lamp with high color rendition allows us to discriminate over a wide range of colors, and the color appearance is similar to the reference light source. A lamp with low color rendition limits that ability and causes colors to appear gray, black, muddy, or identical to other colors.

The problem of color rendering becomes clear when we examine the SPD from several light sources. Figure 8.5 shows the SPDs for daylight and incandescent light. Although the SPDs vary with color temperature, each one of them is relatively smooth and no colors are missing.

Compare the previous SPDs with those in Figure 8.6 for a 5,000K fluorescent and a 3,000K ceramic metal halide. Notice the spikey, irregular SPDs. This gives an indication of the color rendering problems that can occur with these lamps. The spikes indicate that some colors may be overemphasized, while the valleys suggest that adjacent colors may

Kruithof Curve

In 1941, as fluorescent lamps were gaining in popularity, A. A. Kruithof, a lamp engineer with Philips Lighting, wrote an article for lighting specifiers describing the different CCTs available from fluorescent lamps. He supplemented the article with a graph, similar to the one shown in Figure 8.D,

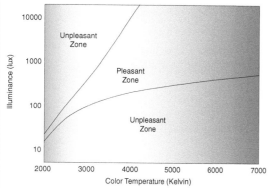

showing the preferred relationship between color temperatures and illuminance levels. The zones of low color temperature/high illumination levels and high color temperature/low illumination levels were deemed to be unpleasant. The area between those two zones is where the color temperature/intensity combinations were considered to be pleasing.

Known as the Kruithof Curve, this information is often cited, and lighting designers frequently use it as a guide. However, Kruithof's research has been criticized for having too small of a sample set (possibly as small as Kruithof and his assistant). Subsequent research has found that the effect is weaker than indicated, or that it does not exist.

Ultimately, a lighting designer selects the color temperature and illumination level for each project based on multiple criteria, not a single graph. Evaluation of real world installations will allow you to determine for yourself how much weight to give any particular criteria or effect.

Figure 8.D The Kruithof Curve Showing Pleasant and Unpleasant Regions.

be underplayed, and that the difference between the two may be distorted due to the large changes in the wavelength intensities.

Clearly, if some light sources distort colors, specifying only the color temperature of a light source is not sufficient. A lighting designer must also have information about the light source's SPD. This gives rise to the need for a color rendering scale.

Color Rendering Index

Color rendering was first quantified for lighting designers in 1965 when the CIE established the Color Rendering Index (CRI). CRI is accepted throughout the lighting industry

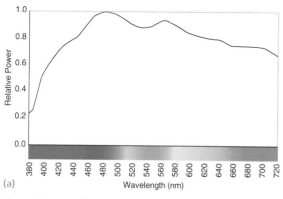
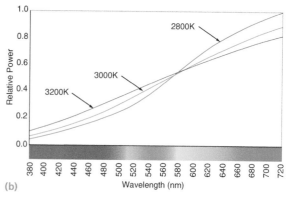

Figure 8.5 Spectral Power Distribution Curves of (a) Daylight and (b) Incandescent Light.

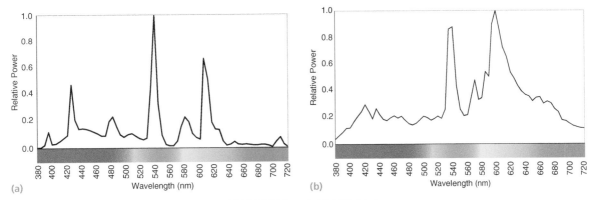

(a)　　　　　　　　　　　　　　　　　　　　　(b)

Figure 8.6 SPD of (a) 5,000K Fluorescent Lamp and (b) 3,000K Ceramic Metal Halide Lamp.

and is the reference standard that lamp manufacturers use to communicate the color rendering ability of their lamps to lighting designers.

CRI is a color fidelity scale that compares the color rendering ability of a lamp being tested to that of a reference light source of the same color temperature. The reference light source is a blackbody radiator for color temperatures less than 5,000K and daylight for color temperatures 5,000K and higher. CRI is a scale from 1 to 100 without units. High CRI indicates that the lamp in question renders colors much like the reference source. A low CRI indicates that the lamp renders colors poorly compared to the reference source.

To determine the General CRI of a lamp, (also identified as Ra or Ra8) a reference light source and the lamp being tested separately illuminate a set of eight basic colors (top row, Figure 8.7). The light that is reflected from the color samples is analyzed, and the deviation between the known light source and the light source being examined is calculated for each color sample. The deviations are then combined to yield a single number between 0

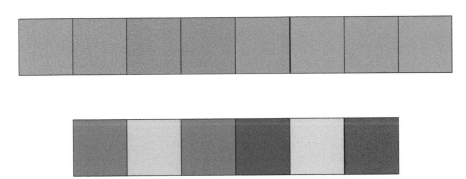

Figure 8.7 Colors Used in Calculating Color Rendition Index (CRI). The Top Eight Colors Are Used to Determine a Basic CRI. The Bottom Six Colors Are Added to Determine a Special CRI.

and 100. Note that in reality there is no need to actually illuminate the color samples. The analysis is entirely mathematical.

Since the CRI calculation results in a single number, we don't know how the light source in question rendered any individual sample color. We don't know if the source muted one or more colors, or if it oversaturated one or more colors. The lack of specific information can be frustrating, but having a single number makes CRI easy to understand and to use. We can gain additional color rendering information by asking the lamp manufacturer for information about the Special CRI (Ri), which is a calculation that includes all six colors in the second line of Figure 8.7. The first eight color samples lack red, so the CRI of test color sample 9 (strong red) is sometimes made available as R9.

How do we work with CRI? First, a CRI difference of one or two points is generally not detectable, even in side-by-side comparisons. A difference of five points is noticeable to most people. A light source with a CRI of 80 produces color shifts that most people notice. Therefore, a CRI of 80 is usually considered the minimum acceptable for applications where color rendering has value. It is also the minimum required qualify for the EPA's Energy Star programs for CFL and LED lamps.

The application, visual tasks, and client expectations combine to indicate the appropriate light source CRI. Warehouse type retail spaces with modest color rendering requirements may only require a CRI of 70+. Big box retail, offices, and classrooms have higher color rendering requirements, and should use light sources with a CRI of 80+. High-end retailers typically require even higher color rendering, and should have CRI of 85+. Healthcare and spaces where color matching is critical will require CRI of 90+.

Problems with Color Rendering Index

It is broadly recognized that CRI is flawed in several respects. First, a low score on one or two color samples can be offset by a high score on other samples, thus masking potential color rendering problems. As a result, two lamps of equal color temperature and CRI can produce different color rendering results. Second, as previously noted, the score tells designers nothing about the light source spectrum or it's deficiencies. While the lighting industry understands these shortcomings, consensus agreement on a replacement system has not yet been reached. CRI continues to be the industry standard.

Other Color Rendering Indices

Part of the problem in finding industry consensus on a solution to the flaws in CRI is the lack of a clear, industry accepted definition of color rendering. The proposed additions to, or substitutions for, CRI fall into two broad categories: color fidelity and color preference.

Color fidelity indices are concerned with measuring the variation between the test light source and one or more reference sources (usually a blackbody radiator or daylight, depending on the color temperature). Thus, light sources that distort object colors in any way (increasing or decreasing color richness, shifting color, etc.) are penalized. The implication is that the reference light sources are the closest to being the "best," "ideal," "most natural," or "truest" at allowing us to see color.

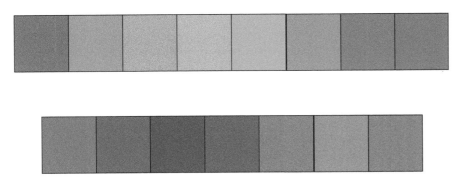

Figure 8.8 Colors Used in Calculating Color Quality Scale (CQS).

Color preference indices dispute the idea that the "best" light sources mimic the color rendering of the color fidelity reference(s). There is evidence that people do not object to, and may even prefer, light sources that slightly increase the saturation of object colors. This information is incorporated into the color preference indices.

The CIE, IES, Lighting Research Center (LRC), and others are all working on solving this problem. Unfortunately, there is no industry-wide timetable for resolution. As of 2014, only one alternative to CRI is actively in use. In 2011 PLASA, an international organization of theatrical equipment manufacturers and distributors, adopted the color quality scale (CQS), which was developed by the Lighting and Color Group of the National Institute for Standards and Technology (NIST). The CQS incorporates aspects of both color fidelity and color preference. It was developed, in part, to correct problems CRI has in evaluating LED systems. CQS uses more color samples in total and more saturated ones as well, and does not penalize light sources that enhance saturation (Figure 8.8). Many theatrical lighting manufacturers now provide both CRI and CQS information.

Color Stability

Another component of color perception is the color stability of the light source used. *Color stability* describes a lamp's ability to continuously emit the same color of light over its entire life. Color stability is a factor that appears later in the life of a lamp as the color characteristics of a lamp change. *Color consistency* describes color matching between identical lamps. Manufacturers are good at controlling the manufacturing process to produce color consistency, especially when their lamps are first energized. However, color differences between manufacturers can be noticeable throughout a lamp's life. A good practice is to use only one lamp manufacturer per project, or at least one manufacturer per lamp technology, to maximize color consistency.

In applications where color perception is not considered to be a significant factor, such as warehouse or roadway lighting, color stability is not a concern. However, in applications where color perception is important, such as museums, retail, and healthcare, lamp

■ *color stability*
A lamp's ability to emit the same color of light throughout its life.

■ *color consistency*
Lamp-to-lamp color matching.

color shifts may produce unwanted changes in color rendering or color appearance. In applications where groups of lamps illuminate an area, such as airports or restaurants, lamp color shifts can produce an undesirable patchwork of different colors of light on floors and walls.

Incandescent lamps have very good color stability and consistency. Fluorescent lamps may have noticeable color variations at the start of their life before they are "seasoned" or "burned in" but those variations will become less apparent, and may disappear, with use. Linear fluorescent lamps are stable when used in a stable environment, which includes most indoor applications. Compact fluorescent lamps are generally less stable than linear lamps and color stability may be an issue, especially with lower quality lamps. Metal halide and ceramic metal halide lamps are known to have color stability problems. Most manufacturers of MH and CMH lamps provide information about the average shift in color temperature, but not the associated shift in CRI. White LEDs exhibit color stability problems that are harder to predict than those of older technologies.

Unfortunately, there is no system for measuring and reporting color stability, so a designer's experience with various lamp technologies becomes an important factor. It's a good idea to periodically revisit old projects to evaluate the color stability of the lamps used. This can provide useful information on future projects.

Metamerism

There is one other color rendering problem in lighting—metamerism. Metamerism is the apparent matching of two or more light sources that have different SPDs.

The appearance of a surface color is dependent on two factors: the SPD of the lamp illuminating the surface and the spectral reflectance properties of the surface itself. On a neutral, white, or pale surface metamerism is usually not a problem and color shift (if any) between metamers is minimal. However, with surfaces that are more colorful or more saturated the likelihood that the metamers (the two or more light sources in question) will produce a matching color appearance diminishes. Colors that were only slightly different under one light source can match or become significantly different under a metamer. This effect is noticeable when comparing incandescent and fluorescent light (as in many retail applications), but is often minor enough to be disregarded by most people. This effect can be quite pronounced under color mixing LED lighting systems.

As an example, let's compare (a) a warm white fluorescent lamp, (b) a warm white HID lamp, (c) an RGB luminaire (red, green, blue LEDs), and (d) an RGBA luminaire (red, green, blue, amber LEDs), all with a CCT of 3,000K (Figure 8.9). Although light sources may have different SPDs (Figure 8.10), the stimulation of our cones and the brain's interpretation of that information can result in what appears to be matching, or nearly matching, colors of white light on white surfaces. However, colored surfaces, especially saturated colors, take on markedly different appearances under the four metamers.

In designs where multiple lamp technologies are used, and that's probably most designs, we must be aware of the possibility of metamers creating confusion about object colors. Our light source decisions should minimize this confusion.

(a)

(b)

(c)

(d)

Figure 8.9 Metamers Have Little Affect on Pale Colors, but Can Shift the Appearance of Saturated Colors.

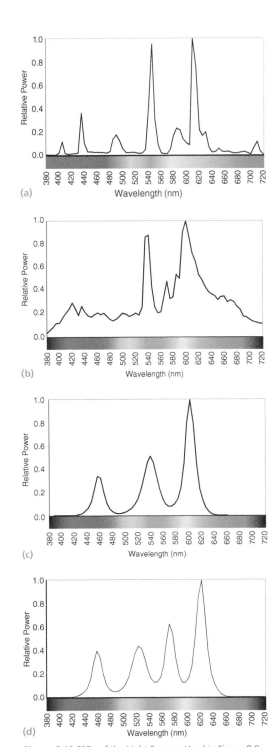

Figure 8.10 SPDs of the Light Sources Used in Figure 8.9.

119

Apparent Color

Which photo in Figure 8.9 is "correct"? That question doesn't have an answer because objects don't have a "correct" or "real" color. Color doesn't exist until our brains process the information received from our eyes. As we've already seen, things such as the color of surrounding objects and the SPD of the light source affect our color perception. The result is that we can't speak of color in absolute terms, but only in relative terms. We can't say we know the true color of an object; we can only say that under a given set of conditions an object has an *apparent color*. We can't truly say what an object's color *is*; we can only say what it *appears to be*.

Figure 8.11 shows examples of a color and materials board illuminated under a range of light sources, color temperatures, and CRIs. The reflective properties of the materials aren't changing, of course. Nonetheless, they appear to be changing their color. What changes from one photo to the next is the color content, the SPD, of the light source.

The lesson for architects and interior designers is that one can only evaluate a color, or color palette, accurately when one uses the light source that will be specified by the lighting designer. Communication and collaboration are the keys to a successful design team. If the lighting designer and interior designer aren't discussing the color palette and the impressions they want the space to have on occupants, the result may be a color palette that doesn't work because the lighting design supports a different set of colors.

■ *apparent color*
The perceived color of an object resulting from the color content of the light source, the object's reflective properties, and the eye's adaptation to the illuminated environment.

Color Constancy

By now you may be asking, "If the color of objects is constantly changing with changing lighting conditions, why don't I notice it?" The answer is *color constancy*, also called chromatic adaptation.

The information we receive about the color of objects changes as the light changes. However, for object color information to be useful to us, it must be relatively stable under different lighting conditions. It doesn't benefit us to take strong note of changes in color, since it is more likely to cause confusion than to be helpful. For example, we should be able to see that a piece of fruit is ripe whether it is seen in full sun, under a cloudy sky, in the green-tinged light under a leafy tree, or in a supermarket with fluorescent lighting. Our vision system has evolved to do just that.

A very observant person, or a person engaged in experimenting with changes in color, will certainly see shifts in object color with changes in the light source. The change we experience during our daily activities, though, is much less than would be predicted, and is frequently disregarded. There are a number of theories that try to explain color constancy, but they all share the idea that when we are processing the color information of an object, our color perception is affected by the color information from the other objects in the scene. That information is used, essentially, to calibrate our color perception so that color shifts are minimized.

■ *color constancy*
The perception of objects as having the same color under differing lighting conditions.

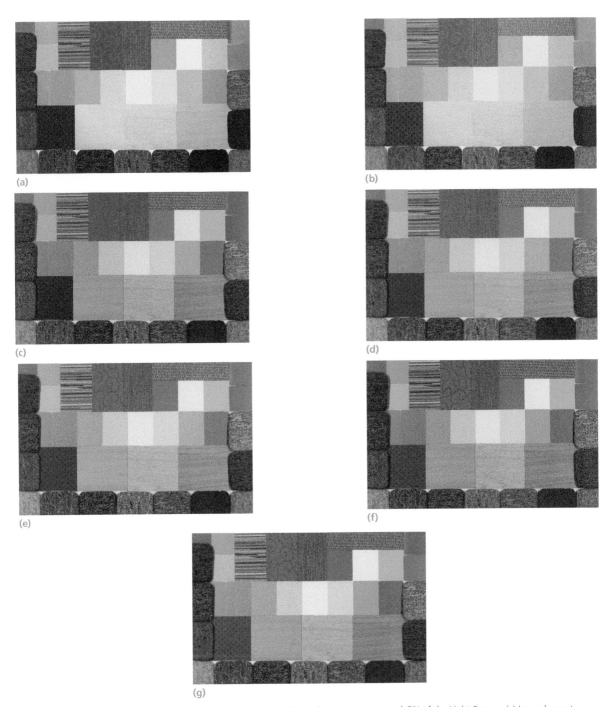

Figure 8.11 Apparent Shifts in Color Resulting from Changes in the Color Temperature and CRI of the Light Source: (a) Incandescent, 2,650K, 99+ CRI; (b) Halogen, 2,750K, 99+ CRI; (c) Fluorescent, 3,000K, 86 CRI; (d) Fluorescent, 3,500K, 85 CRI; (e) Fluorescent, 4,100K, 85 CRI; (f) Fluorescent, 5,000K, 86 CRI (g) Fluorescent, 6,500K, 82 CRI.

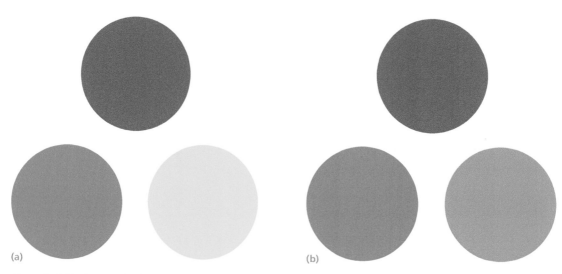

(a)　　　　　　　　　　　　　　　　(b)

Figure 8.12 (a) Primary Colors for Pigment and (b) Light.

Colored Light

Let's now move beyond warm and cool light to talk about spectral, or colored, light. Let's also begin at the beginning with some basic color vocabulary. Please note that if you've studied color theory, you may find that some of the words and definitions change when they are applied to light.

■ *primary color*
One of the base colors used to create all other colors.

The term *primary color* refers to one of the base colors used to create all other colors, or to a color that cannot be created through the mixing of other colors (Figure 8.12). The first thing to know about color in light is that the primary colors are not the same for those of pigments or dyes (also referred to as object color). You've known since you were a young child that the primary colors for pigments that color objects are red, blue, and yellow. The primary colors of light, however, are red, blue, and green! If you've ever adjusted the colors on a television or computer monitor, you may have noticed that you're adjusting RGB (red, green, blue), not RYB (red, yellow, blue). Note that not all color systems use three primaries. The Pantone system, for example, uses 13 primaries plus white and black.

■ *secondary color*
An intermediate color created by mixing equal quantities of two primary colors.

We should note that color wheels and color mixing charts, such as those shown in Figure 8.13, are not representations of the color spectrum, which is linear (see Figure 3.4), but rather they are tools used to explain the interactions of colors and explore color mixing possibilities. The far ends of the visible spectrum, deep blue and deep red, are interpreted by our brain as being similar enough to create a connection and suggest that they are adjacent, even though they are not.

A *secondary color* is an intermediate color created by mixing equal quantities of two primary colors. Of course, changing one of the primary colors between object color and light also changes the secondary colors. As you already know, the secondary colors of pigment are orange, green, and violet. In light the secondary colors are amber, cyan, and magenta (Figure 8.13).

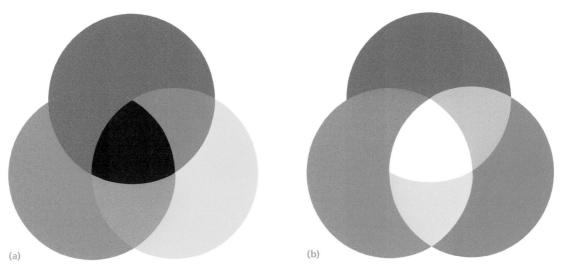

(a)

(b)

Figure 8.13 Primary and Secondary Colors for (a) Pigment and (b) Light.

Hue is the perception of a color as red, green, blue, etc. It is simply the color name.

Chroma is description of the saturation of a color (Figure 8.14). High chroma equals high saturation. Low chroma equals low saturation.

Value describes the relative lightness or darkness of a color, and is equivalent to one of the series of grays between white and black (Figure 8.15). There are additional terms to describe the changes that occur when we add black, white, or gray to a color.

Tint refers to a high value color, or one that has had white added to it. **Tone** refers to a medium value color, or one that has had gray added to it. **Shade** refers to a low value color, or one that has had black added to it. See Figures 8.16 and 8.17.

Complimentary colors are colors that are opposite each other on the color wheel. In pigment a combination of two compliments produces black, while in light they produce white.

■ *hue*
The general color attribute of red, blue, etc.

■ *chroma*
The saturation or purity of a color.

■ *value*
The relative lightness or darkness of a color.

Figure 8.14 High Chroma (left), Low Chroma (right).

Figure 8.15 Gray Scale.

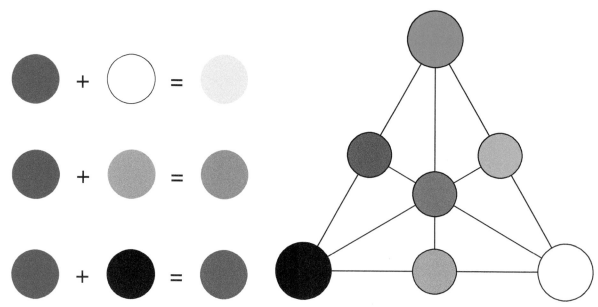

Figure 8.16 Tint, Tone, and Shade.

Figure 8.17 The Relationship between Tint, Tone, and Shade.

Adjacent colors are those colors that are next to each other on the color wheel. They blend into one another seamlessly.

Warm colors are those colors that remind us of fire.

Cool colors are colors of ice and water.

Additive and Subtractive Color Mixing

■ *additive mixing*
Combining the colored light from two sources on a surface producing the appearance of a third color.

There are two methods for creating colored light, and lighting designers use both of them. The first, and the one you have the most experience with, is *additive mixing*. In additive mixing we add two colors together to create a third. With pigments we can, for example, mix blue paint and yellow paint to create green paint. With light, we can combine the light from a red source and a green source to create amber light. Note that we haven't changed the wavelengths by adding red and green together; but when we project red and green on a white surface, and the colors are reflected back to our eye, the resulting effect is the same as if amber light is stimulating our visual system (Figure 8.18).

■ *color gamut*
The range of colors that can be created based on the component colors used.

When discussing additive mixing, such as using RGB LED fixtures, we sometimes talk about the *color gamut*. The color gamut is the range of colors that can be created based on the component colors that are used (in this case red, green, and blue LEDs). The color gamut is usually shown mapped on the CIE 1931 color space. Figure 8.19 shows an example. Colors that are outside of the triangle formed by the three LEDs can't be created by this set of LEDs. In this example, there may be problems rendering deep blue objects because deep blue wavelengths of light are not present.

Figure 8.18 Additive Mixing—Light from Red and Green LEDs Blends to Amber.
LED fixture courtesy of Rosco Laboratories, Inc.

Subtractive mixing with light starts with a white light source. White light, of course, is made up of all colors of light. To "make" colored light from white light we simply take away the colors we don't want and what remains will be the color that we do want.

To make blue light, for example, we want to take away (or subtract) all non-blue wavelengths (Figure 8.20). We do this by using a material that will absorb, or filter out, those wavelengths (usually a piece of glass or plastic), and place it in the white beam of light. The result is simple:

White light – Non-blue light = Blue light.

The blue filter "makes" blue light out of white light.

Of course, the filter doesn't make blue in the sense that it adds anything to the original beam of light. Additive mixing will produce a brighter result than either of the two light sources alone. Subtractive mixing will always result in a loss of intensity relative to the white light source. This fact is part of the appeal of colored LED luminaires. It is more efficient to start with a light source that either produces the color you want or additively mixes to that color, than it is to start with white light and take away the unwanted colors.

■ *subtractive mixing*
Altering the color of light by using a glass or plastic filter to remove unwanted wavelengths.

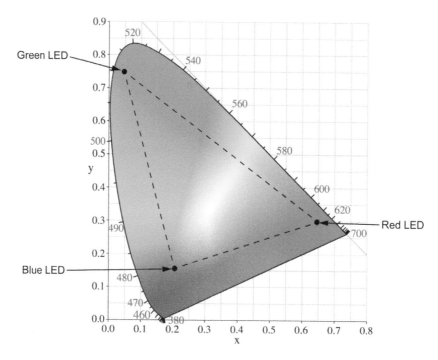

Figure 8.19 Example of an RGB LED Gamut.

Figure 8.20 Subtractive Mixing.

Sources of Colored Light

In addition to the warm/cool variations available from standard lamps, there are many sources of colored light, ranging from subtle tints to bold hues. The light source a designer selects will depend on the color(s) desired, the brightness required, project budget, and whether the color is static or dynamic.

Fluorescent Lamps

Colored, linear fluorescent lamps are available in a limited range from most manufacturers. They are T5 or T8 lamps, usually 4' only, and are typically available only in red, blue, green, and gold. These lamps have the same life as white linear fluorescent lamps and operate on the same ballasts. They are, therefore, an economical, if somewhat limited, means of creating colored light.

Colored compact fluorescent lamps are available in the same limited color range as linear fluorescent lamps. The shapes and wattages available varies. The reader should consult manufacturers' Web sites or catalogs for current options.

Cold Cathode Lamps

Cold cathode lamps are available in the same color temperature range as fluorescent lamps. They are also available in a range of colors that varies by manufacturer. The reader should consult manufacturers' Web sites for available color ranges.

Neon Lamps

In architectural lighting the drawback to neon is its relatively low light output. Neon is excellent for signage, and can be used for color accent, but does not have the light output necessary for use as a general light source.

LED Luminaires

One of the greatest strengths of LED lamps is their ability to produce color. As a result, there is a wide range of luminaires that use multiple-colored LEDs and allow each color to be individually controlled. RGB (red, green, blue) luminaires are the most common, but RGBA (A for amber, see Figure 8.21) and RGBW (W for white), and multiple CCT luminaires are also available and provide the broadest color range available of any lamp technology. Multicolor LED luminaires are manufactured in a range of sizes and shapes, including linear fixtures for cove, soffit, and grazing applications, and round, square, or rectangular configurations for wash applications.

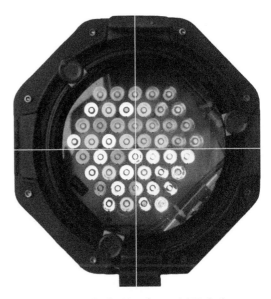

Figure 8.21 Example of a Manufacturer's LED Options. (Clockwise from Top Left) RGBW, RGBA, 3,000K, 3,000K—6,000K.
Courtesy of Altman Lighting.

Colors of White Light LEDs

As discussed in Chapter 7, the standards for measuring and reporting the characteristics of LEDs are still in development. This includes establishing industry-wide color standards and tolerances for white LEDs. Figures 8.E and 8.F are examples of warm and cool LED luminaires from about a dozen manufacturers. As the figures clearly demonstrate, labeling a luminaire as warm, cool, or daylight, or even identifying the CCT do not adequately describe the LED's color characteristics. Until the LED industry matures and settles on a specific set of characteristics that are clearly understood and universally adopted, firsthand evaluation of LED luminaires is the only way to evaluate them.

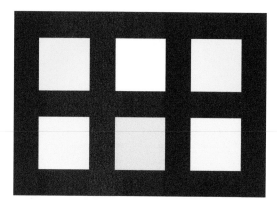

Figure 8.E Light from LED Luminaires Described as Warm White or 3,000K by Their Manufacturers;

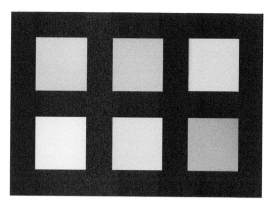

Figure 8.F Light from LED Luminaires Described as Cool White, Daylight, 5,000K, 6,000K, or 6,500K by Their Manufacturers.

Unlike other methods of creating colored light, multicolored LED fixtures can change their color output at any time without making physical changes to the luminaire. Doing so requires a control system (see Chapter 13) and control wiring to deliver the necessary data to each fixture.

Color Filters

White light can be subtractively filtered to achieve the desired color. Some fixture types (especially adjustable accent and track fixtures) are frequently designed to hold color filters. There are three general categories of filters, each with its own characteristics.

Plastic Filters

Plastic filters made for the entertainment industry are available in over 1,000 different colors and dozens of different types of diffusion. The filters are made of thin sheets of polycarbonate or polyester, are inexpensive, and are easy to work with. Plastic filters are readily available in sheets (typically 20″ × 24″), tubes for linear fluorescents, sleeves for compact fluorescents, and rolls (Figure 8.22).

The low cost, ready availability, and ease of use make plastic filters ideal for mock-ups prior to ordering more expensive glass filters. Plastic filters give designers more options than any other method of creating colored light except LEDs.

There are two drawbacks to using plastic filters in architectural applications. The colors can fade in a relatively short time (weeks or months), and they are susceptible to heat damage. Plastic filters work well with fluorescent lamps but they are subject to fading from the lamp's UV output. Although the manufacturers work to limit fading with UV filters and color stabilizers, it is best to assume that the filters will need to be replaced each time the fluorescent lamp is replaced, or more frequently if saturated colors are used. The low melting point of plastic, when compared to glass, makes plastic filters inappropriate for use with most adjustable and track fixtures, as the heat from the face of the lamp will quickly melt the plastic.

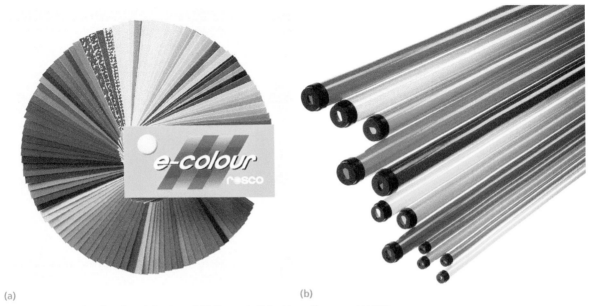

(a)   (b)

Figure 8.22 (a) Color Filter Swatch Book, and (b) Sleeves to Color Linear Fluorescent Lamps.
Courtesy of Rosco Laboratories, Inc.

Colored Glass Filters

Colored glass filters have several advantages over plastic filters. They aren't subject to the same fading; they can be assembled so as to be nearly immune to heat; and, therefore, they have a very long lifetime. Colored glass filters may be tempered for additional heat resistance and impact resistance. The glass is made in sheets and can be cut to almost any size and shape.

Dichroic Glass Filters

Dichroic filters are made by depositing very thin layers of metal oxides onto a glass base. The glass base is placed in a vacuum chamber, and very thin coatings of minerals are deposited using an electron beam. By controlling the materials used, their thickness and the number of layers, the manufacturer can create a filter that reflects specific wavelengths of light while allowing others to pass through. Although the process results in a more expensive filter than traditional glass filters, the resulting colors can be brighter and more vivid. Like colored glass filters, dichroics can be cut to almost any shape.

One unusual characteristic of dichroic filters is that the unwanted wavelengths are not absorbed by the filter, but are reflected back toward the light source. Figure 8.23 is of an amber dichroic filter. It shows how the amber light passes through the filter, while the rest of the spectrum is reflected.

Figure 8.23 Dichroic Filters Pass Some Wavelengths and Reflect the Others.

Another, often undesirable, characteristic is that the color of light passed by the filter changes with the angle of incidence. In wide-angle fixtures the result can be "color fringing" where the color changes near the edge of the beam.

Use of Color

Colored light in the built environment is becoming increasingly inexpensive, flexible, and acceptable. The falling cost of glass color filters, (especially dichroics), the availability of high brightness LEDs, and computer controlled dimming systems have all enabled the use of colored light in a multitude of interior and exterior applications. Color is no longer reserved for casinos, amusement parks, the top of the Empire State Building, and other high energy or landmark projects. Color is now frequently seen as an integral part of architectural and lighting designs that can be used to differentiate a project from its peers and its surroundings, and to brand a building. All of this is an exciting new chapter in the development of the lighting design profession, and presents us with new tools and new design solutions.

Many lighting designers, especially those with a background in engineering or architecture, may have little experience designing with color. The goal of the rest of this chapter is to provide guidelines and information that can form a basis for making appropriate color choices. Unfortunately, there is no single methodology for using color. There are a number of sometimes conflicting ideas, concepts, and beliefs employed by a variety of design professionals. Which one is adopted for a particular project depends, in part, on the project's design goals and the designer's aesthetic.

Colored Light and Vision

Our visual system does not respond equally to all wavelengths or colors of light as discussed in Chapter 4. The $V(\lambda)$ curve shows that under normal (photopic) conditions we have peak response at about 555 nanometers, or to colors in the yellow-green range (see Figure 4.6). We have decreasing response as we move toward the red or blue ends of the spectrum. The result is that, at equal intensities, the average observer will find that yellow light appears to be brighter than red or blue.

This phenomenon can guide us in the use of colored light to affect brightness perception. Using this technique, we could say that within any given color palette those colors that are closer to pale yellow-green tend to appear brighter, while colors farther away from yellow-green tend to appear dimmer. This approach is common in the theatre, and can help an architectural lighting designer select colors to give emphasis to architecture or signage. It may be especially useful with fixtures that can't dim or projects that can't afford dimming.

In Figure 8.24, the performers and the scenic element are separated by less than 4'. However, the blue light on the scenery gives the impression that it is dim and unimportant, while pale amber light on the performers gives the impression that they are brighter, bringing them to the foreground and focusing attention on them. In this scene, the use of color, intensity, and scale focus attention and create perspective to separate the teenagers from the supervision of their parents.

Another interesting phenomenon regarding color perception is that warm colors tend to advance, while cool colors tend to recede, as Figure 8.25 demonstrates. The outlines of the rooms are identical. The only difference is in the color of the far wall, yet nearly everyone perceives the red wall as closer and/or larger than the blue wall.

This technique is related to aerial, or atmospheric, perspective in painting where the background is painted in cooler and paler colors than the foreground to mimic the effect seen in nature.

Figure 8.24 Color Affects Intensity Perception.

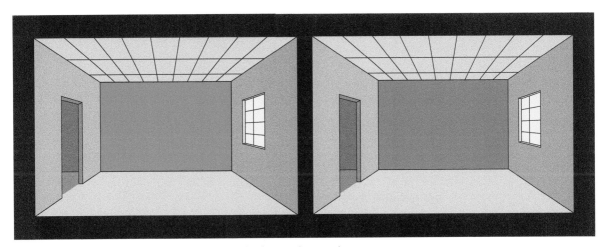

Figure 8.25 Warm Colors Tend to Advance, While Cool Colors Tend to Recede.

(a)

(b)

Figure 8.26 Atmospheric Perspective in Painting and in Nature.
Painting by Alexander Helwig Wyant, 1865, Courtesy of Los Angeles County Museum of Art, www.lacma.org (a); © Mazzzur, Used under license from Shutterstock.com (b).

We see this in the natural world because light from the sky is scattered by dust and moisture in the atmosphere. Distant objects have more air between them and the viewer, and consequently more scattered blue light. The scattered light acts as a veil, softening the outlines and shadows of the distant object and shifting the colors to cooler, paler tints (Figure 8.26).

Our experience of brightness with chromatic (colored) light is different than under white light. This gives rise to some other interesting phenomenon. The first is the Helmholtz-Kohlrausch Effect, which says that we can increase the perception of brightness by increasing the chroma of surfaces or of the light source. This explains why, in environments illuminated with colored light, the perception of brightness is higher than would be predicted by light meter readings.

The Hunt Effect tells us that the chroma of objects increases with higher illuminance, or brightness, levels and decreases with lower illuminance levels. The practical application of this effect is that saturated surfaces are needed to create a colorful environment at low light levels, while at higher light levels object color saturation can be lower.

Color and Meaning

Perhaps you've taken a class or read a book on color and came across a list such as the following:

Purple means Royalty

Blue indicates Stability

Red symbolizes Passion

Etc.

As you may have figured out by now, color is not that simple. Color can have meaning. Color can convey information. Color can affect the viewer's response to what is seen. All of these things are true, but they are not universal. Colors hold different meanings in different cultures, and a color seen alone can have a different meaning when paired with another color. A color seen on one situation (such as on a nation's flag) can have different meaning than when seen in another situation (such as in a casino).

Cultural Preference and Color Connotations

Lighting design is an increasingly global field, with practitioners in New York working in the Middle East and practitioners in London working in China. As practices expand internationally, it is important to understand the meaning of colors in the country or culture in which one is working.

For example, in the U.S. washing a facade with red light may be intended to indicate excitement, but in Russia it is a reminder of communism, and in South Africa it is a color of mourning. Likewise the color blue has different connotations and associations around the world:

North America: Trustworthy, soothing, depression, sadness, conservative, corporate

Western Europe: Sky, fidelity, serenity, truth, reliability, responsibility

Russia: Hope, purity, peace, serenity

China: Sky, water

India: Heavens, love, truth, mercy

Color and Environment

As the previous section shows, we can't use color as the sole environmental signal to the occupants of a space. Blue alone does not create tranquility. Green by itself does not make people think of nature. However, we can use color in concert with other environmental signals to lead people to the experience we want them to have. Thus, blue light plus the sound of crickets is more likely to bring night time to mind, while blue light and a floor covered with sand is more likely to create associations with water and the ocean. There is no such thing as color-coded emotions or universal responses to color, but multiple sensory and environmental signals can be combined to guide impressions.

Even in the absence of other signals, color can still be used to create an environmental experience. In the images found in Figure 8.27, white sheer fabric was stretched over metal frames to create organically shaped enclosures for themed groups of photos. The enclosures were illuminated with colored light to create an individual environment for each group.

(a)

(b)

(c)

Figure 8.27 Using Color to Create an Environment.

The colors were chosen through a process that involved selectively applying certain color associations, along with input from the exhibit designer, lighting designer, and client. Did the viewers automatically associate the color of light with the theme of each group of photos? No, probably not. However, the viewers did understand that there was a reason for each mini-environment, which invited and encouraged them to discover the common theme among the photos.

CASE STUDY   An Environment of Color and Light

Project: A 250-seat music performance venue
Architect: Meridian Design Associates and Luckett & Farley
Stage Rigging: Studio T+L, LLC
Lighting Design: Studio T+L, LLC

Project Requirements

- This performance space for popular music is tucked into the street level corner of an existing building.
- The owner, who owns a group of local radio stations, wanted an intimate venue for exclusive concerts with major music stars for their radio contest winners.
- Key owner requirements were excitement, intimacy, and flexibility.

Project Limitations

- Ceiling height of 18'
- Very small space relative to the owner's expectations

Collecting Relevant Information

1. Review plans and sections already developed by the architect (Figure 8.28). Tour the raw space with the architect. Suggest changes to architectural designs to accommodate performance lighting equipment hung from the ceiling.
2. Consult with electrical engineer to determine amount of power available for the lighting system.
3. Consult with owner to determine caliber of performers (Top 40 artists), frequency of performances (at least once per week), and operational requirements (must be set up for professional lighting operators that the artists may bring along, but also usable by in-house operators for acts that don't bring their own).

Design Development and Implementation

1. With such a small footprint, the designers decided to embrace the space limitations by creating a single environment for both performer and audience, rather than the typical arrangement of a stage separated from the auditorium. Placing the performers and the audience in a shared space will also increase intimacy.
2. For the theatre systems and lighting designers, the unified space meant extending the lighting systems of the stage to cover the seating area, immersing the audience in an environment of light and color.
3. The space is too small for projection screens, and video display walls are beyond the budget. The theatre and lighting designer developed a design for an array of RGB LEDs to create a low-resolution video wall (Figure 8.29). The LEDs are inexpensive "strings" of RGB nodes, 50 nodes to a string. Each node is individually controllable, and therefore can act as a single pixel in the display. The sharp appearance of the LEDs is softened by placing light diffusing panels several inches in front of the LEDs.

continues

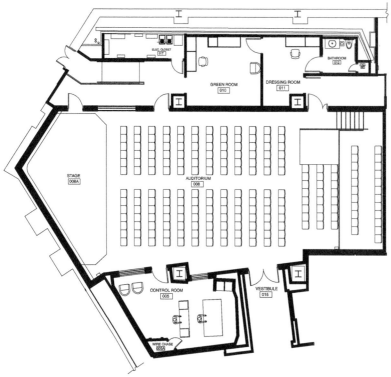

Figure 8.28 Ground Plan.
Courtesy of Meridian Design Associates.

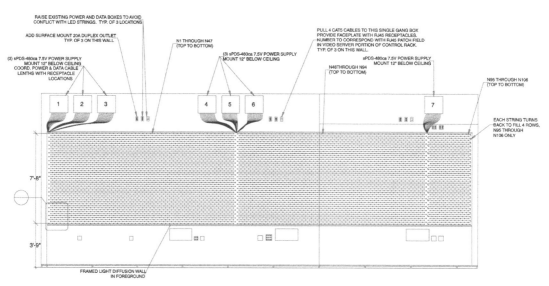

Figure 8.29 Layout of LED Nodes and Power/Data Devices on the Wall behind the Stage.
Courtesy of Studio T+L, LLC.

continues

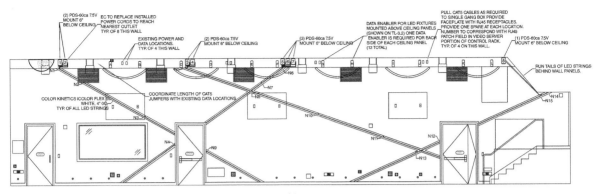

Figure 8.30 Layout of LED Fixtures and Power/Data Devices on the North Wall of the Auditorium. *Courtesy of Studio T+L, LLC.*

Figure 8.31 Testing the Low-Resolution Video Wall and Backlit Ceiling Panels. *Courtesy of Ed McCarthy.*

4. Translucent curved ceiling panels were originally selected for their appearance when they were not illuminated. To extend the light and color of the stage into the audience, these panels are backlit with rows of linear RGB LED fixtures (Figure 8.30). Each foot of fixture is individually controllable. These fixtures are connected to the same control system as the video wall.

5. Over the stage, additional linear LED fixtures are installed to wash the stage in light from above and behind (Figure 8.31). These fixtures visually connect the video wall to the ceiling panels, extending the color and light from the back wall, over the stage, and throughout the auditorium.

6. To further enfold the audience in light and color, the architect designs "slashes" that are cut into the side and rear walls of the room. The slashes are fitted with more of the RGB nodes and are covered with a light-diffusing panel.

7. A video playback system is connected to the stage lighting controller. A single operator has complete control over the stage lighting equipment, and can send color, texture, and/ or video images to the wall behind the performer, varying each parameter as the music changes (Figure 8.32). The color and pattern on the wall is extended and repeated over the side walls and ceiling, immersing the performer and audience in color and light.

8. The designers spent approximately two weeks on-site programming the control system and training the in-house users.

In this installation, some color/song pairs may be preplanned, but it is just as likely that the color combinations are the result of the lighting operator's "in the moment" response to the interaction between the artist, music, and audience. In this application, the spur of the moment use of color is no less valid than a carefully choreographed color sequence.

continues

(a)

(b)

Figure 8.32 Final Design, Changing Color to Change the Environment.
John Brandon Miller.

Projects with extensive control over the color and pattern of the light also require complex control systems. The lighting designer may not have to design the entire control system; sometimes the control system manufacturer will provide assistance. However, the lighting designer must have a clear idea of exactly what the control system is required to do. This is not something that can be figured out on the job site. Control systems are discussed in Chapter 12.

Here are a few final thoughts about the use of color in light. There are as many reasons to use color as to use white light. The use of color should be strongly rooted in the project and in the project's goals. Whatever leads to the decision to use color should also lead to the color palette and to appropriate transitions between colors. That is what we mean by design. If your decision to use color can't be tied to the project concept and goals it may be that you're imposing color rather than using it as a design tool.

Online Resources

International Commission on Illumination (CIE), www.cie.co.at

United States National Committee of the CIE, www.cie-usnc.org

CQS Web page at NIST, www.nist.gov/pml/div685/grp05/vision_color.cfm

Lighting Research Center Lighting Metrics Research, www.lrc.rpi.edu/programs/lightingMetrics/index.asp

SPDs of GE Lamps, www.gelighting.com/na/business_lighting/spectral_power_distribution_curves/

HyperPhysics, Web site from the Georgia State University Department of Physics and Astronomy, http://hyperphysics.phy-astr.gsu.edu/hbase/hph.html

Hyperphysics is also available as an app on iTunes.

Blackbody radiator SPD simulator, phet.coloado.edu

Manufacturers of Colored Glass Filters

Rosco Laboratories, www.rosco.com

Lee Filters, www.leefilters.com

Apollo Designs, www.internetapollo.com

FJ Grey Glass, www.greyglass.net

Manufacturers of Plastic Theatrical Filters

Rosco Laboratories, www.rosco.com

Lee Filters, www.leefilters.com

Apollo Designs, www.internetapollo.com

Manufacturers of Other Glass, Acrylic, and Resin Panels

Bendheim, www.bendheim.com

3Form, www.3-form.com

Designing with Light Resources

Wiley's companion site to *Designing with Light,* www.wiley.com/go/designingwithlight

Author's companion site to *Designing with Light*, www.designinglight.com

References

Cuttle, Christopher, *Lighting by Design, Second Edition*, Boston: Architectural Press, 2008.

Davis, Wendy, *Color Rendering of Light Sources*, The National Institute of Standards and Technology, accessed February 20, 2012, www.nist.gov/pml/div685/grp03/vision_color.cfm.

Davis, Wendy, and Yoshi Ohno, "Color Quality Scale," *Optical Engineering,* March 2010.

De Bortoli, Mario, and Jesús Maroto, "Translating Colours in Web Site Localization," European Languages and the Implementation of Communication and Information Technologies (Elicit) Conference, University of Paisley, 2001.

DiLauria, David, *The Lighting Handbook, Tenth Edition*, New York: Illuminating Engineering Society, 2011.

Gleason, John, "Color Part Three: Dominant/Recessive Qualities," *Lighting Dimensions,* May/June 1988: 84–89.

IES Color Committee, *DG-01 Color and Illumination*, New York: Illuminating Engineering Society, Pre-Print Manuscript.

IES Nomenclature Committee, *RP-16-05 Nomenclature and Definitions for Illuminating Engineering*, New York: Illuminating Engineering Society, 2005.

Kolb, Helga, Ralph Nelson, Eduardo Fernandez, and Bryan William Jones, Webvision, University of Utah School of Medicine, accessed February 13, 2012.

Mahnke, Frank H., and Rudolf H. Mahnke, *Color and Light in Man-made Environments*, New York: Van Nostrand Reinhold Co., 1987.

Pavey, Donald, *Color*, New York: Viking Press, 1980.

Rea, Mark, Lei Deng, and Robert Wolsey, "Lighting Answers: *Full-Spectrum Light Sources,*" Vol. 7, Issue 5, Rev. 1, 2005.

"Rose Color Meanings," Teleflora, accessed February 13, 2012, www.teleflora.com/rose_colors.asp.

CHAPTER 9

Lighting Fixtures or Luminaires

"A man who works with his hands is a laborer; a man who works with his hands and his brain is a craftsman; but a man who works with his hands and his brain and his heart is an artist."

Louis Nizer

After selecting the light source, the second component of controlling light is the lighting fixture or luminaire. The luminaire provides an electrical connection to the lamp, holds the lamp in the correct location within the reflector, houses the ballast/transformer/power supply, and includes hardware for proper installation in the ceiling, wall, or floor.

Unfortunately, there is no industry standard for categorizing or organizing luminaires. Manufacturers organize their Web site or printed catalog according to their product line and marketing strategy. A Web site may organize luminaires by:

- General luminaire type
- Specific use
- Aperture shape and/or size
- Mounting method
- Light distribution pattern (as discussed in Chapter 6)
- Lamp type (as discussed in Chapter 7)

The available variations and options give designers thousands of luminaire configurations to choose from. As you begin to search for a luminaire, you'll have several criteria in mind. Once you see how a manufacturer has organized their Web site or catalog, you'll select the most likely category and begin to search for a luminaire that includes all of your criteria.

A Note of Caution

We've waited until now to discuss lighting equipment because too often, too early in the design process, discussions turn to luminaires and lamps: "What luminaires will be used and how many? What will they cost? How energy efficient is the design?" There is also pressure to provide a finished design as early as possible so that the architect and electrical engineer can incorporate the lighting design information into their documentation.

However, we don't simply pick a luminaire to deliver light. We determine the light that we want to deliver, considering all of the properties of light and the functional and aesthetic requirements of the design, and then select the luminaire and lamp combination(s) that will best achieve those goals. Preliminary lighting ideas should start with the properties of light that are desired, the general lighting techniques to be used, and light levels to be achieved, not with the luminaires that will be used. Once the qualities of light are described and agreed upon, the designer can move on to selecting specific lamps and luminaires.

First, decide what you want the space or project to look like, *then* select the lamps and luminaires that will accomplish those goals.

Luminaire Components

Almost all lighting fixtures share a few basic components. If you understand the purpose and function of these, you will understand every luminaire you encounter. Figure 9.1 illustrates the components.

■ *housing*
The outer enclosure of a luminaire.

The *housing* performs two functions. First, it is the mounting platform for the rest of the luminaire components. Second, it acts as a radiator, dissipating the heat produced inside the luminaire.

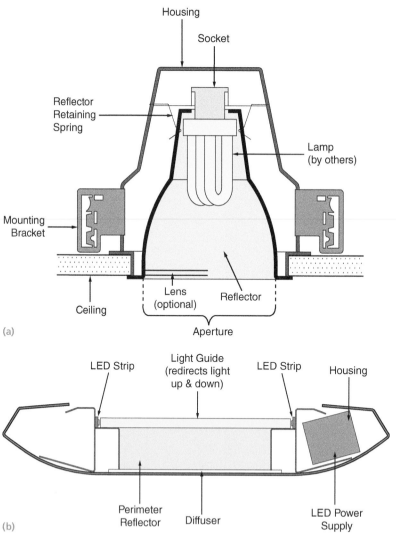

(a)

(b)

Figure 9.1 Typical Luminaire Components.
(a) Courtesy of Edison Price Lighting, Inc., (b) Courtesy of Philips Lighting Company.

The *socket* holds the lamp in the correct location and position, and provides the electrical connection for the lamp.

Reflectors around or above the lamp are used to control the distribution of light through specular, semi-specular, and/or diffuse reflection. The reflector also shields the lamp to prevent glare. Quality luminaires have reflectors that are specifically shaped for the lamp used and the intended distribution pattern, and provide consistent performance from luminaire to luminaire. Reflectors that are simply polished metal (usually aluminum) are referred to as clear because they don't change the color of the light. Other reflector colors are available from most manufacturers, including black, white, gold, and bronze (Figure 9.2).

The opening of the reflector is called the *aperture*. Around the aperture, most reflectors have a ring, called a *flange* or overlap flange, which covers the seam between the ceiling material and the fixture housing. The flange can usually be specified in the same color as the reflector (called self-flanged) or painted white, although some manufacturers are willing to paint the flange a custom color. Flangeless luminaires are also available. They require more careful and time-consuming installation, as patching compound (also called joint compound) needs to be applied around the aperture to fill the gap between the fixture and the ceiling (Figure 9.3).

After light is redirected by the reflector, additional optical control may be provided by lenses, refractors, or diffusers.

A louver or *baffle* is a blade or grid of blades below the lamp that shield the lamp from direct view to prevent glare. The sides of louvers may be curved and reflective to

■ **socket**
The part of a luminaire that provides an electrical connection for the lamp and holds the lamp in the proper position within the luminaire.

■ **reflectors**
The part of a luminaire that partially encloses the lamps and redirects some of their light.

■ **aperture**
The opening in a luminaire through which light exits.

■ **flange**
A ring at the bottom of a reflector that hides the gap between the ceiling material and the reflector.

■ **baffle**
A vertical blade at the aperture of a luminaire used to block light at high angles to prevent glare.

(a) (b) (c) (d)

Figure 9.2 Reflector Colors (a) Clear, (b) Gold, (c) Bronze, (d) Black.
Courtesy of Eaton's Cooper Lighting Business.

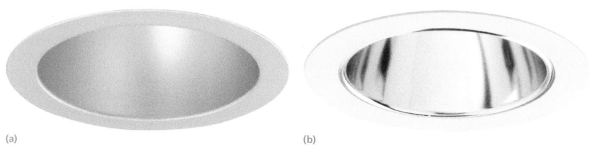

(a)   (b)

Figure 9.3 (a) Self-Flanged Reflector; (b) Flangeless Reflector.
Courtesy of Eaton's Cooper Lighting Business.

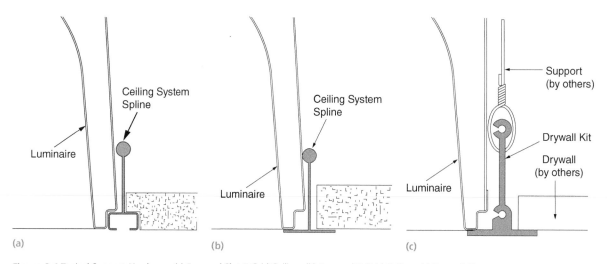

(a)   (b)   (c)

Figure 9.4 Typical Support Hardware: (a) Exposed Slot T-Grid Ceiling; (b) Exposed T-Grid Ceiling; (c) Drywall Kit.
Courtesy of Philips Lighting Company.

add control and increase efficiency, or they may be straight and absorptive to minimize brightness at the aperture.

The support brackets can be outfitted with different types of bars or clips to attach the luminaire to the ceiling or ceiling system (Figure 9.4).

Common Luminaire Types

Downlight

■ *downlight*
A luminaire, from which the light is directed downward.

A *downlight* does exactly what it says: It directs light downward. Downlights always have a direct distribution pattern (see Chapter 6). A downlight may be recessed, surface mounted, or pendant; may use any lighting technology; and may produce a wide, medium, or narrow cone of light (Figure 9.5).

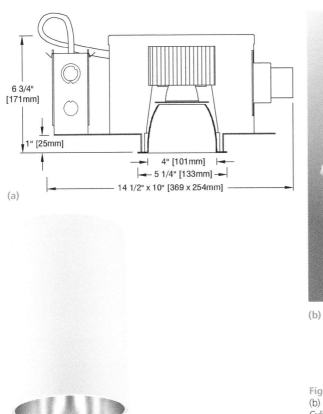

(a)

(c)

(b)

Figure 9.5 Typical Downlights: (a) Recessed LED Downlight; (b) Recessed 2×2 Fluorescent Downlight; (c) Surface Mount HID Cylinder Downlight.
(a) Courtesy of Edison Price Lighting, Inc.; (b) Courtesy of Eaton's Cooper Lighting Business; (c) Courtesy of Philips Lighting Company.

Recessed Adjustable or Accent

A recessed adjustable luminaire is a variation on a downlight that uses a directional lamp (R, PAR, MR, AR, LED), or a lamp set within an adjustable reflector (MH or CMH), on a pivoting arm (Figure 9.6). The arm can hold the lamp facing straight down so that the luminaire acts as a downlight, but can also pivot so that the center of the beam exits the luminaire at up to 45° and rotates up to 358°. These luminaires are frequently seen in retail applications because they can be adjusted to accommodate changing displays from one season to the next. Some adjustable luminaires are semi-recessed, in which case they may tilt as much as 90°.

Wall Washer

A *wall washer* is another special form of downlight (Figure 9.7). The angle and direction of the light is fixed, but it is not directed straight downward. Instead, a specially shaped

■ *wall washer*
A luminaire designed to illuminate a wall.

145

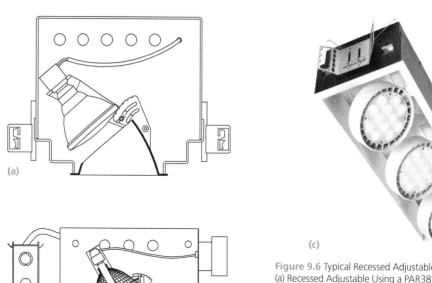

(a)

(b)

(c)

Figure 9.6 Typical Recessed Adjustable Luminaires:
(a) Recessed Adjustable Using a PAR38; (b) Recessed
Adjustable Using T4 CMH and Reflector; (c) Recessed
Multiple Using LEDs.
*(a, b) Courtesy of Edison Price Lighting, Inc.; (c) Courtesy of
Philip Lighting Company.*

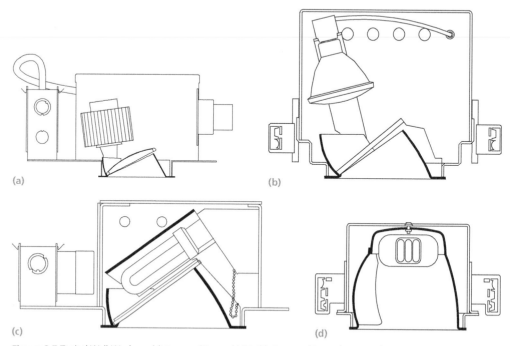

(a)

(b)

(c)

(d)

Figure 9.7 Typical Wall Washers: (a) Recessed Lensed LED; (b) Recessed Lensed PAR38; (c) Recessed Lensed CFL;
(d) Open CFL.
Courtesy of Edison Price Lighting, Inc.

reflector, often paired with a lens, is used to create an asymmetric wash of light to illuminate a wall from top to bottom. Unless a manufacturer's cut sheet indicates otherwise, we make two assumptions about wall wash luminaire spacing. First, the luminaires are placed 2'-6" to 4'-0" from the wall (3'-0" is typical). Second, the center-to-center spacing of the luminaires is the same dimension as the distance from the wall. Additional placement details are discussed in Chapter 11.

Wall Grazer

A *wall grazer* is another specialty downlight. Wall grazing is a lighting technique that projects light at a nearly vertical angle down the face of a wall in interior applications. In exterior applications grazing fixtures are usually installed at the base of a wall and are focused upward. Grazing is often used on textured walls to create high contrast between highlights and shadows on the surface. The result exaggerates the texture and three-dimensional form of the wall material. Wall grazing is also a good way to illuminate a reflective surface like polished stone, because the flat angle of incidence minimizes reflections of the lamp toward the viewer. Wall grazing luminaires use halogen or metal halide reflector lamps, or LEDs, to illuminate the full height of the wall (Figure 9.8). Typical installation details are shown in Chapter 11.

■ **wall grazer**
A luminaire set at the top of a wall that directs light down the face of the wall to illuminate it.

Track

Track and track luminaires comprise the most flexible lighting system (Figure 9.9). Track is typically a straight metal channel with internal wiring: 2', 4', and 8' are common lengths. Track pieces can be joined in a straight line, as well as L, T, and X configurations. Track can be recessed, surface mounted, or pendant, and can be attached to the ceiling or to the wall. Track can have one or more circuits of power, and circuit capacities can range from 20A to 60A. It is important to remember that most manufacturers have a unique internal configuration for their track. Track heads from one manufacturer are unlikely to fit into the track of another.

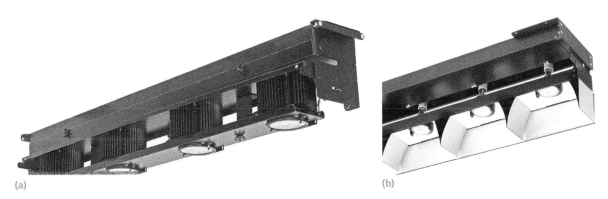

(a)   (b)

Figure 9.8 Typical Wall Grazing Luminaires: (a) LED Lamps without Louvers and (b) PAR Lamps with Louvers.
Courtesy of Edison Price Lighting, Inc.

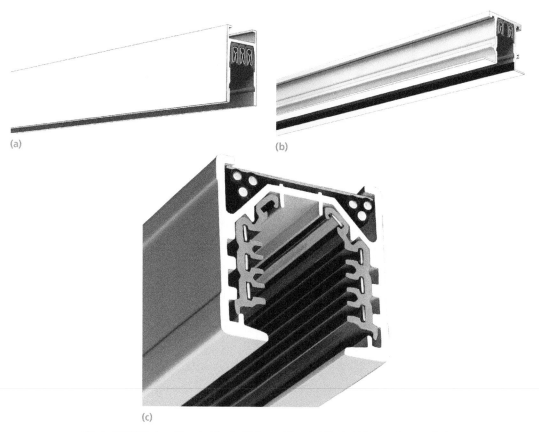

(a)

(b)

(c)

Figure 9.9 (a) Surface Mounted Track; (b) Recess Mounted Track; (c) Surface Mounted, Three-Circuit Track. *(a, b) Courtesy of Edison Price Lighting, Inc.; (c) Courtesy of Eaton's Cooper Lighting Business.*

Variations on track include rod and cable systems, as shown in Figure 9.10.

Track Heads

Track luminaires, often called track "heads" (Figure 9.11), can be attached to the track at any point along its length. Track heads may be direct distribution spotlights, wall washers, or decorative pendants, making this a very flexible lighting system.

A special type of track head is the framing projector (Figure 9.12). It is a scaled down version of a theatrical ellipsoidal reflector spotlight. Framing projectors have internal shutters to precisely shape the beam of light. Two independently adjustable lenses allow for on-site changes of the beam angle and edge softness. An accessory slot near the shutters accept a steel or glass template. Templates are available in thousands of patterns, and can also be custom made to project a corporate logo, for example.

(a)

(b)

Figure 9.10 (a) Rod System and (b) Cable System.
Courtesy of Tech Lighting.

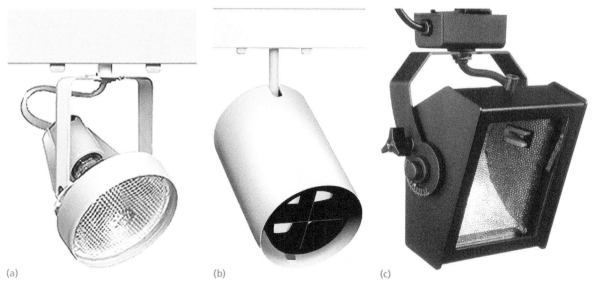

(a)

(b)

(c)

Figure 9.11 (a) Gimble Ring; (b) Cylinder with Cross Baffle; (c) Wall Washer.
(a, b) Courtesy of Edison Price Lighting, Inc.; (c) Courtesy of Altman Lighting.

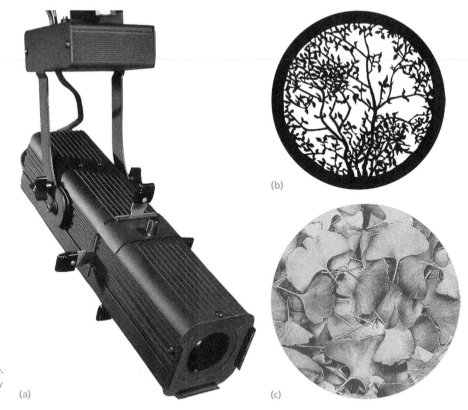

(b)

Figure 9.12 (a) Framing Projector; (b) Steel Template; (c) Glass Template.
Framing projector courtesy of Altman Lighting; Templates courtesy of Rosco Laboratories, Inc.

(a)

(c)

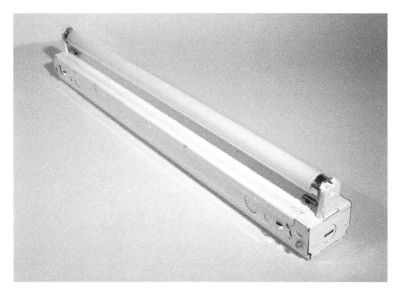

■ *cove lighting*
A technique in which a luminaire is set on a shelf below the ceiling. Light from the luminaire is reflected off of the ceiling and into the space below.

Figure 9.13 Typical Fluorescent Strip.

Fluorescent Strip

A fluorescent strip is a very simple luminaire, consisting of a metal box holding the ballast and sockets, which in turn hold the lamp (Figure 9.13). This workhorse luminaire can be surface mounted on ceilings and walls, or hung on stems, cables, or chain. It is often used in loading docks, utility rooms, and other spaces where light is more important than luminaire appearance. They are also used to backlight luminous ceilings and signage. Accessories include wire cages, reflectors, and diffusers.

Cove Lights

Cove lighting uses a shelf, ledge, or horizontal alcove set below the ceiling with a lip to hide the luminaires sitting on it. The luminaires bounce their light off of the ceiling to create a soft, ambient lighting effect. A cove may be used as a decorative element, creating a line of light at the ceiling but providing little useful light. It may also be used as a major contributor to the overall room brightness. The difference is in the selection of the luminaire and lamp. The simplest cove luminaire is a fluorescent strip (Figure 9.13) or a row of compact fluorescent lamps. Other cove luminaires use LED lamps, and may add reflectors to increase efficiency (Figure 9.14).

Typical installation details are covered in Chapter 11.

(a)

(b)

Figure 9.14 Cove Luminaires: (a) LED Strip; (b) Linear Fluorescent with Reflector.
Courtesy of Philips Lighting Company.

Theatrical Luminaires

Theatrical luminaires can be useful in specialty applications. The barriers to the use of theatrical luminaires are their size and wattage. Theatrical luminaire manufacturers have responded by replacing short life, high wattage (500 to 1,000W is common) quartz lamps with long life, lower wattage metal halide lamps. LED versions of these luminaires are also on available. Only CMH and LED luminaires are discussed here.

Ellipsoidal Reflector Spotlight

Ellipsoidal reflector spotlights (also known by the brand names Source 4, Leko Lite, and Phoenix, among others) are dual lensed luminaires that allow for careful beam shaping and edge softness adjustment (Figure 9.15). The CMH versions place the lamp at the focal point of an ellipsoidal reflector. The reflector directs the light through an area known as a gate. LED versions focus the LEDs toward the gate. At the gate, built-in shutters can be used to shape the beam, and steel or glass templates can be inserted to give texture to the light (Figures 9.12b and 9.12c). The light then passes through two plano-convex lenses. The lenses can slide forward and backward (as a unit in fixed beam angle luminaires and separately in zoom luminaires) to sharpen or soften the beam edge. A color filter slot is located at the front of the luminaire.

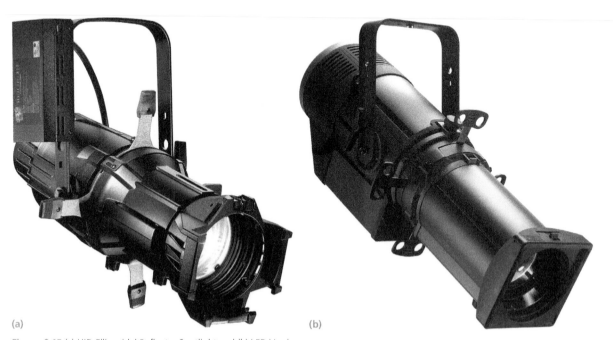

(a)   (b)

Figure 9.15 (a) HID Ellipsoidal Reflector Spotlight and (b) LED Version.
Courtesy of (a) Electronic Theatre Controls; (b) Strand Lighting.

PAR

Theatrical PAR luminaires use larger lamps than common architectural luminaires, usually PAR56 and PAR64 (Figure 9.16). These lamps tend to have a strong punch of light at the center, are oval shaped (not round like the beams of most other luminaires), and have soft, ill-defined edges. The luminaire holds the lamp somewhat loosely so that the lamp can be rotated by hand to orient the oval of light as needed by the designer.

HID PARs typically have an integral reflector and lamp holder with a set of replaceable lenses. The advantage is that one doesn't need to change the entire lamp to change the beam angle, only the lens. The lens is rotatable, and the luminaire retains the oval shaped beam that is characteristic of PAR lamps. LED PARS also have field changeable lenses that produce an oval beam of light.

Striplight

A striplight is a compartmented, multicircuited unit designed to deliver a linear wash of light such as might be used to wash a wall (Figure 9.17). A striplight is generally wired for either three or four circuits. Each circuit typically has its own color, allowing a greater number of colors to be created by blending two or more of the circuits.

LED versions of the striplight using three, four, and even seven colors of LEDs are also available.

(a)   (b)

Figure 9.16 (a) HID Theatrical PAR and (b) LED Version.
Courtesy of Electronic Theatre Controls.

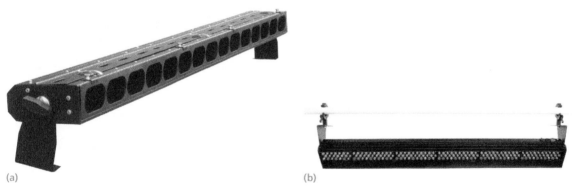

(a)   (b)

Figure 9.17 (a) Incandescent Striplight for MR11 Lamps; (b) Seven-Color LED Striplight.
Courtesy of (a) Altman Lighting; (b) Electronic Theatre Controls.

Luminaire Accessories

Many luminaires, especially those that use a directional lamp (R, PAR, MR, AR) can accept accessories to modify the beam or hide the face of the lens. Options include color filters, spread lenses, beam softening lenses, and UV filters (Figure 9.18). The bright face of the luminaire can be hidden and glare reduced with louvers, open hoods (also called top hats), cross baffle hoods, and barndoors (Figure 9.19).

Mounting Conditions

Another way of describing luminaires is by the way they are mounted and how much of the luminaire's housing or body is visible in the room.

Recessed

Recessed luminaires are those whose entire housing is behind the face of the ceiling, wall, or floor. *Semi-recessed* luminaires are those with a portion of the fixture projecting beyond the face of the ceiling or wall (Figure 9.20).

Surface Mount

Surface mount luminaires are those attached to the surface of the ceiling, wall (Figure 9.21), or perhaps to a piece of furniture. Unlike recessed and semi-recessed luminaires, they can easily be replaced without cutting into or damaging the mounting surface.

Pendant

Pendant refers to any luminaire that is hung from the ceiling (Figure 9.21). It may be purely decorative, like a chandelier, or it may be functional, like a direct/indirect luminaire in an open office. Pendant luminaires may be suspended by one or more metal rods, wire rope, chain, or by the power cord.

■ *recessed*
Describes any luminaire that is installed so that the housing of the luminaire is behind a room surface.

■ *semi-recessed*
A luminaire that is only partly above the ceiling or within a wall.

■ *surface mount*
Describes a luminaire installed on the surface of the ceiling, wall, floor, or piece of cabinetry or furniture.

■ *pendant*
Describes a luminaire hanging from the ceiling.

Figure 9.18 Lenses with Photos of the Affected Beam: (a) No Lens, (b) Beam Softening Lens, (c) Linear Spread Lens.

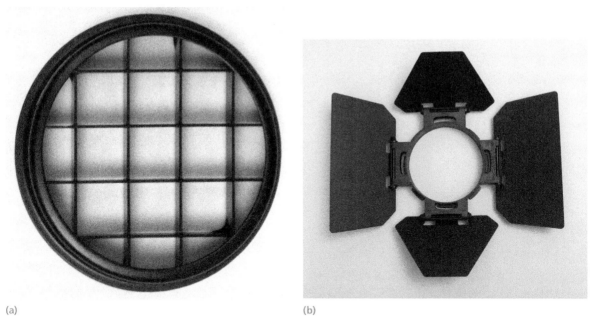

(a)   (b)

Figure 9.19 Accessories: (a) Louver, (b) Barndoor.

Figure 9.20 Recessed and Semi-Recessed Luminaires.

Figure 9.21 Surface and Pendant Luminaires.

Outdoor Luminaires

The considerations discussed in this chapter are illustrated with interior luminaires, but apply equally to exterior luminaires. There is one additional consideration for exterior luminaires; protection from intrusion of water and objects such as dirt and insects. The system for describing the level of protection a luminaire provides is the Ingress Protection (IP) rating. The IP rating consists of two digits, such as IP55. The first digit describes the protection against solid objects.

Category	Protection Level
0	No protection
1	Protected against solid objects over 50 mm, e.g, accidental touch by person's hands
2	Protected against solid objects over 12 mm, e.g, person's fingers
3	Protected against solid objects over 2.5 mm, e.g, tools and thick wires)
4	Protected against solid objects over 1 mm, e.g, tools, thick and thin wires
5	Protected against dust, limited ingress, no harmful deposit
6	Totally protected against dust

The second digit describes the protection against liquids.

Category	Protection Level
0	No protection
1	Protection against vertically falling drops of water, e.g, dripping water
2	Protection against direct sprays of water up to 15° from the vertical
3	Protected against direct sprays of water up to 60° from the vertical
4	Protection against water splashed or sprayed from all directions—limited ingress permitted
5	Protected against low pressure jets of water from all directions—limited ingress permitted
6	Protected against high pressure jets of water and temporary flooding of water, e.g, for use on ship decks—limited ingress permitted
7	Protected against the effect of immersion between 15 cm and 1 m
8	Protects against long periods of immersion under pressure

Luminaire Consideration Summary

The enormous range of luminaire types, and the variations and options for each type, mean that specifying a luminaire can be complicated. When selecting and specifying a fixture we must consider:

- Luminaire purpose
- Light distribution
- Reflector color
- Reflector finish
- Aperture size and shape
- Flange size and color (or flangeless)
- Housing size and dimensions (especially height)
- Lamp type, color characteristics, wattage, and efficacy
- Ballast or transformer type
- Mounting conditions
- Luminaire efficiency
- Luminaire cost

Reading Manufacturer's Literature

Cut sheets, also called specification sheets or spec sheets, are documents prepared by the luminaire manufacturer. They identify and describe the luminaire, and its components, options, and accessories. Cut sheets also include a matrix to aid the designer in compiling the correct product number. The reverse side of the cut sheet typically contains information on the optical performance of the luminaire. Cut sheets are available as PDF downloads from manufacturer's Web sites, or as hard copies in manufacturers' product binders. Figure 9.22 and 9.23 show a typical cut sheet.

Typical Cut Sheet Information

1. Line drawing and/or photo of a complete luminaire
2. Dimensions of housing and aperture

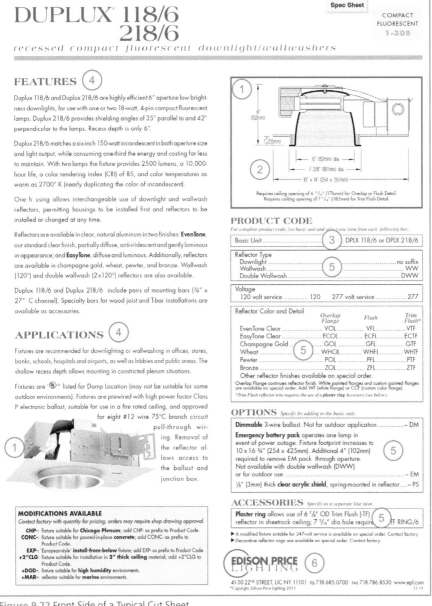

Figure 9.22 Front Side of a Typical Cut Sheet.
Courtesy of Edison Price Lighting, Inc.

DUPLUX 218/6

EDISON PRICE LIGHTING

PHOTOMETRIC REPORT (7)

itl *Report No. 41022. Original Independent Testing Laboratories, Inc. (ITL) test report furnished upon request.*

Luminaire ....recessed compact fluorescent downlight with spun aluminum reflector
Lamps........................two 18-watt double-tube, 4-pin, G24q-2 base, 1250 lumens each
Efficiency 44.0%
Spacing Criteria ....0°-1.5, 90°-1.5, 180°-1.5
Axis orientation............0° plane is parallel to lamps, opposite sockets

Photometric Report for Duplux 118/6 available on request.

ZONAL LUMEN SUMMARY (7)

Zone	Lumens	% Lamp	% Fixture
0 - 30°	445	17.8	40.4
0 - 40°	743	29.7	67.5
0 - 60°	1097	43.9	99.8
0 - 90°	1100	44.0	100.0

CANDLEPOWER DISTRIBUTION *(Candela)* (8)

Vertical Angle	Horizontal Angle 0	45	90	135	180
0	480	480	480	480	480
5	488	484	487	487	481
15	507	518	537	543	530
25	521	523	551	544	547
35	484	479	492	471	466
45	296	317	338	344	339
55	109	111	117	113	113
65	2	2	2	2	2
75	0	0	0	0	0
85	0	0	0	0	0
90	0	0	0	0	0

LUMINANCE DATA *(Candela/m²)* (7)

Vertical Angle	Average 0° Longitude	Average 90° Longitude	Average 180° Longitude
45	22014	25138	25212
55	9994	10727	10361
65	249	249	249
75	0	0	0
85	0	0	0

To convert cd/m² to footlamberts, multiply by 0.2919.

(10) COLOR MULTIPLIERS

EvenTone (V)	.95
EasyTone (EC)	.88
Champagne Gold (G)	.97
Wheat (WH)	.79
Pewter (P)	.81
Bronze (Z)	.58

BALLAST INFORMATION

Voltage	120	277
Input Watts	36	36
Line Current (A)	.34	.14
Power Factor (%)	>99	>99
Min. Starting Temp* (°F)	0	0

Consult lamp manufacturers for specific temperatures.

COEFFICIENTS OF UTILIZATION – ZONAL CAVITY METHOD
Effective Floor Cavity Reflectance 20%

Ceiling Reflectance (%)	80				70				50			30			10			0
Wall Reflectance (%)	70	50	30	10	70	50	30	10	50	30	10	50	30	10	50	30	10	0
Room Cavity Ratio																		
0	52	52	52	52	51	51	51	51	49	49	49	47	47	47	45	45	45	44
1	49	48	47	45	48	47	46	45	45	44	43	43	42	42	42	41	41	40
2	46	43	41	39	45	43	41	39	41	40	38	40	38	37	39	37	36	36
3	43	39	37	34	42	39	36	34	38	35	34	36	35	33	35	34	33	32
4	40	36	33	30	39	35	32	30	34	32	30	33	31	29	32	31	29	28
5	37	33	29	27	36	32	29	27	31	29	27	30	28	26	30	28	26	25
6	35	30	26	24	34	29	26	24	29	26	24	28	25	24	27	25	23	23
7	32	27	24	22	32	27	24	22	26	23	21	26	23	21	25	23	21	20
8	30	25	22	19	30	25	22	19	24	21	19	24	21	19	23	21	19	18
9	28	23	20	18	28	23	20	18	22	20	18	22	19	17	21	19	17	17
10	27	21	18	16	26	21	18	16	21	18	16	20	18	16	20	18	16	15

DUPLUX 218/6 WW

WALLWASH INFORMATION

Distance From Ceiling (Feet)	2'6" From Wall; 2'6" O.C. Below Fixture	Between Fixtures	3' From Wall; 3' O.C. Below Fixture	Between Fixtures
1	14	13	8	8
2	18	18	10	11
3	24	24	15	15
4	23	23	17	17
5	19	19	16	16
6	15	15	13	13
7	12	11	11	11
8	9	9	9	8
9	6	7	7	7
10	5	5	6	5

All vertical footcandles are initial values with no contribution from ceiling or floor reflectances. Computation performed with a total of five wallwashers.

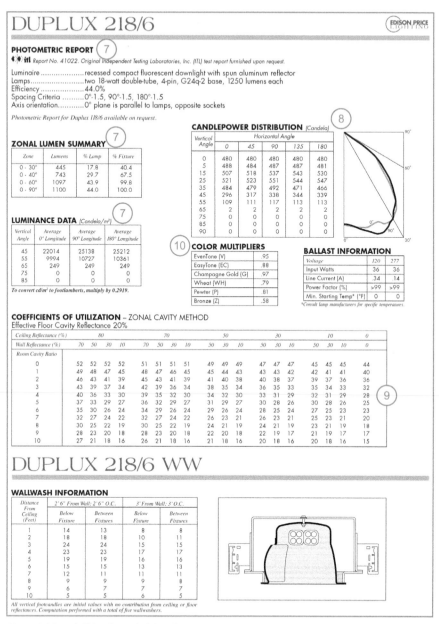

Figure 9.23 Back Side of a Typical Cut Sheet.
Courtesy of Edison Price Lighting, Inc.

3. Base catalog number (to be modified with the addition of options and accessories)
4. Description of luminaire features, optics, ballast/transformer/power supply, etc.
5. Options and accessories
6. Manufacturer's address and other contact information
7. Typical performance information

8. Candlepower distribution. Candlepower distribution curve is more common than the candelas table. This manufacturer provides both.
9. Coefficient of utilization table
10. Reflector color multipliers

We will learn how to read the performance information, called photometrics, in Chapter 13.

Modifying Luminaires

Sometimes an available luminaire is close to what the designer wants, but is not quite right. In those instances, it is worth talking to the manufacturer about modifying the standard luminaire. Many manufacturers are amenable to modifications, and they can usually be done faster and cheaper than a custom luminaire.

Custom Luminaires

When you can't find the perfect luminaire for a project, you may not have to settle for what's available. If the project's budget permits, you may want to design a custom luminaire. Since custom fixtures can become quite expensive, it's often best to begin working with a fabricator as early in the process as possible. Information that the fabricator will need include the overall size, desired materials and finishes, and lamp type(s) to be used. If the luminaire becomes cost prohibitive, the fabricator should be able to suggest cost-saving measures such as substituting a painted finish for a metal finish, substituting acrylic for glass or alabaster, or using other lower priced materials.

Figure 9.24 is an example of an initial sketch provided to a fabricator. The designer was working with a tight budget, so the sketch indicates those aspects of the luminaire that are required by showing detail, and those that are negotiable by omitting detail.

Luminaire Information and Sales

How does the lighting designer get information about luminaires and manufacturers? How do luminaires get ordered and sold? It's much more complicated than most people think! Let's look at a typical design/bid/build process as it pertains to lighting, as shown in Figure 9.25. Let's begin with the lighting designer.

Lighting Designer

The lighting designer is usually under contract to the architect, although sometimes the designer is employed directly by the owner. Lighting designers get information about lamps and luminaires through many channels, including direct email, direct mail, Web

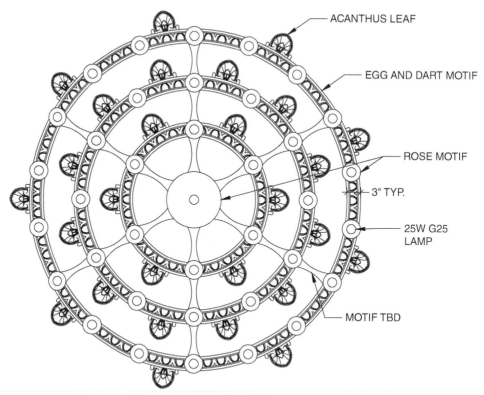

ACANTHUS LEAF

EGG AND DART MOTIF

ROSE MOTIF

3" TYP.

25W G25
LAMP

MOTIF TBD

VIEW FROM BELOW

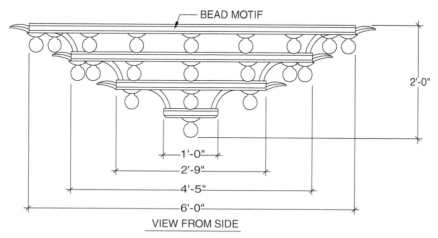

BEAD MOTIF

2'-0"

1'-0"
2'-9"
4'-5"
6'-0"

VIEW FROM SIDE

Figure 9.24 Sketch for a Custom Chandelier.
Courtesy of Studio T+L, LLC.

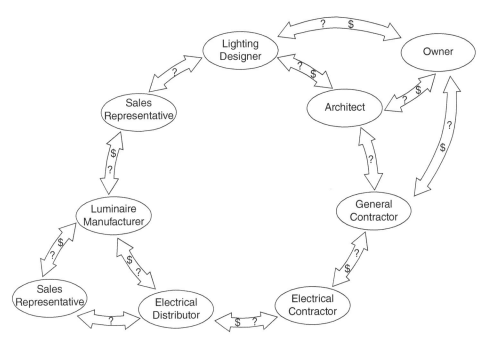

Figure 9.25 Luminaire Information and Sales (Note: Question marks represent exchange of information. Dollar signs represent exchange of money.)

sites, and trade shows. The most important source of information, though, is the sales representative (also known as the sales rep, rep, or sales agent). When the lighting designer needs sample luminaires, luminaire pricing, information on modifications, etc. from the luminaire manufacturer, the designer contacts the sales rep who then contacts the manufacturer on the designer's behalf.

Depending on the project type and contract method established by the owner, the lighting designer may be required to specify one luminaire for each type needed (a one-name, or proprietary, specification) three equal luminaires for each type needed (a three-name specification), or may have to avoid identifying exact luminaires and provide information about the specific performance of the luminaire for each type needed (a performance specification). At the end of the construction documentation phase the lighting designer provides the architect with a reflected ceiling plan or lighting plan, cut sheets, a lighting fixture schedule, and specifications (see Chapter 11 for details about these documents) that clearly and completely describe the lighting design.

Sales Representative

It is expensive and inefficient for every luminaire manufacturer to employ a nationwide sales team. Instead, most manufacturers contract with local or regional firms, which represent a number of manufacturers ranging from as few as a half dozen to 30 or more.

The sales representative's agents call on architects, engineers, interior designers, and lighting designers. They introduce new products, provide information, and generally keep the manufacturers they represent in the minds of the specifiers. The designer does not pay for the information or services of the sales rep. The sales rep's income comes from commissions from the manufacturer that are earned when luminaires are sold to a project.

The sales rep and the manufacturer collaborate to establish pricing for each project. Larger projects with more luminaires will usually pay less per luminaire. This can be frustrating to the designer. It can be hard to estimate the budget for a project when luminaire costs are variable. Another issue with pricing from the sales rep is that it is usually dealer net, distributor net, or DN pricing. This means that the luminaire price given is the price that the electrical distributor will pay the manufacturer. It does not include the electrical distributor's markup for overhead and profit, nor does it include possible markups by the electrical contractor and/or the general contractor. It is up to the lighting designer to estimate the total markup and add that amount to the projected lighting fixture budget.

Another frustration with the sales representative system is that the sales reps are in competition with one another for the sales commission, even those that represent the same manufacturer. It's not uncommon for the sales reps where the project is located to try to convince the electrical distributor and/or the electrical contractor (discussed next) to offer the designer alternative luminaires so that they, not the designer's sales rep, get the commission. See A Note on Substitutions or Alternates for more information on this practice.

Architect

The architect is hired by the owner, and usually hires the lighting designer along with the rest of the specialty consultants (electrical engineer, structural engineer, HVAC engineer, etc.). The lighting designer's documentation (discussed in Chapter 11) is coordinated with the rest of the design team and is integrated into the construction documents with final assembly by the architect.

During design and construction, there are so many people and companies involved that a hierarchy is established and paths of communication must be maintained. The architect is the primary point of contact between the general contractor (GC) or construction manager (CM) and the rest of the design team. Likewise, the GC or CM is the primary point of contact between the architect and owner, and the construction team. All information and communication between contractors and consultants flows through the architect.

General Contractor or Construction Manager

The general contractor (GC) or construction manager (CM) is hired by the owner to erect the building designed by the architect. The GC and CM do not fill the exact same roles, but for the purposes of this discussion we'll treat them the same and refer to them as the GC. It may be surprising to learn that the GC does not directly employ everyone on the construction site. The GC, like the architect, subcontracts much of the work to specialists. One of those specialists is the electrical contractor.

Electrical Contractor

The electrical contractor (EC) is the firm responsible for purchasing and installing all of the power and lighting equipment, and therefore plays a critical role in the execution of the lighting design.

ECs do not have warehouse stock of materials and lighting luminaires. They purchase materials on an as-needed basis. They usually do not purchase directly from manufacturers, but through supply companies known as electrical suppliers.

The EC is usually awarded a contract based on a lump sum bid. Some ECs seek to increase their profit margin by trying to substitute lower priced equipment, including luminaires, for those specified. See A Note on Substitutions or Alternates for more information on the EC's role in substitutions.

Electrical Supplier

The electrical supplier has warehouse stock of common items such as wire and conduit, and standing relationships with manufacturers for materials such as luminaires and control systems. When the EC needs luminaires, they are ordered from the electrical supplier who orders them from the manufacturer. See A Note on Substitutions or Alternates for more information on the electrical supplier's role in substitutions.

Online Resources

Luminaire Search

Lightsearch, www.lightsearch.com

eLumit, www.elumit.com

Advanced Lighting Guide, www.algonline.org

Luminaire Information

Advanced Lighting Guide, www.algonline.org

Lighting Research Center National Lighting Product Information Program—Select Programs, then NLPIP, www.lrc.rpi.edu

Next Generation Luminaire Design Competition, www.ngldg.org

A Note on Substitutions or Alternates

A great source of frustration for the lighting designer is that, despite the designer's contractual requirements for the lighting design documentation (proprietary specification, three-name specification, or performance specification), the EC is not required to provide the specified luminaires. This can give rise to one of several scenarios.

First, in an effort to save money and/or increase profit margins, the EC and/or the electrical supplier will offer alternate luminaires that may not meet the lighting designer's requirements. It becomes the lighting designer's responsibility to review the proposed substitutions and to provide an explanation for each substitute luminaire that is rejected.

Second, the electrical supplier may contact the local sales rep to get pricing for the luminaires. Sales reps near the project probably represent a different mix of manufacturers than the designer's sales rep, and may offer the electrical supplier substitutions for some or all of the luminaires—substitutions that come from the sales rep's other manufacturers. The sales rep does this to increase his or her sales commission, not to serve the project. This process, called "packaging," makes some sense to the electrical distributor since he gets a complete lighting package from one person. It can be frustrating for the lighting designer and bad for the project, though, because the sales rep's substitutions may not meet the project's requirements. Again, the lighting designer must review the proposed substitutions and provide an explanation for each substitute luminaire that is rejected.

In either case, the lighting designer has spent a great deal of time and effort identifying the right luminaire for a given application. It seems always to be the case that the harder the designer works to find just the right luminaire, the more inappropriate is the substitution and the longer it takes to resolve the difference between the two! In many cases, the time spent evaluating substitutions is not reimbursed by the architect or the owner, who see it as part of the lighting designer's job.

The lighting designer knows the project's budget for lighting equipment. In selecting luminaires, quality and performance are balanced against cost, the owner's requirements, and the design goals. The designer has collaborated with the owner, architect, and others to develop the requirements and expectations of the lighting system, and has worked hard to achieve, and perhaps surpass, those expectations. The owner, architect, GC, EC, etc., probably don't know the detailed requirements for the lighting design and may not understand how the specified luminaires fulfill those requirements. It is usually up to the lighting designer to defend the design and protect the owner when substitutions threaten the integrity of the design. Some substitutions are fine and can be readily agreed to. However, substitutions that affect the performance or appearance of the lighting design should be rejected.

Designing with Light Resources

Wiley's companion site to *Designing with Light*, www.wiley.com/go/designingwithlight

Author's companion site to *Designing with Light*, www.designinglight.com

References

DiLaura, David, et al., *The Lighting Handbook, Tenth Edition*, New York: Illuminating Engineering Society, 2011.

Egan, M. David, *Concepts in Architectural Lighting*, New York: McGraw-Hill, 1983.

Gordon, Gary, *Interior Lighting for Designers, Fourth Edition*, Hoboken, NJ: John Wiley & Sons, 2003.

IES Nomenclature Committee, *RP-16-05 Nomenclature and Definitions for Illuminating Engineering*, New York: Illuminating Engineering Society, 2005.

Steffy, Gary, *Architectural Lighting Design, Third Edition*, Hoboken, NJ: John Wiley & Sons, 2008.

CHAPTER 10

Daylighting

> "The sun—the bright sun, that brings back, not light alone, but new life, and hope, and freshness to man—burst upon the crowded city in clear and radiant glory. Through costly-coloured glass and paper-mended window, through cathedral dome and rotten crevice, it shed its equal ray."
>
> Charles Dickens, *Oliver Twist*

Daylighting refers to using sunlight and light from the sky to illuminate building interiors. For centuries, daylighting for building interiors was a given because the other sources of light (candles, torches, etc.) were dim, dirty, and expensive. In the twentieth century electric lighting came to dominate our thinking about lighting design. Today, with ever tightening power allowances in the energy conservation codes and the realization that daylighting provides many benefits in addition to free illumination, daylighting has been added to the areas of expertise of lighting designers. While it is not possible or desirable to incorporate daylighting into every building or building type, daylighting should be considered where appropriate.

The Benefits of Daylighting

Research has demonstrated many benefits from illuminating interior spaces with daylight and the resulting views to the outside.

Reduced energy costs: Although daylighting won't completely eliminate the need for electric lighting, especially because many buildings are occupied at night, combining daylighting with proper design of the electric lighting and control systems can reduce a building owner's energy costs by 35 percent.

Increased occupant satisfaction: The variations in light intensity, direction, and color that come with weather, time of day, and change in seasons provide a connection to the outside. Most people appreciate the connection, and express greater satisfaction in spaces with daylighting and views to the outside. In addition, the variations in patterns of light and shadow add dynamic visual interest to a space.

Increased worker/student productivity: Workplaces and schools where there is daylighting have demonstrated reduced absentee rates, increased productivity, reduced fatigue, and improved occupant health.

Increased sales: Many types of retailers have shown increased sales after the installation of skylights.

Improved health: Hospital patients have been shown to recover faster in rooms that provide a view to the outside. Daylighting may support circadian entrainment, which is discussed in Chapter 16.

Planning for Daylighting

Daylighting is not a strategy that is implemented solely by the lighting designer. Although the lighting designer may be the one to suggest it, the support and collaboration of the entire design team is needed to successfully design and execute a daylighting scheme. The owner must also be onboard, because successful daylighting has implications for the building facade and the interior design.

During programming, the design team and owner should discuss the possibility, requirements, and options for daylighting by asking questions such as:

- Is daylighting important to the owner or users, and if so, why?
- Is daylighting important in all spaces? Which spaces require daylighting, and which do not?
- In spaces with daylighting, are exterior views also important?

If the answers to these questions lead to the inclusion of daylighting in the building design, the design team can move forward together with that understanding.

During schematic design and design development, the architect and interior designer, with input from the lighting designer, will arrange the building exterior, orientation, and interior to take advantage of daylighting opportunities. The architect will seek to orient the building to take advantage of daylighting by aligning the long axis of the building (if there is one) parallel with east/west. This presents the maximum building face to direct, daylong sunlight along the south face (in the northern hemisphere), and indirect, northern light along the north face.

The interior designer should select materials and finishes that have high reflectance values to maximize inter-reflection, which will help daylight to penetrate deeper into the building. Workstation partitions should be low so as not to block or absorb the daylight. The layout of private and open offices and other types of spaces should be arranged and designed to minimize obstructions to daylight. For example, many people would assume that private offices (with their important occupants) should be at the perimeter of the building to provide views. However, since a typical private office has solid, opaque walls, daylight cannot penetrate to the interior of the building.

Alternative strategies include shifting private offices to the interior of the building and/ or using a transparent or translucent material for partition walls so that light can pass through them.

Solar Angles

The position of the sun changes with the time of day, the season, and the latitude, yet the position of the sun is critical for many daylighting strategies. What's a design team to do? At a minimum the team should examine the angle and intensity of the sun at its highest and lowest angles, which on the summer solstice (June 21) and the winter solstice (December 21).

The sun's position is located by two angles (Figure 10.1). The solar altitude is the angle above the horizon. The solar bearing, or azimuth, is the angle measured clockwise from north. Knowing the location of the sun, we can calculate the horizontal and vertical angle at which sunlight is striking the building. A more detailed study of the sun's affect on our design may include adding the fall and spring equinox (March 21 and September 21), and looking at other times of day.

There are other ways of examining a daylighting strategy. One is with scale models. Once the sun's position is known, a model is placed in a heliodon (a device that accurately emulates the motion and intensity of the sun in scale). The exterior and interior can then be studied and photographed.

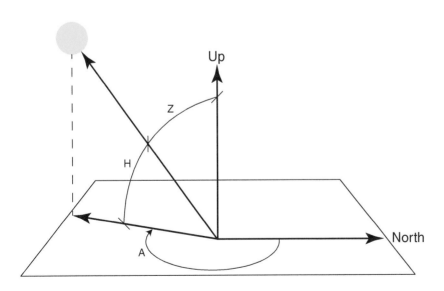

A = Azimuth angle, measured clockwise from North
H = Elevation angle, measured up from the horizon
Z = Zenith angle, measured from vertical

Figure 10.1 Solar Angle.

Computer simulation software is also available as stand-alone software, as an add-on to CAD software such as Revit, and within the illuminance calculation software used by most lighting designers (see Chapter 14). In each case, the building's longitude and latitude is entered into the software along with the north/south orientation and the date and time to be studied. The software, depending on its capabilities, can then display illuminance data; color, black and white, or false color perspectives; and even generate a walk-through or fly-by video clip.

Building Orientation

Each face of a building receives distinctly different types of daylight. The following information is generalized for a building in the northern hemisphere at mid-latitude (20–60°).

North Face

The north face of a building receives the most consistent illumination (from the northern sky). The diffuse illumination is the easiest to control across the day and year-round, and provides the best opportunity for large windows without the risk of the large heat gain associated with direct sunlight. Direct sunlight, if any, will strike the north face in the early morning or late evening at times close to the summer solstice.

South Face

The south face of a building receives the greatest variation of daylight over the course of a day and year. During the summer, the high angle of incident sunlight may be managed with blinds or a modest overhang to block direct sun while still admitting light from the sky. The low angle sunlight in the winter results in the deepest penetration of light into the building, but also the highest likelihood of discomfort glare. This light is best managed by operable blinds or shades.

Below 20° latitude the north and south faces may see similar lighting conditions but at opposite time of the year. The north face may receive direct sunlight in the summer and northern skylight in the winter, while the south face may receive direct sunlight in the winter and southern skylight in the summer.

East Face

The east face receives direct sunlight in the morning at an angle that increases from horizontal to vertical as the sun rises overhead. The direct morning sunlight can be limited by operable blinds or shades. Once the sun is high enough in the sky to stop direct penetration, the remaining light from the sky is similar to northern light.

West Face

The west face is the opposite of the east face, receiving north sky-like light in the morning and direct sunlight of a decreasing angle from noon to sunset.

Glazing

Glazing refers to the part of the wall, window, or skylight that is made of glass or another light admitting material. There are many glazing products available with a wide range of light transmitting characteristics. New materials are always coming to market, so the reader is advised to keep up with developments by consulting trade publications and other sources.

Glazing Characteristics

Visible Light Transmittance

The visible light transmittance of a material (denoted as VT or Tvis) is the percentage of light that passes through it. With north-facing glazing, windows used for views typically have a high VT. South-facing glazing may require a lower VT to control the light intensity and minimize heat gain from direct sunlight.

Insulating Properties

Glazing typically has lower insulating values than exterior wall assemblies. Large amounts of glazing in a building that utilizes daylighting can increase heat gain in summer and heat loss in winter, possibly negating the energy savings gained by the daylighting design. The insulating properties of window assemblies are rated using a U-factor, which is a measurement of the conduction of heat through the assembly. A lower U-factor indicates less conduction, and, therefore, better insulating properties.

Solar Heat Gain

Visible light represents approximately 46 percent of the energy of direct sunlight. The rest of the energy is found in the infrared (47 percent) and ultraviolet (7 percent) regions of the spectrum. The solar heat gain coefficient (SHGC) is a percentage of the solar energy that passes through a glazing assembly. In southern climates, glazing that passes much of the visible spectrum but blocks IR and UV is generally preferred. In northern climates the heat gain from IR and UV may offset heating requirements during winter days.

Designing Daylighting

The greatest challenge to daylighting is the extreme variability of the light that is captured or admitted into the building. Direct sunlight should be avoided because it is usually too bright and adds too much heat to the interior of the building. The intensity of daylight changes with the time of day, the weather, and the seasons. The angle, too, changes with the time of day and the seasons. The steep angle of the summer sun and the shallow angle of the winter sun must both be accounted for. That angular shift is greater at higher latitudes (farther away from the equator). All of these factors make daylighting a challenge. Part of the solution to that challenge is an electric lighting system that is designed to support daylighting, and a control system that allows the electric lighting to take over in a seamless and reliable manner.

Broadly speaking, there are two types of daylighting: toplighting and sidelighting. Toplighting refers to light that enters through skylights, *roof monitors*, or *clerestories*. *Sidelighting* refers to light that enters through windows in the walls. *Toplighting* is a more effective daylighting solution, since it minimizes or eliminates direct sun and can cover the entire floor area evenly. Sidelighting, however, is the more common strategy. After all, only the top floor of any building has a roof and can use *skylights*.

Toplighting

There are two approaches to toplighting. The first, when the roof and ceiling are minimally separated, is to use skylights and/or roof monitors. The second, when there is a larger separation between the roof and the ceiling, is the use of a light tube. Roof monitors are part of the overall shape of the building and will affect its appearance from the outside. Skylights and light tubes can be integrated into the roof without affecting the building's appearance.

Skylights are apertures in the roof that admit light from the sky. The aperture is usually covered with a diffusing glass or plastic to improve the even distribution of light into the building. Dome-shaped skylights collect more daylight than do flat skylights. Splaying the interior of the skylight provides more even distribution and softens the contrast between ceiling and skylight. Adding a diffuser to the bottom of the skylight creates the broadest distribution (Figure 10.2).

To provide even illumination, skylights should be evenly distributed and should cover between 2 percent and 6 percent of the roof. The exact number of skylights will depend on their size, the illuminance target, the skylight's efficiency, and desired uniformity. Spacing between skylights generally should not exceed 1.5 times the height of the space illuminated, or the uniformity will become unacceptable (Figure 10.3).

Light tubes, or light pipes, are used to overcome separation between the roof and the space being illuminated. Light pipes are made of highly reflective material that can efficiently conduct light 20' or more, even around bends (Figure 10.4).

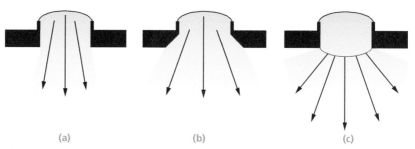

(a)　　　(b)　　　(c)

Figure 10.2 Distribution from Skylights: (a) Straight-Sided Skylight; (b) Splayed Skylight; (c) Skylight with Bottom Diffuser.

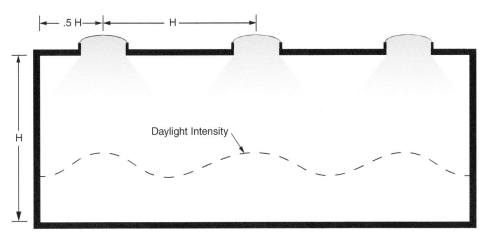

Figure 10.3 Skylight Placement and Illuminance Curve.

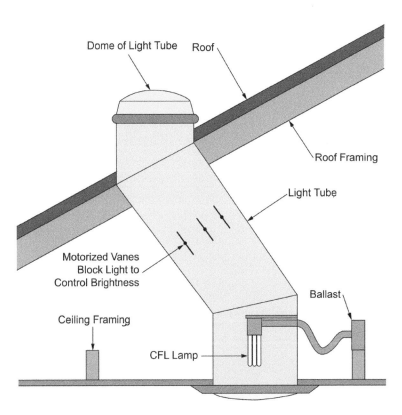

Figure 10.4 Light Pipe Bringing Light into an Interior.

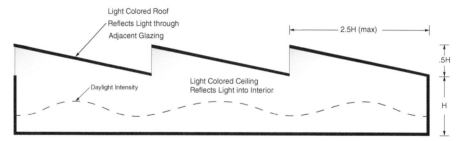

Figure 10.5 Clerestory and Sawtooth Roof Monitor.

The light emitted from skylights and light pipes can be controlled by the addition of a manual or motorized set of vanes or louvers. These will block some of the light as they are rotated from parallel to the light's direction of travel to perpendicular. At night the skylight's opening into the room will be a dark hole with no light below it. However, small luminaires can be installed in the light tube to compensate for the absence of daylight.

Sawtooth roof monitors and clerestories (Figure 10.5) fall between skylights, which admit light from above, and windows, which admit light from the side. The light from sawtooth monitors and clerestories is admitted at or near the ceiling, but has a partial sideways distribution. Although they can be oriented in any direction, they are often designed to face north, admitting light from the sky and sunlight reflected off of the roof.

Another toplighting strategy is the use of "pop-up" roof monitors (Figure 10.6). These monitors have glazing on more than one side. The additional glazing admits more daylight than clerestories, and the resulting light is less directional. However, they can have the added complication of admitting direct sunlight if not carefully shielded or shaded.

Sidelighting

The simplest form of sidelighting is the window (Figure 10.7), although effective daylighting through windows is not simple. When sidelighting with simple windows, the general rule of thumb is that the daylight will penetrate into the room a distance 1.5 to twice the head height of the window.

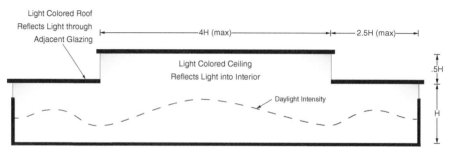

Figure 10.6 Clerestory and Roof Monitor.

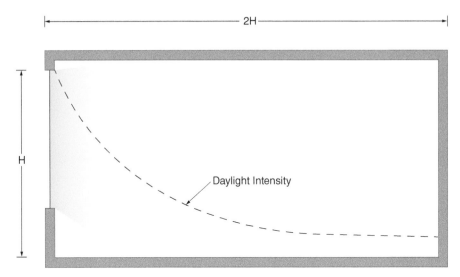

Figure 10.7 Light through a Window.

Figure 10.7 shows that using a window alone gives a fairly rapid drop-off in illuminance level. One method of forcing light deeper into the room is with the addition of a light shelf (Figure 10.8). A light shelf is a horizontal platform that reflects incoming sunlight to the ceiling, where it is reflected and diffused deeper into the room. It splits the window into two halves. The upper half is glazed to admit light, and the lower half is glazed for views.

The top of the light shelf should be a highly reflective material to maximize the light that is redirected, although specular materials should be avoided because they can create excessively bright ceiling areas that may be a source of glare. A light shelf can be inside, through, or outside the window, depending on the architecture and building orientation. Light shelves that are outside or through the window have the added benefit of shading the lower portion of the

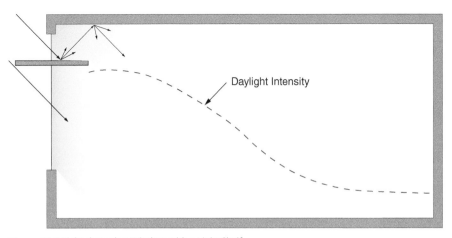

Figure 10.8 Light through a Window with a Light Shelf.

window, reducing heat gain from direct sunlight. Light shelves are typically installed at heights of 7'-6" or more, so ceiling heights of 9' or higher are required. Variations on this simple light shelf include tilting the shelf and sloping the ceiling, or using curved instead of flat surfaces, to increase the amount of light redirected and the depth the light travels into the room.

Another variation is a mirrored louver system. This may be permanently installed or it may be user operable. Similar to venetian blinds, but mirrored on the top of the slat, users can lower the blinds and adjust the angle of the slats to maximize the light reflected toward the ceiling.

The presence of a daylighting system affects the design of the electric light system. The energy code ANSI/ASHRAE/IES Standard 90.1, for instance, (see Chapter 14) includes formulas for determining how much of the floor area is affected by daylighting system and the electric lighting system's response (light sensors, dimming, etc).

Shading Strategies

As previously mentioned, we don't want direct sunlight entering a building. Direct sunlight is far too bright (up to 100,000 lx or 10,000 fc) in contrast to the rest of the interior illuminance levels, and causes discomfort and glare. It also adds heat to a building's interior. So, while we are trying to maximize our use of light from the sky and reflected sunlight, we are also trying to block direct sunlight. Some of the most common shading techniques include exterior shelves, shutters or awnings, interior drapes or blinds, and louvers or blinds inside double glazing systems.

Exterior shelves are solid, horizontal opaque elements that are integral to the architecture of the building. They block direct sunlight and light from the sky. Shutters (Figure 10.9) are systems of framed slats that are angled to block direct sunlight, but often have gaps between them to admit a portion of the light from the sky. Shutters can be permanently affixed to a building's exterior or may be on the interior and be user adjustable. Awnings (Figure 10.10) are typically fabric or aluminum assemblies attached to a building's exterior. Like light shelves, they are opaque.

Online Resources

Advanced Buildings Daylighting Pattern Guide, http://patternguide.advancedbuildings.net/home

Advanced Lighting Guide—Daylighting, www.algonline.org

Daylighting Collaborative, www.daylighting.org

Energy Efficiency & Renewable Energy (U.S. Department of Energy), www.eere.energy.gov

Solar Calculator by National Oceanic & Atmospheric Administration, www.esrl.noaa.gov/gmd/grad/solcalc/

Whole Building Design Guide, www.wbdg.org/resources/daylighting.php

Figure 10.9 Typical Shutters to Keep Direct Sunlight from Entering the Building.
© *Paul Matthew Photography, used under license from Shutterstock.com.*

Figure 10.10 Typical Awning Blocking Sunlight.
© *Alexander Chakin, used under license from Shutterstock.com.*

Designing with Light Resources

Wiley's companion site to *Designing with Light,* www.wiley.com/go/designingwithlight

Author's companion site to *Designing with Light,* www.designinglight.com

References

ASHRAE Standing Standard Project Committee 90.1 *ANSI/ASHRAE/IESNA Standard 90.1-2010 Energy Standard for Buildings Except Low-Rise Residential Buildings*, Atlanta: American Society of Heating, Refrigeration and Air-Conditioning Engineers, Inc., 2004.

Boubekri, Mohamad, *Daylighting, Architecture and Health*, Oxford, UK: Elsevier Ltd. 2012.

"Daylighting," Advanced Lighting Guidelines, New Buildings Institute, accessed January 23, 2013, /www.algonline.org/index.php?daylighting.

DiLaura, David, et al., *The Lighting Handbook, Tenth Edition,* New York: Illuminating Engineering Society, 2011.

Egan, M. David, *Concepts in Architectural Lighting*, New York: McGraw-Hill. 1983.

IESNA Daylighting Committee, *IESNA RP-5-99 Recommended Practice of Daylighting*, New York: Illuminating Engineering Society, 1999.

Meshbert, Gary, and Craig DiLouie, "Estimating Energy Savings from Controls," *Lighting Design + Application,* August 2013, 18–22.

CHAPTER 11

Documenting the Design

"The details are not the details. They make the design."

Charles Eames

A design is not developed and documented all at once. It is a process that goes through several clear steps, or phases. Along the way there are pauses for coordination among the design disciplines, budgeting, and review by the owner. Owner or user feedback at each step helps to assure that the design is meeting their needs.

Phases of the Architectural Design Process

At the beginning of any project, before the design professionals are hired, there is a need. The future owner needs new office space, classroom space, retail locations, etc. Once the future owner is convinced that the need is real and must be acted upon, a design team is hired and the project begins.

    The design of a building and all of the components that make up the building will usually follow a well-understood series of steps. While the steps in the process are somewhat fixed, the methods used and the materials produced, especially in the early steps, vary according the owner's needs and the working methods of the design team.

Programming Phase

The design team's first task is to analyze and understand the owner's needs for the building. How many types of spaces are needed and the quantity of each, what activities will occur, are there any special requirements, and are all questions to be asked and answered. The process usually results in the development of a spreadsheet called the building program, which identifies every room in the project and each room's requirements for size, adjacencies, mechanical needs, finishes, etc. The more information that can be included in the building program the better. The design team may also include rough floor plans, massing sketches of the building, and drafts of other materials. The architect will usually go through the programming phase without a lighting designer.

The building program is presented to the owner for review and questions. Once the owner is satisfied that the building program includes all of the necessary components, it is approved and the team moves on to the next phase.

Schematic Design Phase

Armed with the building program, the design team can begin to make basic design decisions. During schematic design (SD) the design team develops and refines an idea or set of ideas about how to meet the programming needs, both technically and aesthetically. Those ideas are explored and documented in a variety of ways: sketches, diagrams, preliminary ground plans, outlines, and narratives. The schematic design conveys the broad strokes of the building, and is the foundation for the rest of the design work.

During schematic design the lighting designer will gather information from the owner, users, architect, and interior designer related to the use of the spaces, the desired feeling/impression that the spaces should create or support, and initial thoughts about the color and materials palettes. That information will shape the lighting designer's initial ideas about the types of lamps, warmth or coolness of the light, types of fixtures, and the distribution patterns of light. By the end of schematic design, the lighting designer will usually provide the design team with a narrative and budget, and may include cut sheets for preliminary fixture choices, preliminary details for special installations, and control system information. At the completion of SD an updated budget is prepared and the budget, along with the other documentation, are delivered to the owner and distributed to the entire design team for review.

Design Development Phase

During design development (DD) the design team takes the SD documents to the next level of refinement with additional design work, drawings, details, and finishes. This is when the mechanical, electrical, plumbing, and structural drawings begin to be developed. As the design progresses, the lighting designer makes the following decisions:

- The lamps and fixtures to be used
- The arrangement or layout of the luminaires—the lighting plan
- Any required electrical and control devices
- Any details of special installations or custom fixtures
- Suggestions of modifications to the architectural or interior designs that may improve the lighting, and therefore the project

Often, the DD process stops at 50 percent and/or 90 percent for budgeting and design team coordination. At the completion of DD an updated budget is prepared and the budget, drawings, and specifications are delivered to the owner and distributed to the entire design team for review.

The lighting designer's contribution to design development includes lighting plans, cut sheets, and a fixture schedule (although they may be preliminary or only partially complete), drawings or sketches of construction and installation details (such as coves), and modified or custom fixtures. If there is a control system, a control riser and control narrative will also be prepared. The budget is refined or revised. Code compliance calculations or documentation may be started in collaboration with the electrical engineer. Preliminary specifications may also be required.

Construction Documentation Phase

In the construction documentation (CD) phase, the design team coordinates and completes all of the drawings and specifications that the contractor will use to bid on and to construct the building. During the CD phase there are often pauses at 50 percent and 80–90 percent for coordination and budgeting.

At the end of construction documentation the lighting designer will have fully completed the lighting plans, drawings of modified and/or custom fixtures, the fixture schedule, cut sheets, specifications, and the control riser, dimming schedule, and controls narrative (if required). All special construction or installation details will have been fully coordinated with the architect.

As discussed in Chapter 1, lighting design is not a licensed profession, which means we cannot certify that the work shown on the drawings complies with building and safety codes. That certification must come from a licensed professional such as the architect or electrical engineer. Therefore, our drawings may not appear as stand-alone drawings in CD documentation. Sometimes, the information contained in our drawings is incorporated into the drawings of the architect and electrical engineer. Either way, once the final CD documents are assembled, they are sent out to contractors for bidding.

Bidding Phase

Once construction documents are completed, interested and qualified contractors will have the opportunity to review the drawings and specifications to prepare their bids. While reviewing the drawings they may have questions about the design intent or construction methods. If so, the design team will receive, and respond to, these questions in writing. Once the bids have been received by the owner, the design team may be asked to review them to confirm that they are equal, that they cover the entire project, and that the bid totals are reasonable.

Construction Administration Phase

The design team's responsibilities continue through construction. This phase of a project is called construction administration or contract administration (CA). During CA the entire design team provides information and oversight by regularly attending meetings, answering contractor questions, and making periodic visits to inspect the progress of the work.

The two most important aspects of CA are shop drawings, or submittals, and site visits. Contractors don't purchase and install any important materials without first getting those materials approved, even though they are identified in the drawings and specifications. For lighting designers, this means that the EC sends cut sheets for each luminaire that he intends to purchase and install. This package is called the lighting shop drawings or the lighting submittals. The lighting designer will review each luminaire submitted and approve it, approve it with comments, or reject it. If a luminaire is rejected, the EC offers another for approval. This is a critical time for the lighting designer. Errors in reviewing the submittal can result in luminaires of the wrong color or with the wrong ballast, for example. Inappropriate substitutions can affect distribution and light levels, so a careful review of proposed substitutions is important.

Site visits are made periodically to inspect the progress of the work. Site visits are followed up with written reports and punch lists of items that are incomplete, complete but unsatisfactory, or incorrect.

At the end of CA, the lighting designer will return to the site to focus all focusable fixtures, and to work with a control system technician to record light levels and program control system operations. The lighting designer may also instruct the users on the lighting system's operation and instruct the maintenance staff on relamping and focusing.

Design Documentation

A beautifully thought out design is of little value if it can't be communicated to those who will be constructing the building. There are several standard documents that the lighting designer produces or initiates to communicate everything about the lighting design to the rest of the design team and to the contractor. Those documents are the following:

- Reflected Ceiling Plan or Lighting Plan
- Luminaire Cut Sheets
- Luminaire or Lighting Fixture Schedule
- Specifications

- Installation Details
- Illuminance Calculations, which are covered in Chapter 13

Reflected Ceiling Plan or Lighting Plan

The reflected ceiling plan (RCP) is the plan view drawing that shows the location of each luminaire at the ceiling, and may show luminaires mounted in or on the walls as well. It is best to think of the drawing as a lighting plan, and understand that the cutline through the room or building is at the ceiling. This approach eliminates any possible confusion about "reflecting," and clarifies the purpose of the drawing, which is to show the location and type of all luminaires. For the sake of brevity, we will refer to this drawing as the RCP for the rest of this book.

Figure 11.1 is the RCP for the conference room that was discussed in Chapter 2. Note that, unlike the lighting plan shown in the Chapter 10, this RCP is a complete page that follows the rules of good drafting and contains a title block, detail markers, notations of scale, date, page/drawing number, etc.

Luminaire Symbols

The range of luminaires, and their options and variations, is so vast that it is impossible to develop a set of symbols that can denote all of the information about a given luminaire. There are, however, several rules-of-thumb and conventions that are used across the lighting industry.

Rule #1: Draw the Luminaire. Symbols should represent the general proportions, orientation, and shape of surface and pendant mounted luminaires, and the aperture for recessed luminaires. Since the cutline of the drawing is at the ceiling, we can't see the housing of a recessed luminaire, we only see the aperture of the reflector. For recessed luminaires, the purpose of RCP is to show aperture in the right location. Remember that the housing might not be centered around the aperture.

Rule #2: Simplicity and Clarity. Most luminaires are circles, squares, and rectangles when seen in plan view, so most of the symbols used on an RCP should be, too. It's acceptable to simplify a symbol. For example, a chandelier with eight arms can be drawn as a circle of the appropriate diameter. Remember that the symbols will be on drawings that are often in small scales (say 1/8″ = 1′-0″), so a symbol that is too fussy becomes illegible when printed.

Rule #3: Stay in Scale. Don't create symbols that are larger or smaller than the luminaire or aperture. The one exception to this rule is small aperture luminaires such as 2″ aperture MR16 downlights. With these luminaires the symbol may turn into a dot when printed at a small scale. If that is the case, the symbol may be enlarged until it is clear.

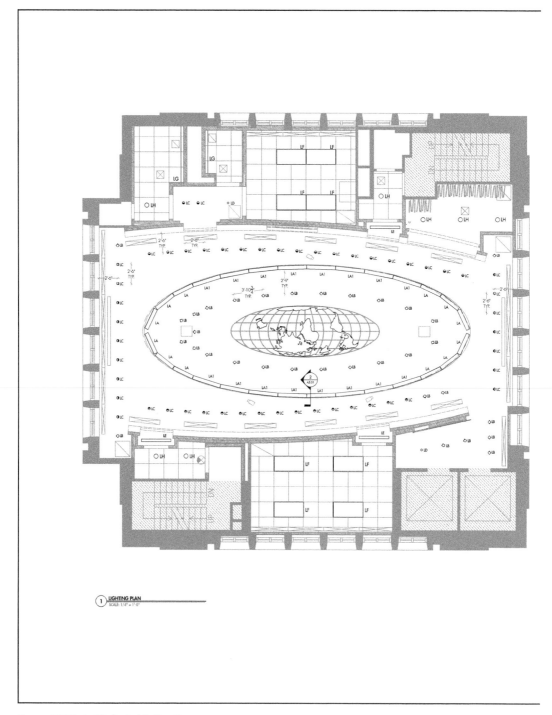

Figure 11.1 Typical Reflected Ceiling Plan.
Courtesy of Big Show Construction Management.

NOTES

1. FIXTURE INFORMATION CAN BE FOUND ON THE CUT SHEETS IN SECTION 265113.
2. "FOCUSING REQUIRED" WHEN NOTED REQUIRES THE CONTRACTOR TO PROVIDE ALLOWANCE FOR MANPOWER, SCAFFOLDING, AND TOOLS TO ADJUST, AIM, OR INSTALL FIXTURES AND ACCESSORIES PER THE LIGHTING CONSULTANT'S DIRECTION. THIS WORK WILL BE PERFORMED DURING EVENING HOURS IF THE LOCATION OF THE WORK RECEIVES DAYLIGHT DURING NORMAL WORKING HOURS. THE CONTRACTOR IS TO LOCK, (IF THE FIXTURE ALLOWS) BUT NOT OVER-TIGHTEN, ALL FIXTURES SO THAT THE LAMPHOLDERS WILL NOT MOVE DURING SUBSEQUENT RELAMPING.

SYMBOLS AND ABBREVIATIONS

S_A DUAL TECHNOLOGY OCCUPANCY SENSOR WATTSTOPPER DW-100

S_B DUAL TECHNOLOGY OCCUPANCY SENSOR WATTSTOPPER DW-200

S_C PIR TECHNOLOGY OCCUPANCY SENSOR WATTSTOPPER PW-100

S_D PIR TECHNOLOGY OCCUPANCY SENSOR WATTSTOPPER PW-200

◯ LA — FIXTURE TYPE

③ — NOTE# OR DETAIL
AL-1 — PAGE

AP - APERTURE
OAL - OVERALL LENGTH
NIC - NOT IN CONTRACT
EC - ELECTRICAL INSTALLER
AFF- ABOVE FINISHED FLOOR
BOF- BOTTOM OF FIXTURE
TBD - TO BE DETERMINED

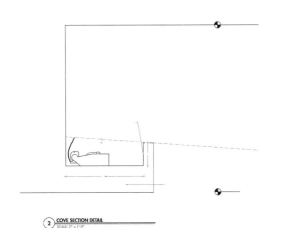

2 COVE SECTION DETAIL
SCALE: 3" = 1'-0"

WORK ON THIS SHEET IS ASSOCIATED WITH SECTION 265113 UNLESS OTHERWISE NOTED.

Consultants:
BIG SHOW CONSTRUCTION MANAGEMENT
231 WEST 29TH STREET, #504
NEW YORK, NY 10001
PHONE: (212) 206-6443
FAX: (212) 206-7225

STUDIO T+L LLC
123 7TH AVENUE#283
BROOKLYN, NY 11215
PHONE: (718) 788.0588
FAX: (718) 768.2170

EJC ENGINEERING, PLLC
136-21 ROOSEVELT AVENUE, SUITE 211
FLUSHING, NY 11354
PHONE: (718) 353.8010
FAX: (718) 353.4007

Issued:

Issue no.	Date	Issue name
1	8/8/08	CD SET SUBMISSION

Seal:

PROJECT NAME WITHHELD
PROJECT ADDRESS WITHHELD

Lee H. Skolnick Architecture + Design Partnership
7 West 22 Street
New York, New York 10010
212 989 2624 Fax 212 727 1702
www.skolnick.com

Ownership And Use Of Documents

These Drawings and specifications including the ideas, design and arrangements represented therein, are the property of the designer and/or client. No part thereof shall be copied, disclosed to others or used in connection with any work or project other than for which they have been prepared without the express written consent of the designer and/or client. All drawings and digital files loaned by the designer are declared to show design intent only and shall not be used for fabrication, construction or installation. These drawings and digital files are to be used solely for bidding purposes and as a guide for the preparation of shop drawings. Shop drawings and finish samples must be submitted for all work of this contract. All fabrication, construction, finishing and installation shall conform to approved shop drawings and finish samples.

Drawing title:
10TH FLOOR LIGHTING PLAN

Date: 8/1/08
Scale: AS NOTED
Drawn By: JL

A5.01

Downlight Symbols

Downlights (Figure 11.2) probably have the widest range of sizes and options. However, the symbols remain relatively simple.

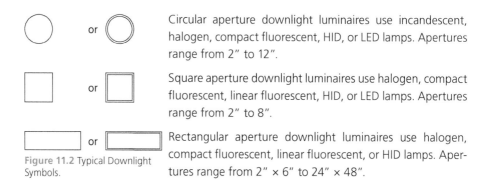

Circular aperture downlight luminaires use incandescent, halogen, compact fluorescent, HID, or LED lamps. Apertures range from 2" to 12".

Square aperture downlight luminaires use halogen, compact fluorescent, linear fluorescent, HID, or LED lamps. Apertures range from 2" to 8".

Rectangular aperture downlight luminaires use halogen, compact fluorescent, linear fluorescent, or HID lamps. Apertures range from 2" × 6" to 24" × 48".

Figure 11.2 Typical Downlight Symbols.

Adjustable or Accent Symbols

Adjustable or accent luminaires (Figure 11.3), including track luminaires, should always indicate the direction of focus. The symbol may use an arrowhead, an arrow, or a line as an indicator. All accent luminaires use halogen, HID, or LED lamps.

Circular aperture accent luminaire apertures range from 2" to 8".

Square aperture accent luminaire apertures range from 4" to 8".

Rectangular aperture accent luminaire apertures range from 2" × 6" to 6" wide in long continuous rows. The lamps in a multi-lamp luminaire do not have to be the same. It may be necessary to label each lamp in a multi-lamp fixture.

Figure 11.3 Typical Adjustable or Accent Symbols.

Wall Wash Symbols

Wall wash luminaires (Figure 11.4) may use halogen, compact fluorescent, linear fluorescent, HID, or LED lamps and can be shown in two ways. First, the blacked out side of the symbol is on the room side of the luminaire. The open half of the luminaire faces the wall. Alternately, an arrowhead may indicate the direction of light. If so, a line or arrow should be used for adjustable luminaires to avoid confusion.

Circular aperture wall wash luminaires range from 5" to 8".

Square aperture wall wash luminaires range from 4" to 6".

Rectangular aperture wall wash luminaires range from 6" × 2' to 8" × 4'.

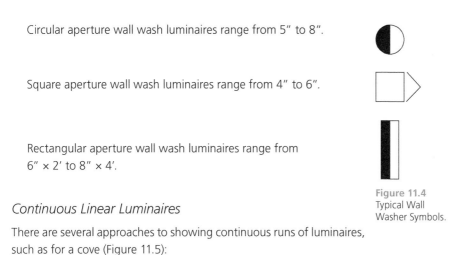

Figure 11.4
Typical Wall
Washer Symbols.

Continuous Linear Luminaires

There are several approaches to showing continuous runs of luminaires, such as for a cove (Figure 11.5):

Continuous run showing the exact length, possibly allowing the contractor to determine individual luminaire lengths

Continuous run without dimensions, requiring the contractor to take measurements in the field

Continuous run showing each luminaire

Continuous run showing each luminaire

Staggered luminaires

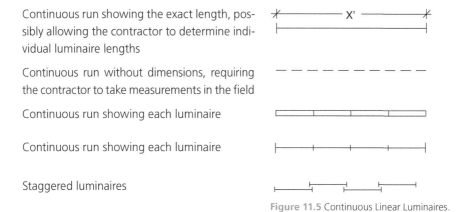

Figure 11.5 Continuous Linear Luminaires.

Pendants, Sconces, Floor and Table Lamps

Pendant and sconce luminaires may be shown on the RCP if it can be done clearly. If they conflict with or overlap symbols for recessed and ceiling surface mounted luminaires a separate drawing may be needed. Portable luminaires such as table and floor lamps may also be shown if their location is known, and may also need to be shown on a drawing separate from the RCP. Symbols are shown in Figure 11.6.

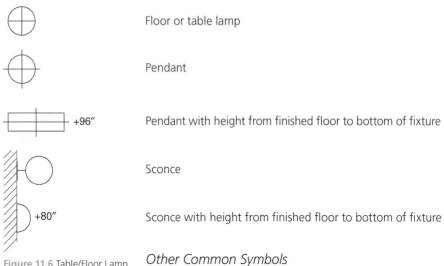

Floor or table lamp

Pendant

Pendant with height from finished floor to bottom of fixture

Sconce

Sconce with height from finished floor to bottom of fixture

Figure 11.6 Table/Floor Lamp, Pendants, Sconces.

Other Common Symbols

Outlets and switches (Figure 11.7) are usually addressed by the electrical engineer. However, if the lighting designer requires them or their location is critical, such as to power table or floor lamps, the electrical engineer should be given instructions.

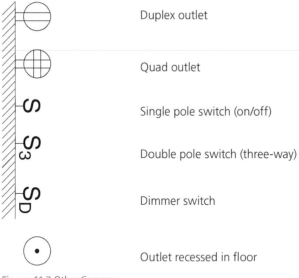

Duplex outlet

Quad outlet

Single pole switch (on/off)

Double pole switch (three-way)

Dimmer switch

Outlet recessed in floor

Figure 11.7 Other Common Symbols.

Luminaire Designations

With symbols are relatively simple circles, squares, and rectangles, how does the designer identify the luminaire when the symbol could apply to more than one luminaire in the design? We use an alphanumeric label attached to each instance of a symbol. Anyone can reference that label on another document, the luminaire schedule, to find information about the luminaire. As with luminaire symbols, there is no single, industry standard way to label luminaires, but there are strong rules-of-thumb and industry conventions.

Rule #1: The first character is always a letter. On small projects luminaires may simply be labeled A, B, C, etc. On larger project there may be variations of a luminaire type. In that case, they might be A1, A2, etc., but would never be 1A, 2A.

Rule #2: All luminaires of the same type get the same label with no additional information. If a room has 12 type A luminaires, each one is labeled A. There is no need to give each luminaire a unique label (such as A(1), A(2)). Doing so will only create confusion with the variations described in Rule #1.

Rule #3: Every change in a luminaire requires a new label. A label denotes a luminaire as a complete package: reflector color, lamp wattage, etc. Any change in that package, such as using a different reflector color or a different beam spread, requires a new, unique label to prevent confusion for those ordering, manufacturing, and installing the luminaires.

In my office we use the three-character code, shown in Table 11.1.

Table 11.1 A Luminaire Designation Matrix

Purpose/Type/Mounting	Lamp	Variation Number
A—Accent/Adjustable	A—A, AR	1, 2, 3, etc.
B—Bollard	B—B	
C—Cove	C—C, CA, CFL	
D—Downlight	E—Electroluminescent	
E—Exposed (bare lamp)	F—F, Fluorescent	
F—Flood	G—G	
G—In-Grade	H—HID	
H—Step, Aisle	L—LED	
L—Landscape	M—MR	
M—Mirror	P—P, PS, PAR, Plasma	
P—Pendant	Q—Induction	
Q—Sconce	R—R	
R—Existing, for repair or refurbishment	S—S	
S—Surface	T—T	
T—Track and Track Heads, Theatre	V—Various (luminaire uses more than one lamp type)	
U—Underwater	X—No Lamp (as with track)	
V—Valence, Soffit		
W—Wall Wash, Wall Graze		
X—Exit Sign		
Y —Torchiere		
Z—Custom		

Developing the RCP

When planning the arrangement of luminaires, we obviously want to put the light where it is needed. Our other goals are to properly space the luminaires and to arrange them sensibly.

Spacing Criteria

Spacing criteria are the ratio of (1) the distance from the work plane to the luminaire and (2) the maximum distance between luminaires to maintain even illumination on the horizontal work plane. Note that the spacing criteria are a ratio (such as 1:1.5), not fixed dimensions. As the ceiling height increases, so too does the distance between luminaires. The formula to determine the maximum horizontal spacing for a luminaire is:

(vertical distance between luminaire and work plane) × (spacing criteria) = maximum horizontal spacing

■ *spacing criteria*
The maximum distance that luminaires may be spaced while still providing uniform illumination on the work plane.

For example, if the spacing criteria or spacing ratio of a luminaire is 1:1.5 (which is often given as simply 1.5), and if the luminaires are 10' above the work plane we calculate as follows:

$$10' \times 1.5 = 15'$$

The luminaires can be placed up to 15' apart. However, if they are 8' above the work plane, they can only be placed up to 12' apart to maintain even illumination.

Note that while the illumination may be even, it may not be what is needed. Spacing criteria address even illumination, but do not guarantee a specific brightness. Illuminance calculations will be required to confirm that the light level goal is being met. Calculations are covered in Chapter 13.

Laying Out Luminaires

When the designer begins to place luminaires on the RCP, the spacing criteria are already known because the luminaires have been selected. The next consideration is often the grid upon which the luminaires will be aligned. Let's look at a few luminaire layouts.

In a tile ceiling system the dimensions of the ceiling grid dictate the placement of the luminaires. Since we locate luminaires in the center of a tile or in place of a tile, a 2' × 2' grid, for example, only permits luminaires to be placed on increments of 2'.

In Figure 11.8a, for example, the designer is using 2 × 2 fluorescent luminaires that fit into the 2' × 2' grid. In Figure 11.8b, the designer is using 6" recessed downlights centered in the tiles. Both of these layouts clearly intend to provide even illumination throughout the room. Both layouts must adhere to the grid of the ceiling tile system. We don't place luminaires off-center in a tile because it will look unbalanced. We don't cut the ceiling grid to accommodate a luminaire because the grid supports the luminaires and we don't want to weaken that support.

In Figure 11.8c, the designer is using rows of pendant fluorescent fixtures and is giving emphasis to one end of the room. We can infer that that end of the room is important because of the extra luminaires. Perhaps a teacher or speaker occupies that end, along with a whiteboard.

Since the ceiling tile dimensions are known, it is often not necessary to provide dimensions to locate the luminaires. These basic rules apply to all tile ceiling systems, regardless of the tile dimensions.

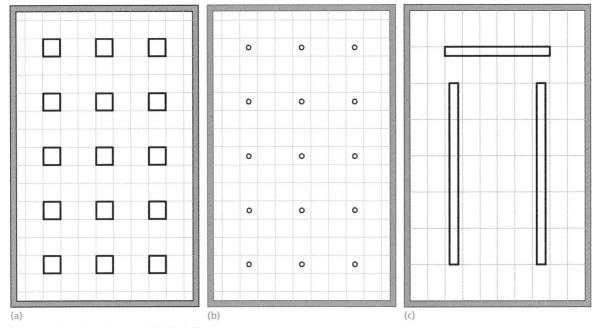

(a)   (b)   (c)

Figure 11.8 Luminaire Layouts with Tile Ceilings.

If there is no ceiling grid, either because the ceiling is dry-wall or because the ceiling structure is left exposed, the lighting designer will want to establish a grid, which is normally aligned with the architecture. We work from a grid for several reasons. First, the room occupants' experience helps to establish their expectations. We see fixtures aligned on a grid in most spaces, so we expect to see luminaires arranged on a grid in new spaces. When that expectation is met, it doesn't draw attention to itself. Luminaires arrayed on a grid go unnoticed and that is usually what we want: to pay attention to the results of the lighting, not the source of the lighting.

Second, most spaces are rectilinear, so laying out luminaires on a grid that relates to the space makes the most sense spatially and aesthetically, and is likely to provide the best coverage. In trying to establish the layout grid, look for architectural centerlines, such as doors, windows, and columns as shown in Figure 11.9. Other features to consider are bump-outs or jogs in walls and the furniture layout, especially if it is off-center or asymmetrical to the architecture. Luminaires may align on the grid formed by the axes of the architecture, straddle the grid lines, or fit into the boxes of the grid.

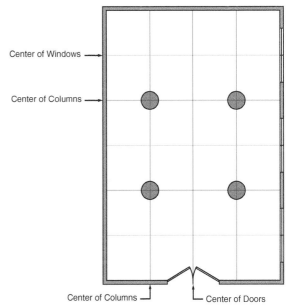

Figure 11.9 Architectural Axes That May Aid in Laying Out the Lighting Grid.

A LAYOUT PROCESS

Let's take a look at this process by examining a simple conference room (Figure 11.10). After talking to the owner about the purpose of the conference room and the types of people who will use it, we have determined the practical

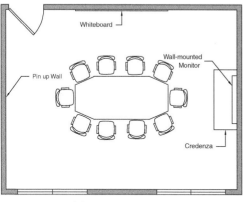

Figure 11.10 Ground Plan.

design criteria. First, illuminate the table to a brightness level appropriate for general office work and reading of small print. Second, illuminate the vertical whiteboard and the pinup wall to an appropriate level. Third, ensure that people's faces are illuminated. Decorative lighting is desirable, but not required. The rest of the room must also be illuminated, but slightly lower light levels are acceptable. We want to minimize reflected glare on the computer monitor, although since it is on an adjustable mount, glare is not a major concern. In this exercise let's assume that north is at the top of the page.

In a commercial office space, where power consumption is an issue, we would probably select a fluorescent or LED downlight. A luminaire with a 6" aperture is fairly common, and there are many options over a wide range of prices for us to choose from. Experience suggests that an 18W CFL downlight is a good beginning. We can see on the manufacturer's luminaire documentation (Figure 11.11) that the spacing criteria are 1.2. The conference room has a table at the standard height of 30" and a ceiling height of 10'. The distance between the two is 6'-6", so the maximum horizontal spacing for even illumination is 7'-9".

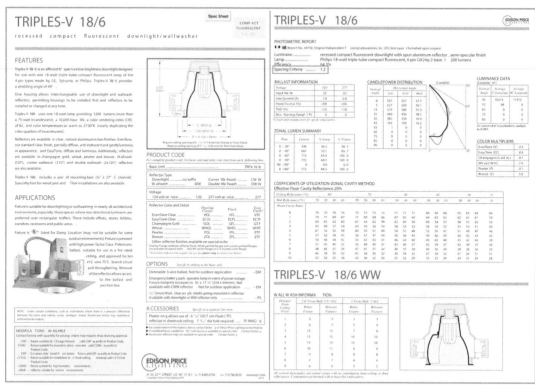

Figure 11.11 Spacing Criteria on Luminaire Documentation.
Courtesy of Edison Price Lighting, Inc.

continues

Begin by looking for major axes in both directions (Figure 11.12). There are major axes at the centerlines of the room in both directions. There are additional axes at the center of both windows. Finally, there is an axis running through the center of the door.

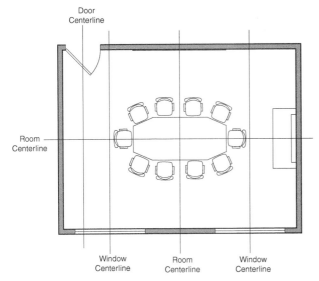

Figure 11.12 Major Room Axes.

Additional north-south axes can be established by dividing the distance between two adjacent axes in half (Figure 11.13). Likewise, additional east-west axes can be established by dividing the distance between the centerline and the wall in half. We've discarded the door centerline because it doesn't seem to relate to the rest of the room in a useful way.

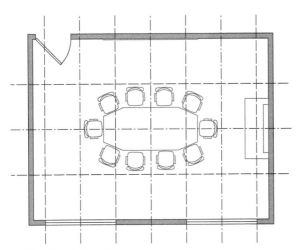

Figure 11.13 Axes Expanded into a Grid.

continues

The simplest layout would place luminaires at the intersection of the axes as shown in Figure 11.14. A luminaire is not required at every intersection, so in this case only every other north-south axis is used, which is within the luminaire's spacing criteria.

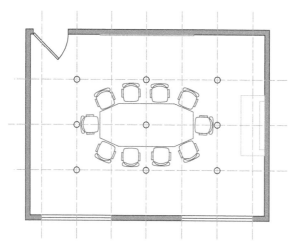

Figure 11.14 Preliminary Layout.

It's sometimes difficult to understand how much light is in a room just by looking at an RCP, even for experienced professionals. Figure 11.15 is a computer generated rendering of the room illustrating the results of the layout. As you can see, the center of the room is well illuminated, but the walls somewhat dark, which doesn't work well, especially for the whiteboard. Perhaps we can put more light on the walls by spreading out the luminaires.

Figure 11.15 Rendering of Preliminary RCP.

continues

Figure 11.16 shows that the distance between the east-west axes has been subdivided again to create more grid points for the luminaires, which have now been spread out.

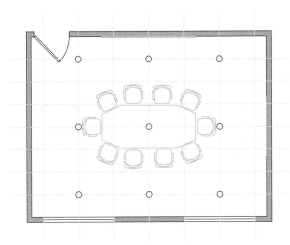

Figure 11.16 RCP, Version 2.

The luminaires are now somewhat more evenly distributed but, as the rendering in Figure 11.17 shows, problems remain. With only nine luminaires, overall brightness of the room may not meet the design criteria. The luminaires are now too close to the whiteboard wall, and we are beginning to see hot spots of light on the wall, also called scallops, which is not desirable in this instance. We'll have to try again.

Figure 11.17 Rendering of RCP, Version 2.

continues

The RCP in Figure 11.18 begins by creating a new grid. First, the center of the east and west windows are drawn. The arrangement of three luminaires east-to-west is not working well, so let's try using four luminaires. Let's also disregard the previous north-south axes and simply divide the distance between the east and west windows into three equal lengths.

Instead of placing the east-west rows of lights on the centerline of the room, we'll use the additional axes developed in Figure 11.16 to split the centerline. The layout now has more luminaires to increase the illuminance level, and those luminaires are better distributed throughout the room. Finally, the room is a little boring, so let's add two decorative wall sconces on either side of the credenza.

As we can see in Figure 11.19, adding luminaires has brightened the room, which is good, but we still have scallops of light on the whiteboard wall, which is not good. There are probably scallops on the other walls, too, but

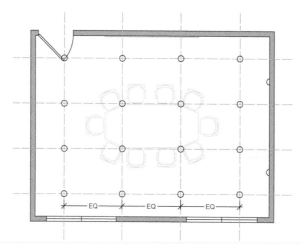

Figure 11.18 RCP, Version 3.

Figure 11.19 Rendering of RCP, Version 3.

continues

the rendering doesn't show them well from this vantage point. We want even lighting on the walls, especially the whiteboard, so let's try using a system of wall washers instead.

With the layout in Figure 11.20 we are washing the whiteboard and pinup walls with light to ensure that it is evenly illuminated and clearly visible. Wall washing luminaires are typically arranged so that the distance from wall to luminaire is also the separation distance between luminaires. Fortunately, the grid we've been developing can quickly be adapted to place the fixtures at an appropriate distance from the wall. The same distance is then applied to the on-center spacing of the wall washers.

Downlights from a matching family of luminaires are distributed around the perimeter of the room on grid points that align with the wall washers. Instead of simple downlights over the table, let's add a decorative pendant that matches the sconces and also provides sufficient light. Wall sconces have been shifted to align with the rows of luminaires in the ceiling.

We can see how the new layout is working in Figure 11.21. This is looking better! The wall washers are providing smooth, even lighting on the whiteboard and pinup walls. The pendant is providing the right amount of light on the

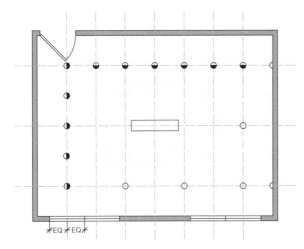

Figure 11.20 RCP, Version 4.

Figure 11.21 Rendering of RCP, Version 4.

continues

table. Some designers may object to the hot spot of light on the ceiling over the pendant and search for one that has a different upward distribution. However, we'll stop here and move on to other issues.

The final RCP (Figure 11.22) does not show the alignment axes. It also usually does not show furniture or other features on the floor, however for continuity and clarity we'll continue to show them here. The RCP should have a label next to every luminaire symbol and sufficient dimensions for the contractors to install the luminaires in the correct locations.

Keep in mind that the process we've just gone through, starting with the architectural grid, is one way to approach a layout. Other projects may have a different emphasis or criteria that could suggest another approach. For example, in a space with very specific lighting requirements in specific locations it may be better to first place the critical fixtures where they need to be. The next steps would be to work outward through the rest of the space, addressing each one of the other lighting criteria and developing the layout of the luminaires separate from the architecture.

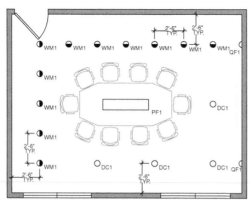

Figure 11.22 Final RCP.

Luminaire Cut Sheets

Let's continue with the conference room we've been working on. As part of the design documentation we must provide cut sheets (which we discussed in Chapter 9). How do we show the connection between the shapes and labels on an RCP and the luminaire cut sheets? It's simple; we label each cut sheet page with a header and/or footer containing the relevant information.

In my office we use the footer shown in Figure 11.23. With this footer every cut sheet page contains the lighting designer and a contact number, the project name, the specification section, the luminaire type and, since there is usually more than one page for a luminaire, the page number and total number of pages for that luminaire type. This information can be added to the PDFs of the manufacturer's cut sheets with a variety of programs. We use a template we've made in Adobe InDesign.

The cut sheets for our conference room, then, are shown in Figures 11.24 through 11.27.

Luminaire or Fixture Schedule

The fixture schedule is a table that lists all of the significant information about each type of luminaire. The schedule serves two purposes. First, it is a descriptive document that identifies: the luminaire type; the manufacturer; the catalog code for the luminaire; important physical and optical characteristics; additional information such as mounting height; and lamp information. The electrical contractor relies on the fixture schedule when preparing the lamp and luminaire budget, and when submitting an order to the electrical supplier. If there is a discrepancy between the fixture schedule and the cut sheets, the contractor will follow the fixture schedule.

The luminaire schedule is also a defensive document. As discussed in Chapter 9, it is common for contractors to offer substitute luminaires for the designer to approve. The catalog number of the luminaire identifies what options the designer wants on the specified luminaire, but says nothing about what the designer is willing to accept in a substitution. We use the Description and Remarks column of the schedule to clearly call out the significant (or minor but important) components, functions, options, and any other information we deem to be relevant. If a contractor's proposed substitution is not acceptable, we can refer to the schedule, in effect saying, "These aspects of the luminaire are so important I took the time to write them down for everyone to see." This clarifies the requirements for substitutions (they must possess all of the characteristics described) and keeps our rejection of substitutions from seeming arbitrary.

Company Name	Project Name	Type _____
Phone Number	Specification Section	Page _____ of _____

Figure 11.23 Typical Cut Sheet Footer.

TRIPLES-V 18/6

recessed compact fluorescent downlight/wallwasher

Spec Sheet

COMP ACT
FLUORESCENT
1-1 25

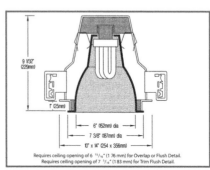

Requires ceiling opening of 6 ¹⁵/₁₆" (176 mm) for Overlap or Flush Detail.
Requires ceiling opening of 7 ³/₁₆" (183 mm) for Trim Flush Detail.

FEATURES

Triples-V 18/6 is an efficient 6" aperture low brightness downlight designed for use with one 18-watt triple-tube compact fluorescent lamp of the 4-pin types made by GE, Sylvania or Philips. Triples-V 18/6 provides a shielding angle of 40°.

One housing allows interchangeable use of downlight and wallwash reflectors, permitting housings to be installed first and reflectors to be installed or changed at any time.

Triples-V 18/6 uses one 18-watt lamp providing 1200 lumens (more than a 75-watt incandescent), a 10,000-hour life, a color rendering index (CRI) of 82, and color temperatures as warm as 2700°K (nearly duplicating the color qualities of incandescent).

Reflectors are available in clear, natural aluminum in two finishes: EvenTone, our standard clear finish, partially diffuse, anti-iridescent and gently luminous in appearance; and EasyTone, diffuse and luminous. Additionally, reflectors are available in champagne gold, wheat, pewter and bronze. Wallwash (120°), corner wallwash (210°) and double wallwash (2x120°) reflectors are also available.

Triples-V 18/6 includes a pair of mounting bars (¾" x 27" C channel). Specialty bars for wood joist and T-bar installations are also available.

APPLICATIONS

Fixture is suitable for downlighting or wallwashing in nearly all architectural environments, especially those spaces where non-directional luminaires are preferred over rectangular troffers. These include offices, stores, lobbies, corridors, restrooms and public areas.

Fixture is ℅UL™ listed for Damp Location (may not be suitable for some outdoor environments). Fixture is prewired with high power factor Class P electronic ballast, suitable for use in a fire rated ceiling, and approved for ten #12 wire 75°C branch circuit pull-through wiring. Removal of the reflector allows access to the ballast and junction box.

NOTE: Under certain conditions, such as installations where there is a pressure differential between the room and ceiling cavity, amalgam based fluorescent lamps may experience reduced lumen output.

MODIFICATIONS AVAILABLE
Contact factory with quantity for pricing; orders may require shop drawing approval.

CHP- : fixture suitable for Chicago Plenum; add CHP- as prefix to Product Code.
CONC- : fixture suitable for poured-in-place concrete; add CONC- as prefix to Product Code.
EXP- : 'European-style' install-from-below fixture; add EXP- as prefix to Product Code.
+2"CLG : fixture suitable for installation in 2" thick ceiling material; add +2"CLG to Product Code.
+DOD- : fixture suitable for high humidity environments.
+MAR- : reflector suitable for marine environments.

PRODUCT CODE

For complete product code, list basic unit and select one item from each following box.

Basic Unit	TRPV 18/6

Reflector Type			
Downlight ....no suffix		Corner Wallwash	CWW
Wallwash	WW	Double Wallwash	DWW

Voltage			
120 volt service	120	277 volt service	277

Reflector Color and Detail	Overlap Flange	Flush	Trim Flush*
EvenTone Clear	VOL	VFL......	VTF
EasyTone Clear	ECOL	ECFL......	ECTF
Champagne Gold	GOL	GFL......	GTF
Wheat	WHOL	WHFL......	WHTF
Pewter	POL	PFL......	PTF
Bronze	ZOL	ZFL......	ZTF

Other reflector finishes available on special order.
Overlap Flange continues reflector finish. White painted flanges and custom painted flanges are available on special order. Add WF (white flange) or CCF (custom color flange).
*Trim Flush reflector trim requires the use of a plaster ring Accessory (see below).

OPTIONS
Specify by adding to the basic unit.

Dimmable 3-wire ballast. Not for outdoor application	– DM
Emergency battery pack operates lamp in event of power outage. Fixture footprint increases to 10 x 17 ½" (254 x 444mm). Not available with CWW reflector. Not for outdoor application	– EM
⅛" (3mm) thick clear acrylic shield, spring-mounted in reflector. Available with downlight or WW reflector only	– PS

ACCESSORIES
Specify as a separate line item.

Plaster ring allows use of 6 ⅞" OD Trim Flush (-TF) reflector in sheetrock ceiling; 7 ³/₁₆" dia hole required	TF RING/ 6

▶ For combinations of the Options above, contact factory or Edison Price Lighting representative.
▶ A modified fixture suitable for 347-volt service is available on special order. Contact factory.
▶ Decorative reflector rings are available on special order. Contact factory.

EDISON PRICE
LIGHTING

41-50 22ᴺᴰ STREET, LIC NY 11101 TEL 718.685.0700 FAX 718.786.8530 www.epl.com
°Copyright, Edison Price Lighting 2009 06:10

Studio T+L, LLC	CONFERENCE ROOM	TYPE: __DC1__
718.788.0588	Section 265113	Page __1__ of __2__

Figure 11.24 DC1 Cut Sheets.
Courtesy of Edison Price Lighting, Inc.

TRIPLES-V 18/6

 EDISON PRICE LIGHTING

PHOTOMETRIC REPORT

itl Report No. 44758. Original Independent Testing Laboratories, Inc. (ITL) test repor t furnished upon request.

Luminaire .... recessed compact fluorescent downlight with spun aluminum reflecto r, semi-specular finish
Lamp .... Philips 18-watt triple-tube compact fluorescent, 4-pin GX24q-2 base, 1200 lumens
Efficiency .... 64.3 %
Spacing Criteria .... 0°-1.2, 90 °-1.1

BALLAST INFORMATION

Voltage	120	277
Input Wa tts	22	22
Line Current (A)	.19	.08
Power Fa ctor (%)	>98	>98
THD (%)	<10	<10
Min. Starting Temp* (°F)	0	0

*Consult lamp manufacturers for specific temperatures.

CANDLEPOWER DISTRIBUTION

(Candela)

Vertical Angle	Horizontal Angle		
	0.0	45.0	90.0
0	557	557	55 7
5	627	589	56 1
15	575	580	55 3
25	489	456	48 2
35	385	354	34 9
45	143	158	16 2
55	1	0	0
65	0	0	0
75	0	0	0
85	0	0	0
90	0	0	0

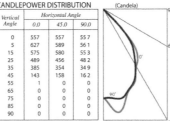

LUMINANCE DATA

(Candela/ m²)

Vertical Angle	Average 0° Longitude	Average 90° Longitude
45	10215	1157 2
55	88	0
65	0	0
75	0	0
85	0	0

To consult cd/m² to footlamberts, multiply by 0.2919.

COLOR MULTIPLIERS

EvenTone (V)	.9 5
EasyTone (EC)	.8 8
Champag ne G old (G)	.9 7
Wh eat (W H)	.7 9
Pewter (P)	.8 1
Bronze (Z)	.5 8

ZONAL LUMEN SUMMARY

Zone	Lumens	% Lamp	% Fixture
0 - 30°	436	36.3	56.5
0 - 40°	661	55.1	85.7
0 - 60°	772	64.3	100.0
0 - 90°	772	64.3	100.0
90 -180°	0	0.0	0.0
0 -180°	772	64.3	100.0

COEFFICIENTS OF UTILIZATIO N – ZONAL CAVITY METHOD
Effective Floor Cavity Reflectance 20%

Ceiling Reflectance (%)	80				70				50			30			10			0
Wall Reflectance (%)	70	50	30	10	70	50	30	10	50	30	10	50	30	10	50	30	10	0
Room Cavity Ratio																		
0	76	76	76	76	75	75	75	75	71	71	71	68	68	68	65	65	65	64
1	73	71	69	67	71	69	68	66	67	65	64	64	63	62	62	61	61	59
2	69	65	62	60	67	64	62	59	62	60	58	60	58	57	58	57	56	55
3	65	60	57	54	63	59	56	54	58	55	53	56	54	52	55	53	51	50
4	61	56	52	49	60	55	51	49	54	51	48	52	50	47	51	49	47	46
5	57	52	48	45	56	51	47	44	50	46	44	49	46	44	48	45	43	42
6	54	48	44	41	53	47	43	41	46	43	40	45	42	40	45	42	40	39
7	51	45	40	37	50	44	40	37	43	40	37	42	39	37	42	39	37	36
8	48	42	37	34	47	41	37	34	40	37	34	40	36	34	39	36	34	33
9	46	39	35	32	45	38	35	32	38	34	32	37	34	32	37	34	31	31
10	43	36	32	30	42	36	32	30	35	32	29	35	32	29	34	31	29	28

TRIPLES-V 18/6 WW

WALL WASH INFORMATION

Distance From Ceiling (Feet)	2'6" From Wall; 2'6" O.C.		3' From Wall; 3' O.C.	
	Below Fixture	Between Fixtures	Below Fixture	Between Fixtures
1	5	5	3	3
2	8	7	5	4
3	13	13	7	6
4	15	15	10	10
5	13	13	10	10
6	10	11	9	9
7	9	8	8	8
8	7	7	6	6
9	6	6	5	5

All vertical footcandles are initial values with no contribution from ceiling or floor reflectances. Computation performed with at least five wallwashers.

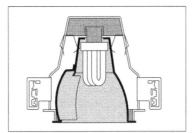

Studio T+L, LLC	CONFERENCE ROOM	TYPE: __DC1__
718.788.0588	Section 265113	Page __2__ of __2__

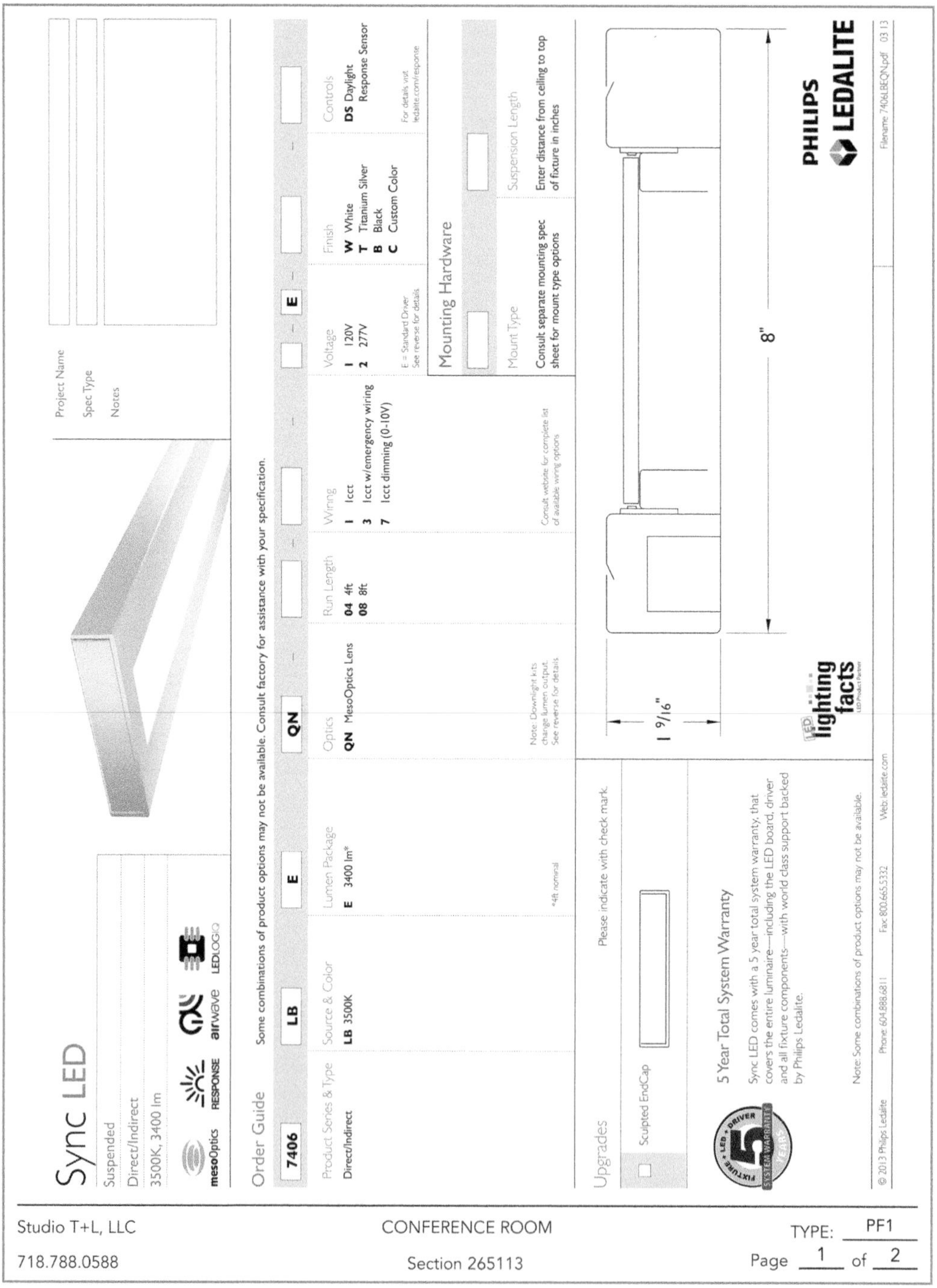

Sync LED

Suspended
Direct/Indirect
3500K, 3400 lm

mesoOptics RESPONSE airwave LEDLOGIQ

Project Name
Spec Type
Notes

Order Guide

Some combinations of product options may not be available. Consult factory for assistance with your specification.

7406	LB	E	QN	–	–	– E –	–	
Product Series & Type	Source & Color	Lumen Package	Optics	Run Length	Wiring	Voltage	Finish	Controls
Direct/Indirect	LB 3500K	E 3400 lm*	QN MesoOptics Lens	04 4ft 08 8ft	1 1cct 3 1cct w/emergency wiring 7 1cct dimming (0-10V)	1 120V 2 277V	W White T Titanium Silver B Black C Custom Color	DS Daylight Response Sensor
		*4ft nominal	Note: Downlight kits change lumen output. See reverse for details		Consult website for complete list of available wiring options	E = Standard Driver See reverse for details		For details visit ledalite.com/response

Mounting Hardware

Mount Type	Suspension Length
Consult separate mounting spec sheet for mount type options	Enter distance from ceiling to top of fixture in inches

Upgrades

Please indicate with check mark.

☐ Sculpted EndCap

5 Year Total System Warranty

Sync LED comes with a 5 year total system warranty, that covers the entire luminaire—including the LED board, driver and all fixture components—with world class support backed by Philips Ledalite.

FIXTURE + LED + DRIVER 5 SYSTEM WARRANTY YEARS

Note: Some combinations of product options may not be available.

1 9/16"
8"

LED lighting facts LED Product Partner

PHILIPS LEDALITE

© 2013 Philips Ledalite Phone 604.888.6811 Fax 800.665.5332 Web: ledalite.com Filename: 7406LBEQN.pdf 03 13

Studio T+L, LLC
718.788.0588
CONFERENCE ROOM
Section 265113
TYPE: PF1
Page 1 of 2

Figure 11.25 PF1 Cut Sheets.
Courtesy of Philips Lighting Company.

Sync LED

Suspended - Direct/Indirect - 3500K, 3400 lm

Photometry — MesoOptics Lens

Report No	ITL75737	CRI	83	Power Factor	0.94 @ 120
Efficacy	101.7 mwW	R9	23	Peak/Zenith Ratio	3.9:1
Total Lumens	3264 lm	InputWatts	32.1	Peak Candela/Value	944 @ 112.5

*Meets RP-1-04 recommendations for VDT-intensive spaces.

*IESNA LM-79-08 specifies the entire luminaire as the source resulting in a fixture efficiency of 100%.

lighting facts

Light Output (Lumens)	3264
Watts	32
Lumens per Watt (Efficacy)	102
Color Accuracy	83
Light Color	3500 (Bright White)
Warranty**	Yes

**See www.lightingfacts.com/products for details.

1000 cd

--- 0
— 45
— 90

72% Up / 28% Down

Fixture photometry has been conducted by a NVLAP accredited testing laboratory in accordance with IESNA LM-79-08. Lumen maintenance of the LEDs used in this fixture has been tested by the LED manufacturer in accordance with IESNA LM-80-08.

IES files for this and other photometric options can be downloaded online at ledalite.com

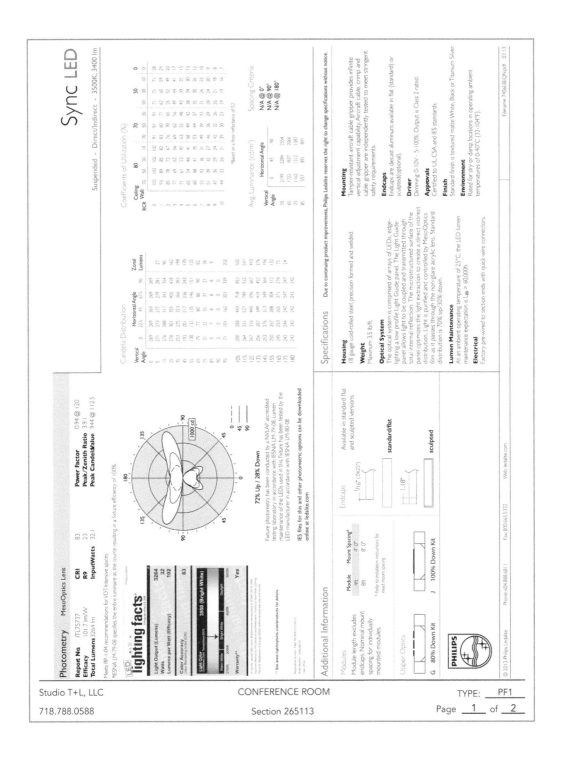

Coefficients of Utilization (%)

Ceiling	80			70			50			0
Wall	70	50	30	70	50	30	50	30	10	0
RCR										
0	102	102	102	91	91	91	71	71	71	28
1	93	89	85	83	82	62	60	59	24	
2	85	78	72	67	76	65	55	52	49	20
3	77	69	62	56	69	62	49	44	41	17
4	71	61	53	47	63	55	43	39	35	15
5	65	54	46	42	58	49	38	34	30	12
6	60	48	41	35	53	44	33	30	26	12
7	55	43	36	31	49	39	31	26	23	10
8	51	39	32	27	45	36	29	24	20	9
9	47	35	28	24	42	32	26	22	18	8
10	44	33	26	22	39	30	23	21	16	7

*Based on a floor reflectance of 0.2

Candela Distribution

Vertical Angle	Horizontal Angle					Zonal Lumens
	0	22.5	45	67.5	90	
0	269	269	269	269	269	27
5	271	273	277	279	281	27
15	276	288	317	343	354	90
25	278	301	355	405	428	163
35	253	275	321	366	383	198
45	193	201	217	236	243	170
55	130	122	135	146	151	125
65	75	77	80	88	90	62
75	31	31	35	77	77	38
85	0	0	0	8	8	9
95	71	101	162	301	339	202
105	200	258	443	718	853	502
115	264	331	527	789	932	547
125	267	316	440	596	667	410
135	256	287	349	419	453	276
145	253	275	313	349	364	196
155	250	267	288	304	312	132
165	245	253	265	271	274	75
175	243	244	247	247	247	24
180	242	242	242	242	242	

Avg Luminance (cd/m²)

Vertical Angle	Horizontal Angle		
	0	45	90
55	2199	2284	2554
65	1722	1837	2066
75	1162	1312	1387
85	557	891	891

Spacing Criteria

N/A @ 0°
N/A @ 90°
N/A @ 180°

Due to continuing product improvements, Philips Ledalite reserves the right to change specifications without notice.

Specifications

Housing
18 gauge cold-rolled steel, precision formed and welded.

Weight
Maximum 3.5 lb/ft.

Optical System
The optical system is comprised of arrays of LEDs, edge-lighting a low profile Light Guide panel. The Light Guide panel allows light to be coupled and transmitted through total internal reflection. The microstructured surface of the panel optimizes the light extraction to create a direct indirect distribution. Light is purified and controlled by MesoOptics film as it passes through the non-glare acrylic lens. Standard distribution is 70% up / 30% down.

Lumen Maintenance
At an ambient operating temperature of 25°C, the LED lumen maintenance expectation is L₇₀ > 60,000h.

Electrical
Factory pre-wired to section ends with quick-wire connectors.

Mounting
Tamper-resistant aircraft cable gripper provides infinite vertical adjustment capability. Aircraft cable, crimp and cable gripper are independently tested to meet stringent safety requirements.

Endcaps
Endcaps are diecast aluminum; available in flat (standard) or sculpted(optional).

Driver
Dimming 0-10V - 5-100%. Output is Class 2 rated.

Approvals
Certified to UL, CSA and IES standards.

Finish
Standard finish is textured matte White, Black or Titanium Silver.

Environment
Rated for dry or damp locations in operating ambient temperatures of 0-40°C (32-104°F).

Filename 740eLBEQN.pdf 03.13

Additional Information

Modules
Module length excludes endcaps. Nominal mount spacing for individually mounted modules.

Module	Mount Spacing*
4ft	4' 0"
8ft	8' 0"

*Refer to installation instructions for exact mount spacing.

Upper Optics

Available in standard flat and sculpted versions.

standard/flat
1/16" (0625")

sculpted
1.18"

Endcaps

G 80% Down Kit
J 100% Down Kit

© 2013 Philips Ledalite   Phone: 604.888.6811   Fax: 800.665.5332   Web: ledalite.com

PHILIPS

Studio T+L, LLC

718.788.0588

CONFERENCE ROOM

Section 265113

TYPE: PF1

Page 1 of 2

203

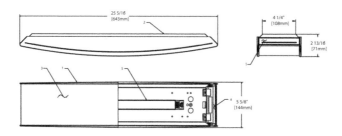

LIGHTOLIER® Brisa™ Linear Bow Surface Mount **FB5114U**

Page 1 of 2   Wall/Ceiling Mounted T5 Fluorescent ADA Compliant

Fixture Ordering Information
Single Lamp

Catalog No.	Description	Finish	Wattage	Volts	Lamp
FB5114U	Linear Bow Surface Mount	Satin aluminum	14W	120-277V	(1) T5
FB5114UEM	Linear Bow Surface Mount w/Emergency	Satin aluminum	14W	120-277V	(1) T5

Multi Lamp

Catalog No.	Description	Finish	Wattage	Volts	Lamp
FB5214U	Linear Bow Surface Mount	Satin aluminum	14W	120-277V	(2) T5

Diffuser Ordering Information

Catalog No.	Description	Finish	Dimensions (Nominal)
FBA5	Acrylic Bow Diffuser	Opal	5" X 24"
FBG5	Glass Bow Diffuser	Opal	5" X 24"

Features
1. Housing Sides and ends: Die-cast aluminum.
2. Back Pan: Stamped 18ga. (0.048") sheet metal.
3. Diffuser: Bowed opal glass or opal acrylic
4. Optics: Internal white acrylic diffuser covers slots on housing sides and ends

Mounting
Fixture Mounts directly to 4" octagonal junction box.

Electrical
5. Ballast

A. Electronic 120V-277V	1 Lamp		2 Lamp	
Voltage	120V	277V	120V	277V
Total Input Watts	19W	19W	34W	34W
Max. Line Current (Amps)	0.16A	0.07A	0.29A	0.13A
Power Factor	>0.98	>0.98	>0.98	>0.90
THD	<20%	<20%	<10%	<10%
Min. Starting Temp.	0°F,	-18°C	0°F,	-18°C

B. Emergency(1-lamp fixture only)
Bodine LP550 emergency battery pack with integral test light and switch

6. Luminaire-Ballast Disconnect: Meets NEC 410.130(G) and CEC Disconnect Requirements.

Lampholders
Fluorescent: Mini Bi-Pin, G5 Base

Lamping (by others)

General Electric	Osram/Sylvania	Philips
(1) 14W T5 Linear Fluorescent		
F14W/T5/*/ECO	FP14/*	F14T5/*/ALTO
*Manufactures Color Temperature Designation		

Finish
Satin Aluminum

Labels
cULus Listed. Suitable for Damp Locations.
ULus Listed, Suitable for Dry Locations for Emergency Units only.

Job Information	**Type:**
Job Name:	
Cat. No.:	
Lamp(s):	
Notes:	

631 Airport Road, Fall River, MA 02720 • (508) 679-8131 • Fax (508) 674-4710
We reserve the right to change details of design, materials and finish.
www.lightolier.com © 2009 Philips Group • B0209

Lightolier is a Philips group brand

PHILIPS

Studio T+L, LLC	CONFERENCE ROOM	TYPE: __QF1__
718.788.0588	Section 265113	Page __1__ of __2__

Figure 11.26 QF1 Cut Sheets.
Courtesy of Philips Lighting Company.

LIGHTOLIER®

Brisa™ Linear Bow Surface Mount **FB5114U**

Wall/Ceiling Mounted T5 Fluorescent ADA Compliant

FB5214U-FBG5

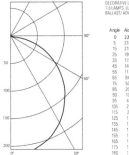

90° · 50 · 60° · 100 · 150 · 200 · 0° · 30°

DECORATIVE LUMINAIRE CAT. # FB5214U-FBG5 2-14W PHILIPS T-5 LAMPS. LUMEN RATING = 1200 LMS. BALLAST/ ADVANCE ICN-2S28

Candlepower Summary

Angle	Along	22.5	45	67.5	Across	Output Lumens
0	220	220	220	220	220	
5	218	219	219	218	219	21
15	210	211	210	210	210	60
25	196	197	196	195	195	90
35	175	175	174	173	173	109
45	148	148	147	146	146	114
55	117	117	116	115	115	104
65	84	84	83	82	81	82
75	50	50	49	49	48	52
85	20	20	19	17	16	21
90	10	10	10	9	7	6
95	4	4	4	4	4	5
105	2	2	2	3	3	2
115	2	1	2	2	2	2
125	1	1	1	2	2	1
135	1	1	1	1	1	1
145	1	1	1	1	1	1
155	1	1	1	1	1	1
165	1	1	1	1	1	0
175	1	1	1	1	1	0
180	1	1	1	1	1	

Coefficients of Utilization

Ceiling	80%				70%				50%			30%			10%			
Wall	70	50	30	10	70	50	30	10	50	30	10	50	30	10	50	30	10	0
RCR	Zonal Cavity Method - Effective Floor Reflectance = 20%																	
0	.33	.33	.33	.33	.32	.32	.32	.31	.31	.29	.29	.29	.28	.28	.28	.28	.28	.27
1	.30	.29	.28	.27	.29	.28	.27	.26	.27	.26	.25	.26	.25	.24	.25	.24	.24	.23
2	.27	.25	.23	.22	.27	.25	.23	.22	.24	.22	.21	.23	.21	.20	.21	.20	.19	.19
3	.25	.22	.20	.18	.24	.22	.20	.18	.21	.19	.18	.20	.19	.17	.19	.18	.17	.16
4	.23	.20	.17	.16	.22	.19	.17	.15	.19	.17	.15	.18	.16	.15	.17	.16	.15	.14
5	.21	.17	.15	.13	.20	.17	.15	.13	.18	.15	.13	.16	.14	.13	.15	.14	.13	.12
6	.19	.16	.13	.11	.19	.15	.13	.11	.15	.13	.11	.14	.12	.11	.14	.12	.11	.10
7	.18	.14	.12	.10	.17	.14	.11	.10	.13	.11	.10	.13	.11	.10	.12	.11	.09	.09
8	.16	.13	.10	.09	.16	.12	.10	.08	.12	.10	.08	.12	.10	.09	.11	.09	.08	.08
9	.15	.11	.09	.07	.15	.11	.09	.07	.11	.09	.07	.10	.09	.07	.10	.08	.07	.07
10	.14	.10	.08	.07	.14	.10	.08	.06	.10	.08	.06	.09	.08	.06	.09	.08	.06	.06

Room Cavity Ratio

Determined In Accordance With Current IES Published Procedures
Luminaire Input Watts = 33.0

Zonal Lumens and Percentages

Zone	Lumens	% Lamp	%Luminaire
0-30	170	7.12	25.60
0-40	279	11.66	41.95
0-60	497	20.73	74.56
0-90	653	27.23	97.93
40-90	373	15.57	55.98
60-90	155	6.50	23.37
90-180	13	.58	2.07
0-180	667	27.80	100.00

** Efficiency = 27.8%**

Certified Test Report no. 3577FR
Computed by LSI Program **TEST-LITE**
SC=1.3

Prepared For:
Lightolier
Fall River, MA

TESTED ACCORDING TO IES PROCEDURES. TEST DISTANCE EXCEEDS FIVE TIMES THE GREATEST LUMINOUS OPENING OF LUMINAIRE.

Job Information **Type:**

631 Airport Road, Fall River, MA 02720 • (508) 679-8131 • Fax (508) 674-4710
We reserve the right to change details of design, materials and finish.
www.lightolier.com © 2009 Philips Group • B0209

Lightolier is a Philips group brand

PHILIPS

Studio T+L, LLC	CONFERENCE ROOM	TYPE: __QF1__
718.788.0588	Section 265113	Page __1__ of __2__

DARKLITE WASHLITE MR/4

recessed low voltage wallwasher

Spec Sheet

LOW
VO LTAGE
2-241

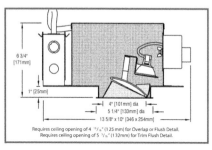

6 3/4"
[171mm]

1" [25mm]

4" [101mm] dia
5 1/4" [133mm] dia
13 5/8" x 10" [346 x 254mm]

Requires ceiling opening of 4 ¹³/₁₆" (125 mm) for Overlap or Flush Detail.
Requires ceiling opening of 5 ³/₁₆" (132mm) for Trim Flush Detail.

FEA TURES

Darklite Washlite MR/4 is a 4" aperture lensed wallwasher designed for use with 12-volt MR-16 flood lamps (75-watt maximum; see note below). The integral electronic transformer delivers 11.8 volts, to lengthen lamp life. Recess depth is only 6¾".

The optical assembly consists of a lamp holder, an internal reflector, a 40° x 70° glass spread lens and an external reflector. Precise optical design provides uniform illumination on vertical surfaces up to the ceiling line and minimizes aperture brightness. The optical assembly provides 360° horizontal rotation and may be removed from the fixture housing as a unit for easy relamping.

The 4" aperture matches our 4" low voltage, compact fluorescent, A, PAR and HID lamped downlights, wallwashers and accent lights.

W ith a 75-watt lamp, Darklite Washlite MR/4 accepts one of four available Optical Accessories including a UV filter and various color filters. With a 50-watt lamp, an additional five Optical Accessories are available.

Reflectors are available in three clear natural aluminum finishes — semi-specular (C), slightly diffuse (V) or fully diffuse (EC) — as well as champagne gold or black Alzak`. Other reflector finishes are available on special order .

Darklite Washlite MR/4 includes a pair of mounting bars (¾" x 27" C channel). Specialty bars for wood joist and T-bar installations are also available.

APPLICATIONS

Fixture is recommended for wallwahing in stores, offices, museums, restaurants, showrooms, residences and hotels.

Fixture is ⒸⓁᵤₛ listed for Damp Location. Fixture includes an integral electronic transformer protected by a thermal auto-reset switch. Fixture is prewired with thermal protector, suitable for use in a fire rated ceiling and approved for ten #12 wire 90°C branch circuit pull-through wiring. Removal of the reflector allows access to the transformer and junction box.

▶ To minimize socket/lamp problems we recommend the use of lamps by GE, Sylvania, Philips or Ushio. In addition, in areas of high ambient temperatures the lamp should be limited to 50 watts.

▶ Important installation note: If controlled by a dimmer, use dimming equipment compatible with the design (electronic or magnetic) of the fixture transformer.

MODIFICATIONS	AVAILABLE	▼ See next page

PRODUCT CODE

For complete product code, list basic unit and select one item from each following box.

Basic Unit			DLWLMR/ 4

Reflector Color and Detail	Overlap	Flush	Trim Flush*
Semi-specular Clear	COL	CFL	CTF
Slightly diffuse Clear	VOL	VFL	VTF
Fully diffuse Clear	ECOL	ECFL	ECTF
Champagne Gold	GOL	GFL	GTF
Black	BOL	BFL	BTF

Other reflector finishes available on special order .

Standard reflector flange continues reflector finish. White painted flanges and custom painted flanges are available on special order. Add WF (white flange) or CCF (custom color flange).
*Trim Flush reflector trim requires the use of a *plaster ring* Accessory (see below).

OPTIONS   *Specify by adding to the basic unit.*

Integral 1 20/12 volt magnetic transformer by Q-Tran` with anti-buzz choke and toggle for dimmed vs. switched use (factor y set to switched)	– QT120
Integral 277/12 volt magnetic transformer by Q-Tran Same features as above	– QT277
Integral 277/12 volt electronic transformer	– SS277
No transformer . With leads and thermal protector for 12-volt ser vice from remote transformer (by others)	– NXFMR

OPTICAL A CCESSORIES   *Specify as separate line items.*

All are 2 ⅜" (60mm) dia. Lenses and filters are glass; screens are aluminum.

UV filte r	UVF/2.375
color filters	
Daylight Blue	DAY/2.375
Surprise Pink	PNK/2.375
amber	AMB/2.375
blue *(50-watt max. lamp)*	BLU/2.375
green *(50-watt max. lamp)*	GRN/2.375
red *(50-watt max. lamp)*	RED/2.375
33% light reduction screen *(50-watt max. lamp)*	SCR33/2.375
50% light reduction screen *(50-watt max. lamp)*	SCR50/2.375

A CCESSORIES   *Specify as a separate line item.*

Plaster rin g allows use of 4 ⁷/₈" OD T rim Flush (-TF) reflector in sheetrock ceiling; 5 ³/₁₆" dia hole required	TF RING/ 4

EDISON PRICE
LIGHTING

41-50 22 ᴺᴰ STREET, LIC NY 11101 TEL 718.685.0700   FAX 718.786.8530   www.epl.com
`Copyright, Edison Price Lighting 2009   ` Darklite, Wa shlite are registered trademarks of Edison Price Lighting   05:1 0

Studio T+L, LLC	CONFERENCE ROOM	TYPE: __WM1__
718.788.0588	Section 265113	Page __1__ of __2__

Figure 11.27 WM1 Cut Sheets.
Courtesy of Edison Price Lighting, Inc.

DARKLITE WASHLITE MR/4

MODIFICATIONS AVAILABLE

Contact factory with quantity for pricing; orders may require shop drawing approval.

CHP-: 50-watt fixture suitable for Chicago Plenum; add CHP- as prefix to Product Code.

EXP-: 50-watt 'European-style' install-from-below fixture; add EXP- as prefix to Product Code.

+TR: fixture prepared for top re-lamping; add +TR to Product Code.

+DOD: fixture suitable for high humidity environments; add +DOD to Product Code.

+MAR: reflector suitable for marine environments; add +MAR to Product Code.

PHOTOMETRIC REPORT

(LTL) Luminaire Testing Laboratory Report No. 08113. Original test report furnished upon request.

Luminaire .... recessed incandescent with internal wallwash reflector
and 40° x 70° spread lens

CANDLEPOWER DISTRIBUTION

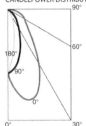

WALL WASH INFORMATION

50-watt MR16 halogen FL40 (EXN), 880 lumens (estimated)

Distance From Ceiling (Feet)	2'6 From Wall; 2'6" O.C.		3' From Wall; 3' O.C.	
	Below Fixture	Between Fixtures	Below Fixture	Between Fixtures
1	12	10	8	6
2	13	12	9	8
3	12	12	9	8
4	11	11	8	8
5	9	9	7	7
6	7	7	6	6
7	6	6	5	5
8	5	5	4	4
9	4	4	4	4

All vertical footcandles are initial values with no contribution from ceiling or floor reflectances. Computation performed with a total of ten wallwashers.

WALL WASH INFORMATION

75-watt MR16 halogen FL (EYC), 1410 lumens (rated)

Distance From Ceiling (Feet)	2'6" From Wall; 2'6" O.C.		3' From Wall; 3' O.C.		3'6" From Wall; 3'6" O.C.		4' From Wall; 4' O.C.	
	Below Fixture	Between Fixtures	Below Fixture	Between Fixtures	Below Fixture	Between Fixtures	Below Fixture	Between Fixtures
1	20	16	12	10	8	7	6	5
2	20	19	14	13	11	9	8	7
3	20	18	14	13	10	10	8	7
4	17	17	13	13	10	9	8	7
5	15	14	12	12	9	9	8	7
6	12	11	10	10	9	8	7	7
7	10	9	9	8	7	7	6	6
8	8	8	7	7	6	6	6	6
9	6	6	6	6	6	5	5	5
10			5	5	5	5	4	4

All vertical footcandles are initial values with no contribution from ceiling or floor reflectances. Computation performed with a total of ten wallwashers.

Studio T+L, LLC	CONFERENCE ROOM	TYPE: WM1
718.788.0588	Section 265113	Page 2 of 2

A fixture schedule for the luminaires shown previously and developed by Studio T+L, LLC is shown next.

		CONFERENCE ROOM 100% CD Luminaire Schedule Studio T+L, LLC	
Type	**Manufacturer and Catalog Number**	**Description and Remarks**	**Lamp**
DC1	Edison Price TRPV 18/6-120-VOL-DM	**Compact Fluorescent Downlight** Triple CFL open downlight. Housing is nominally 9" high × 10" wide × 14" long, with an integral, 3-wire dimming ballast for 18W triple tube CFL lamp. Reflector is clear, natural aluminum with semi-specular finish, self-overlap flange, 6" aperture, and provides a 40° cutoff. Contractor shall coordinate mounting hardware with ceiling type and thickness.	PL-T 18W/835/4P/ALTO Philips Lighting
PF1	Ledalite 7406 LB E QN-04-1-1-C	**Pendant** Semi-indirect LED linear pendant. Housing is formed steel nominally 48" long × 8" wide × 1-9/16" high with two rows of LEDs edge lighting a light guide. LEDs are 3500 K with a total luminous output of over 3200 lm, CRI of greater than 82, and L80 of 60,000 hrs. at 25C. Dimming is via a 0-10VDC signal to the driver. Finish is polyester powder coat in a color to be selected by the architect. Contractor shall install so that bottom of luminaire is 84" AFF.	NA
QF1	Lightolier FB5214U/FBG5/DIM	**Wall Sconce** Surface mount T5 linear fluorescent sconce. Housing is nominally 25-5/16" high × 5-5/8" wide × 2-13/16" deep with integral 3-wire ballast for (2) 14W T5 lamps, die-cast aluminum sides and ends, 18 ga. back, and internal white acrylic diffuser. Removable front diffuser is opal glass. Contractor shall install so that bottom of luminaire is 48" AFF.	(2) F14T5/835/ALTO Philips Lighting
WM1	Edison Price DLWLMR/4-VOL	**Wall Washer** MR16 lensed wall washer. Housing is nominally 6-3/4" high × 10" long × 13-5/8" wide with integral 75W, 12-volt electronic transformer. Removable optical assembly (for relamping) consists of lamp holder, aluminum internal and external reflectors, and 40° × 70° glass spread lens that rotates through 360° and has a 4" aperture with self-overlap flange. Reflector finish is slightly diffuse clear. Contractor shall coordinate mounting hardware with ceiling type and thickness.	35MRC16/IRC/ALU/ FL36 Philips Lighting
Date		**Section 265113**	**Page 1 of 1**

Components of a Fixture Schedule

1. Document header should include project name, project phase, lighting designer, and the words "Lighting Fixture Schedule" or "Luminaire Schedule."
2. Column 1—Luminaire type or designation
3. Column 2—Luminaire manufacturer and complete catalog/product number
4. Column 3—Luminaire description and all relevant or significant features; this may include housing size, aperture size, reflector color and finish, lamp type, distribution type, type of ballast/transformer/power supply, installation height, lens type, accessories required, materials used, finishes, and any other information that the designer deems important.
5. Column 4—Lamp code, manufacturer, and voltage if applicable
6. Document footer identifying the date, specification section, and page number

Specifications

Specifications are text documents that call out, in great detail, the requirements for a construction project. Most specifications are in the MasterFormat by the Construction Specifications Institute (CSI), which covers everything from site conditions and materials used to installation methods and documentation provided to the owner. The MasterFormat CSI specification sections related to lighting are shown in Table 11.2.

Table 11.2 MasterFormat Sections Related to Lighting

MasterFormat 2012 Section Number	Description
260923	Lighting Control Devices
260933	Central Dimming Controls
260936	Modular Dimming Controls
260943	Network Lighting Controls
265000	Lighting
265100	Interior Lighting
265113	Interior Lighting Luminaires, Lamps and Ballasts
265600	Exterior Lighting
265626	Landscape Lighting
265636	Flood Lighting

Specifications typically have three sections:

Part 1 addresses general information about the project and the section by identifying related specification sections, setting requirements for submittals and warranties, and setting minimum qualifications for those involved in the installation.

Part 2 describes the products. For lamps and luminaires this includes materials used, fixture fabrication, requirements for ballast and transformer types and efficiency, reflector performance, and luminous output.

Part 3 covers the execution of the specification section by listing delivery and installation requirements, the contractor's and lighting designer's responsibilities for aiming and adjusting luminaires and for programming control systems, and the use of luminaires for lighting during construction.

A well-written specification can help to preempt problems during bidding and construction, such as attempts to substitute inappropriate luminaires. The Lighting Industry Resource Council (LIRC), an affiliate of the IALD, has written a pamphlet called *Guidelines for Specification Integrity*, which describes actions that may be taken by the lighting designer to protect the specification, and therefore the design. A link can be found in the Online Resources at the end of this chapter.

Layout and Installation Details

When the architecture must accommodate a luminaire or lighting treatment, the lighting designer draws the detail, or at least the first draft of the detail, for the installation. This is done as early in the design process as possible so that the architect and other design professionals can integrate the information into their drawings. The final details will appear in the architect's drawings with other construction details.

Wall Washing

Washing a wall with light illuminates the entire vertical surface from ceiling luminaires mounted a few feet from the wall (see wall wash luminaires in Chapter 9). Illuminated vertical surfaces can be useful because they help to establish boundaries and brighten a room. Washing a wall, as opposed to grazing it (which is described next), minimizes highlights and shadows, thus reducing the apparent texture and three dimensionality of a wall surface. Wall washing luminaires can use a wide range of lamps. Wall washers may have lensed apertures for precise light distribution on the wall, or open apertures with the lamp and reflector distributing the light on the wall and into the room.

Wall washers are designed to work as a row of luminaires set 2'-6" to 4'-0" from the wall. The optics are also designed so that even illumination is achieved when the distance from the wall to the center of one luminaire is the same as the distance between luminaire centerlines (Figure 11.28). For example, if the luminaires are set 3'-0" from the wall, they should be spaced 3'-0" on-center.

Wider spacing between luminaires will result in a scallop effect on the wall. Tighter spacing will increase the wall illuminance. When laying out a wall wash system, the location of the first luminaire and last luminaires is at the same spacing increment from the start and end points of the illuminated wall as the spacing of the rest of the row (Figure 11.29). If you're unsure

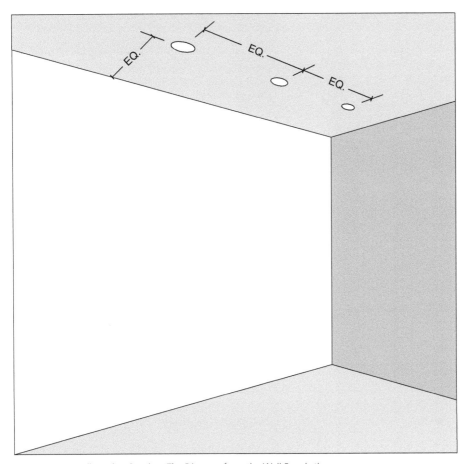

Figure 11.28 Wall Washer Spacing: The Distance from the Wall Equals the On-Center Spacing.

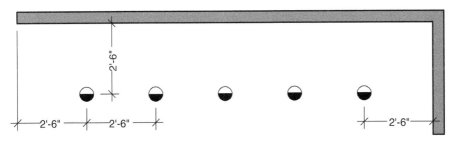

Figure 11.29 Locating the First and Last Wall Wash Luminaires by Dimensions.

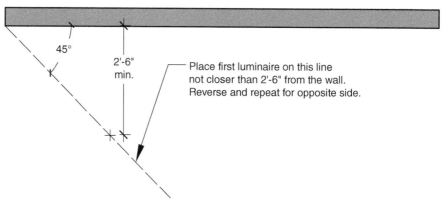

45°

2'-6"
min.

Place first luminaire on this line
not closer than 2'-6" from the wall.
Reverse and repeat for opposite side.

Figure 11.30 Locating the First Luminaire by Angle.

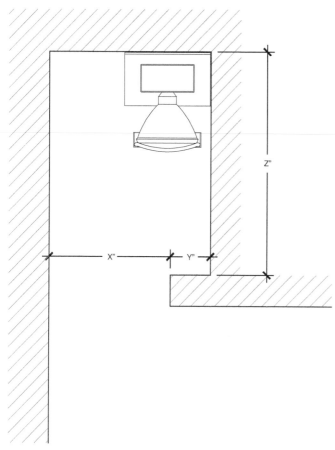

Z"

X"   Y"

Figure 11.31 Installation Detail of Typical Wall Grazing Luminaire.
Dimensions Vary by Lamp Type and Wall Height.

of the distance from the wall, or if the wall is an awkward length, you can place the first fixture by drawing a line at 45° to the wall in the direction of the row of luminaires, and placing the first fixture along that line at any appropriate distance from the wall (Figure 11.30).

Wall Grazing

A wall grazer is typically installed at the top of a wall in interior settings (see wall grazing luminaires in Chapter 9). In exterior applications grazing fixtures are often installed at the base of a wall and are focused upward. Both installations create a strong gradient of light on the wall by placing narrow beams of light at regular intervals along a wall and skimming the light along the face of the wall. As with dedicated cove luminaires, most manufacturers provide guidelines for designing the recess that holds and hides the wall grazing luminaire (Figure 11.31).

A softer version of wall grazing typically uses fluorescent luminaires. Rather than projecting the light down the face of the wall, linear fluorescent lamps are used to create a softer effect

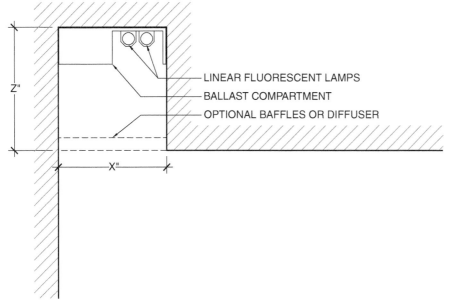

Figure 11.32 Installation Detail for Recessed, Linear Fluorescent Luminaire. Dimensions Vary by Luminaire Configuration and Manufacturer.

that only covers the top portion of the wall. Often, the fluorescent lamps are shielded by a diffuser or louvers to prevent direct view of the lamps. This effect can be created with simple fluorescent strips (Figure 11.32). Reflectors can increase output from the soffit. There are also luminaires designed for this purpose (Figure 11.33).

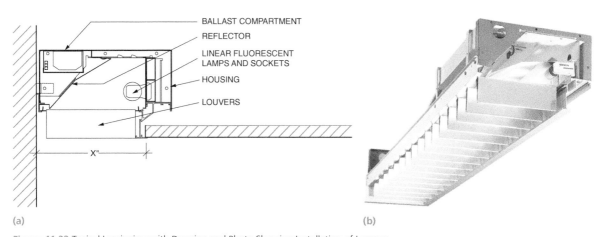

(a)

(b)

Figure 11.33 Typical Luminaires with Drawing and Photo Showing Installation of Louvers.
Courtesy of Philips Lighting Company.

Accent Lighting

Luminaires used for accent lighting may be recessed, semi-recessed, surface mount, or pendant. The feature that they all share is that they are adjustable. Recessed adjustable luminaires typically have a tilt range of 0° to 30°, although some tilt as far as 45°. Surface mount adjustable and track luminaires usually tilt to 90°.

Unlike wall washers, accent luminaires are not set back from the surface being illuminated by a specific distance. Experience has shown that the most pleasing accent angles range from 30° to 45° from vertical. The best way to determine the correct location is by looking at a section, as shown in Figure 11.34.

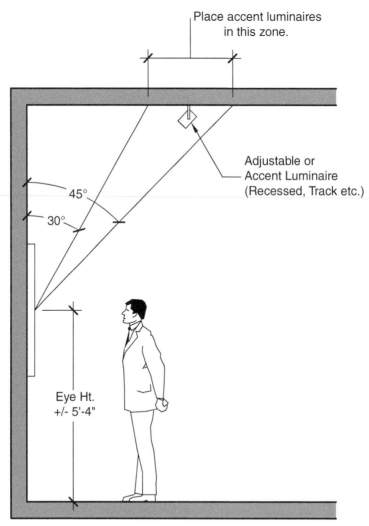

Figure 11.34 Accent Lighting Angles.

Coves

The simplest and least expensive cove light source is a fluorescent strip (Figure 11.35). Here are the guidelines for designing a cove using a fluorescent strip:

1. Lip to ceiling opening is 12" minimum.
2. Center of lamp to wall is 5" mininum.
3. Center of lamp to lip is 2" mininum.
4. Align top of lip with top of lamps. Lip may be lower but confirm that lip shields lamps from view.
5. Paint inside of cove matte white or color of ceiling.

   The same guidelines apply to a cove using LED, compact fluorescent, or cold cathode luminaires.

   Using the cove described in Figure 11.35 with fluorescent strips installed end to end may produce "socket shadow" as shown in Figure 11.36. Socket shadow is a vertical shadow line in the cove and on the ceiling caused by the end caps of the fluorescent lamps and

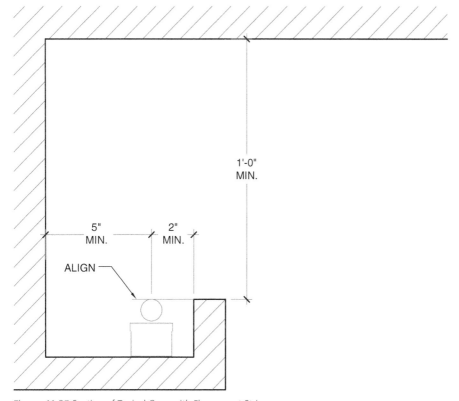

Figure 11.35 Section of Typical Cove with Fluorescent Strip.

Figure 11.36 Socket Shadow from End to End Installation of Fluorescent Strips.

the lamp sockets. Socket shadow is normally not produced by LED or cold cathode lamps. Socket shadow can be eliminated by either staggering the fluorescent strips (Figure 11.37) or by using a luminaire with a housing that staggers the lamps.

There are also specialty cove luminaires that use asymmetric reflectors with linear fluorescent lamps to direct light across the ceiling (Figure 11.38). Other luminaires take advantage of the directed beam of LEDs (Figure 11.39). Both of these luminaires are more expensive than fluorescent strips, but are also more efficient. In most cases the manufacturer's cut sheet or Web site will provide guidelines to determining the dimensions for the cove holding their luminaires based on the angle that the reflector directs the light and the luminaire dimensions.

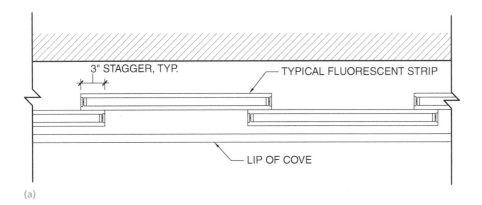

3" STAGGER, TYP.　　　　　TYPICAL FLUORESCENT STRIP

LIP OF COVE

(a)

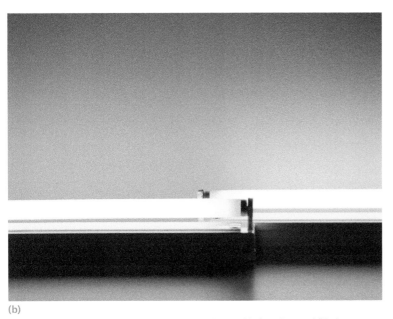

(b)

Figure 11.37 Staggering Fluorescent Strips in a Cove—(a) Plan View and (b) Photo.

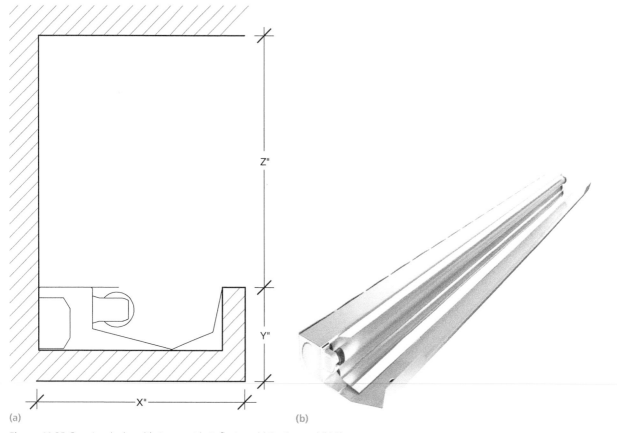

(a)

(b)

Figure 11.38 Cove Luminaire with Asymmetric Reflector—(a) Section and (b) Photo.
Courtesy of Philips Lighting Company.

Figure 11.39 LED Cove Luminaire.
Courtesy of Philips Lighting Company.

Scallops

Downlight luminaires placed close to a wall will produce "scallops" of light on the wall (so called because they are reminiscent of the edge of the shell of a scallop). Scallops can be used to give a pattern to an otherwise unadorned wall. It's relatively easy to calculate a scallop pattern:

1. In a section of the room, draw the luminaire and its beam spread. The beam spread is found on the luminaire cuts sheet as discussed in Chapter 9.
2. Move the luminaire's position so that the beam intersects the wall at the desired height (Figure 11.40).
3. On an elevation of the same wall, mark the beam/wall intersection at the centerline of the luminaire.
4. Repeat the beam angle lines, this time radiating from the point on the wall determined in step 3 (Figure 11.41).
5. Draw a line midway between both sets of angled lines. Round off the intersection of the new lines so that the arc crosses the beam/wall intersection point (Figure 11.42).
6. Space luminaires and resulting scallops to create the desired rhythm on the wall (Figure 11.43).

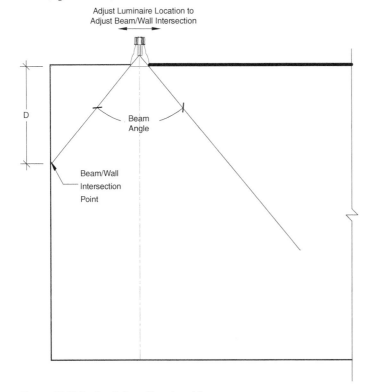

Figure 11.40 Scallop Pattern Steps 1 and 2.

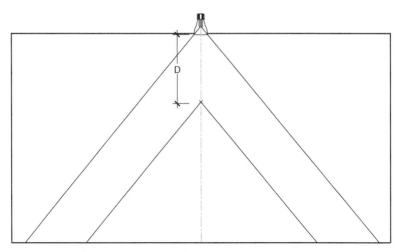

Figure 11.41 Scallop Pattern Steps 3 and 4.

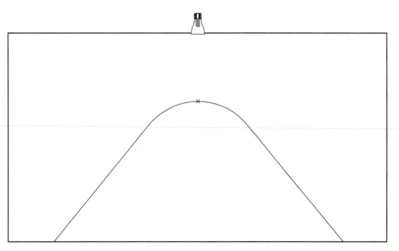

Figure 11.42 Scallop Pattern Step 5.

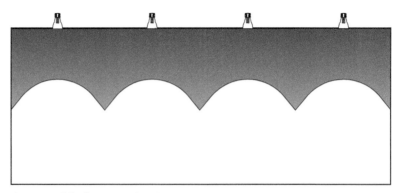

Figure 11.43 Scallop Pattern Step 6.

Care must be taken to coordinate the placement of scallops with patterns of texture, placement of artwork, and apertures in the wall. The softness of the shadow edge will depend on the lamp and reflector.

Luminous Ceilings

Luminous ceilings are made of a translucent material. Light comes through the material from luminaires located behind it, not through fixtures penetrating the ceiling plane, as with a typical hard ceiling. Luminous ceilings can be used as a decorative ceiling feature, or they can cover the entire space to produce an even, shadowless illumination. There are several options when considering a luminous ceiling.

First, several ceiling system manufacturers offer translucent panels in addition to their standard 2' × 2' and 2' × 4' acoustic ceiling panels. The panels are available in a variety of colors, textures, and designs, but the ceiling's support grid remains visible. Second, some manufacturers use larger sheets of translucent material and nearly invisible support systems. Third, other manufacturers specialize in the translucent material and offer technical assistance, but don't make the ceiling support system, leaving the final decision up to the design team.

As with other designs, the first question to ask when considering a luminous ceiling is, "What do I want the space to look like?" If the luminous ceiling will be the main, or only, source of light, then deep colors and heavy textures with low transmission values can be ruled out. If the ceiling is a decorative element, a broader range of materials can be considered. One approach to determining the luminous ceiling system is as follows:

1. How much light is needed in the room and on visual tasks?
2. How much of the space will be covered by the luminous ceiling?
3. What should the ceiling look like? Is a visible support grid acceptable? Is a color other than white desirable and/or acceptable? Is a texture desirable and/or acceptable?
4. What building systems will be integrated into the ceiling? Possible systems include fire detection, fire suppression, HVAC, and emergency lighting.
5. What ceiling system(s) satisfies the requirements of the previous questions?
6. What is the transmission percentage of the panels under consideration? Transmittance can range from greater than 80 percent to less than 10 percent.
7. How diffusing are the panels under consideration? How far behind the panels will the light sources need to be so that they are not apparent?
8. How much light does the lighting system need to produce to achieve the desired light levels when considering the losses due to absorption of the translucent material?
9. In considering the answer to the previous question, are either linear fluorescent or linear LED luminaires clearly a better choice?
10. Do budget or maintenance considerations affect the luminaire choice?

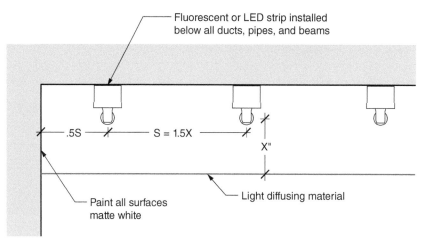

Fluorescent or LED strip installed
below all ducts, pipes, and beams

.5S — S = 1.5X —

X"

Paint all surfaces
matte white

Light diffusing material

Figure 11.44 Typical Luminous Ceiling Section.

As these steps suggest, a luminous ceiling is most likely to be lit with linear fluorescents or linear LEDs. OLEDs may soon become competitive in cost and light output. Figure 11.44 is a typical section when lighting a luminous ceiling with linear fluorescent or LED luminaires. Following are details about the installation:

1. Luminaires are installed at the same elevation, and below all ducts, pipes, and beams.
2. The distance from the ceiling material to the luminaire is as determined by the ceiling system and its requirements.
3. Begin calculations by spacing luminaires 1.5 times the distance between the ceiling and the bottom of the luminaires. Spacing may be closer to increase light levels.

Online Resources

Construction Specifications Institute, www.csinet.org

IALD/LIRC Guidelines for Specification Integrity, www.iald.org/council/Guidelinesfor-SpecificationIntegrity.asp

Manufacturers of Luminous Ceilings or Materials

3form, www.3-form.com/collaborate/light_design/

Armstrong, www.armstrong.com/commceilingsna/products/ceilings/infusions-lay-in/_/N-cZ1z141ql

Barisol, www.barrisolusa.com

Newmat, www.newmat.com

USG, www.usg.com/content/usgcom/en/products-solutions/products/ceilings/specialty-ceilings/tran slucentsluminousinfillceilingpanels.html

Designing with Light Resources

Wiley's companion site to *Designing with Light,* www.wiley.com/go/designingwithlight

Author's companion site to *Designing with Light,* www.designinglight.com

References

DiLaura, David, et al., *The Lighting Handbook, Tenth Edition*, New York: Illuminating Engineering Society, 2011.

Egan, M. David, *Concepts in Architectural Lighting*, New York: McGraw-Hill, 1983.

Gordon, Gary, *Interior Lighting for Designers, Fourth Edition*, Hoboken, NJ: John Wiley & Sons, 2003.

IES Computer Committee, *DG-3-00 Application of Luminaire Symbols on Lighting Design Drawing*, New York: Illuminating Engineering Society, 2000.

IES Nomenclature Committee, *RP-16-05 Nomenclature and Definitions for Illuminating Engineering*, New York: Illuminating Engineering Society, 2005.

MasterFormat Numbers and Titles, Alexandria: The Construction Specifications Institute, 2012.

Steffy, Gary, *Architectural Lighting Design, Third Edition*, Hoboken: John Wiley & Sons. 2008.

CHAPTER 12

Lighting Controls

"The day when we shall know exactly what "electricity" is, will chronicle an event probably greater, more important than any other recorded in the history of the human race. The time will come when the comfort, the very existence, perhaps, of man will depend upon that wonderful agent."

Nikola Tesla

Lighting controls take many forms, from simple on/off switches to advanced systems controlling entire buildings. You may think of lighting controls as a means of turning lights on and off, and that's true, but that's not all they do. Lighting control systems can also monitor the amount of daylight entering a space and make adjustments to the electric lighting and/or window shading systems to maintain appropriate light levels, and they can monitor occupancy of a space and turn lights off when a space is not in use. Controls simplify a complex lighting system for the users, and can reduce building owners' energy costs.

Electricity and Electrical Engineering

Before we discuss controls, we should have a basic understanding of electricity. Electricity is the movement of electrons through a material that is conducive to such movement (hence the word "conductor"). The movement of electrons is called the *current*, and can take two forms: Electrons can flow in one direction, which is called direct current or DC; they can oscillate back and forth, which is called alternating current or AC. DC is the type of electricity supplied by batteries and solar panels. AC is the type of electricity powering most devices in our homes, stores, and offices. Figure 12.1 shows the constant DC output of a typical solar panel (in blue) and the AC wave of typical building power. As you can see, the AC wave alternates between being positive and negative, with each cycle occurring in 1/60th of a second.

When a complete path exists for electricity to travel (say through the wires of your home, through a switch, and through a lamp that is producing light), we refer to that as a closed circuit (Figure 12.2). An open circuit is a path that is interrupted, for example, by turning the switch to the off position.

The pressure behind the flow of electricity is measured in *volts* (V). In North America most electrical devices are designed to operate on a nominal 120V, although certain devices are designed for other voltages. For example, it is more efficient to transmit

■ *current*
The flow of electricity past a given point.

■ *volts*
The "force" or "pressure" of electricity.

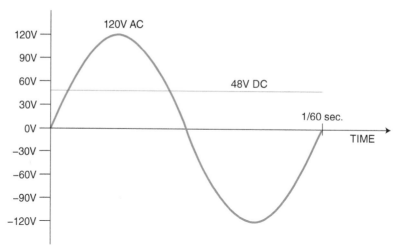

Figure 12.1 Alternating and Direct Current.

■ *amperes*
The amount of electricity moving past a given point in a circuit during a specific period.

■ *watts*
The rate of energy consumption by an electrical device.

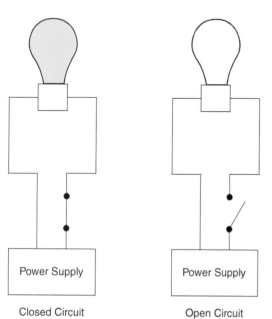

Closed Circuit   Open Circuit

Figure 12.2 Closed Circuit (Left) and Open Circuit (Right).

electricity at higher voltage, so in large buildings it is common to use 277V for the lighting system.

The current is measured in *amperes* or amps (A). A lighting designer's biggest concern with amps involves the upper limit that is allowed by a protective device such as a fuse or circuit breaker, which are rated in amps.

Energy is consumed as work is done (by creating light with a fluorescent lamp, for instance). That consumption is measured in *watts* (W) and is often referred to as the "connected load" or the "load" on a circuit.

The formula that expresses the relationship between volts, amps, and watts is:

$$W = V \times A$$

The proceeding statement is true; if voltage is steady (usually at 120V), then amperage varies with wattage. However, lighting designers aren't necessarily concerned with changes in amperage, but with wattage maximums. In other words, how many luminaires can be connected to one switch or dimmer?

All electrical circuits have protective devices (fuses or circuit breakers) that disconnect the electrical power under unsafe conditions, such as placing too great a load on the circuit. Once we know the maximum amperage rating of a circuit or device, we can use that number as A, and express the allowable wattage range as:

$$W \leq V \times A$$

The National Electric Code (NEC), and good electrical engineering practice, say that we only load a lighting circuit to 80 percent of its rating, making the following a more accurate expression of our limitations per circuit:

$$W \leq .8(V \times A)$$

This tells us that a circuit protected by a 20A circuit breaker can have a load of up to 1,920W of lighting equipment on it, a 15A circuit up to 1,440W, etc. We need to keep this information in mind as we plan our lighting controls and decide which luminaires we want working together on a single circuit, switch, or dimmer.

In Figure 12.2 we show a supply of electricity, a consumption of electricity (by the lamp), and a return path of the unused electricity. The supply wire is often called the "hot" wire, and the return is called the "neutral." The neutral has less current flowing through it than does the hot. Therefore, the primary feed of electricity into the building's service panel may utilize two or three supply wires and one neutral. Common building power supplies are:

- 120/240V, single-phase, three-wire: This means two 120V supply wires and one neutral. This is common in single-family homes and small commercial buildings.
- 120/208V, three-phase, four-wire: This means three supply wires and one neutral.
- 277/480V, three-phase, four-wire: This means three supply wires and one neutral.

The second two are common in larger commercial buildings. When selecting dimming systems, it's important to make sure that the dimmers are compatible with the building power supply, or that the electrical engineer can include equipment to convert the building's power supply to one that is compatible with the dimmers.

Another electrical engineering concern is resistance, which is the opposition to the flow of electricity, and is present in the wiring and in all electrical devices. In wiring, resistance increases as the length of the wire increases, and decreases as the wire's diameter is made larger. Resistance can result in voltage drop, meaning that the voltage at the end of a wire is lower than it is at the beginning. Since electrical engineers want to deliver full voltage to electrical devices, it is common to specify larger diameter wires (with lower resistance and thus less voltage drop) for long runs from the building's main service panel to smaller, local panels placed throughout the building. The circuit breakers in these panels will then feed the nearby switches, outlets, and equipment. We may need to coordinate the electrical requirements of the lighting system with the electrical engineer's design of the local panels.

The Need for Controls

As energy-related building codes have expanded, the amount of energy that is allotted to lighting has been steadily reduced and is close to as low as it can go without affecting design and aesthetics (many lighting designers argue that it *is* affecting design and aesthetics). By strictly controlling when lights are on, dimmed, and off, lighting control systems are the next logical step in reducing the energy consumption of a lighting system. Lighting controls, in one form or another, are now required by the U.S. government, all state energy codes, and all green construction codes and voluntary programs. Clearly this is a topic lighting designers must understand.

The reason energy controls are required, is that the energy savings from controls can be significant. For example, researchers at the Lawrence Berkeley National Laboratory analyzed over 80 papers and studies on the benefit of lighting controls. They found average energy savings of 24 percent for occupancy sensors, 28 percent for daylighting, 31 percent for personal tuning in offices and workstations, 36 percent for building-wide controls, and 38 percent for combining multiple approaches.

Basic Controls

Switches and Wall Box Dimmers

■ **dimmers**
An electrical device that controls lamp intensity by regulating the flow of electricity to the lamp.

■ **wall box**
A wall mounted switch or dimmer.

The simplest lighting control is the on/off switch. The switch provides two light levels—all or none. If we want to be able to fine-tune the light levels, we can replace switches with *dimmers*. Dimmers installed in the wall in place of switches are called *wall box* dimmers. Switches and dimmers are available in a wide range of styles and colors (Figure 12.3).

Types of Dimmers

While we don't need to delve deeply into the engineering of dimming technology, it is still important for lighting designers to know what technologies exist and their key characteristics. Each type of dimmer affects the sine wave cycle of electricity differently,

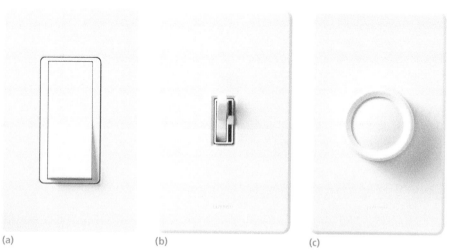

(a) (b) (c)

Figure 12.3 (a) Paddle or "Decora" Switch, (b) Toggle Switch with Sliding Dimmer, (c) Rotary Dimmer. *Courtesy of Lutron Electronics Company, Inc.*

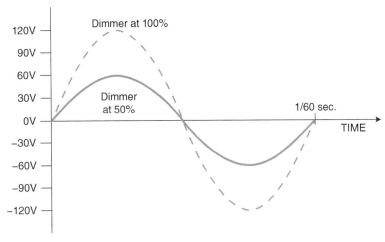

Figure 12.4 Resistance Dimming.

which in turn affects the devices that are being dimmed. Dimmers and the devices they control (lamps, ballasts, transformers, and power supplies) must be matched to avoid dimmer or device failure, voiding of equipment warranties, and other undesirable outcomes.

Resistance Dimming

The oldest and simplest form of dimming is resistance dimming. In resistance dimming electricity passes through a coil of copper wire, providing a high amount of potential resistance to the flow of the electricity. An adjustable arm makes contact with the coil, at which point the electricity passes through the arm and out to the lamp. If the arm contacts the copper coil at the beginning, there is very little electrical loss to resistance and the lamp is bright (Figure 12.4). If the arm is adjusted to contact the coil at the end there is a great deal of resistance and the lamp is dim or even off.

Resistance dimming is very inefficient and generates considerable heat. It has been completely replaced in lighting applications by other technologies.

Forward Phase Dimming

Forward phase dimmers control the intensity of the lamp by varying the "on" point in each half of the cycle (Figure 12.5), thus controlling the amount of power delivered to the lamp. Forward-phase dimmers are typically either triac (triode alternating current switch) or SCR (silicone controlled rectifier) dimmers. Triac dimmers are the most common wall box dimmer, while SCRs are typically used in large, centralized dimming systems. Forward phase dimming is the most used dimming technology because it is inexpensive and reliable. The potential disadvantages of forward phase dimming are a humming or buzzing sound from the lamp filaments, and potential *electromagnetic interference* with nearby, sensitive equipment such as audio systems.

■ *electromagnetic interference*
High frequency interference (electrical noise) caused by electronic components or lamps that interferes with the operation of electrical equipment.

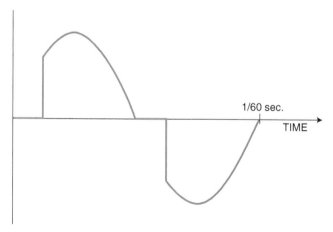

Figure 12.5 Forward Phase Dimming.

Reverse Phase Dimming

Reverse phase dimmers are, as one would expect, the opposite of forward phase dimmers. They control lamp intensity by varying the "off" point in each half of the cycle (Figure 12.6). Reverse phase dimmers are typically used to dim electronic transformers in low voltage fixtures, and electronic ballasts in fluorescent fixtures. When designed to dim electronic transformers they are often referred to as electronic low voltage (ELV) dimmers. They are slightly more expensive than forward phase dimmers. Forward phase dimmers typically use insulated gate bipolar transistor (IGBT) technology.

Sine Wave Dimming

A newer technology, sine wave dimming, modifies the entire sine wave of the electrical cycle much like a resistance dimmer. The advantages are that sine wave dimmers

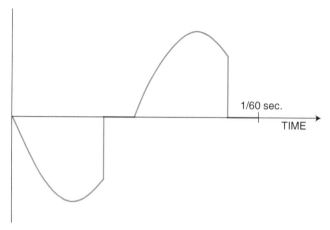

Figure 12.6 Reverse Phase Dimming.

can dim a wider range of devices, they do not cause incandescent filaments to hum or buzz, and they do not introduce *harmonics* into the building's electrical system as with forward and reverse phase dimming. The drawback to sine wave dimmers is their higher cost, although some of that may be offset because equipment to handle the harmonics is not required.

Dimming Ballasts

Linear and compact fluorescent lamps can be dimmed with specially designed dimming ballasts when paired with the correct type of dimmer. In many applications, smooth dimming from 100 percent down to 0 percent of output is not necessary, so ballasts are usually described by their lowest output level, as in "10 percent dimming" or "5 percent dimming." Once the lowest output level is reached, the ballasts will not be able to maintain the arc inside the tube and the lamp will stop producing light.

Manufacturers label their ballasts according to the minimum light output; however, our eyes do not respond to brightness in a linear manner, so the labeling on dimming ballasts can be confusing:

Ten percent dimming ballasts will dim the measured lamp output to 10 percent of the full output. However, this will be perceived as a reduction to 32 percent of full output.

Five percent dimming is perceived as a reduction to 22 percent of full output.

1 percent dimming is perceived as a reduction to 10 percent of full output.

New fluorescent lamps may flicker when installed on a dimming system. This can be due to the initial distribution of mercury inside the lamp, or to impurities that remain inside the lamp during manufacturing. In either case, lamps that are to be used on a dimming system should be "seasoned" by operating them at full output for several hours before dimming. The National Electrical Manufacturers Association (NEMA) recommends 12 hours of seasoning. One good practice is to change the lamps in groups (called group relamping) and then leave the group on at full power overnight.

There are several ways of controlling dimming ballasts. As previously mentioned, reverse phase dimmers can be used with two-wire ballasts, which refers to two wires (hot and neutral) between the dimmer and the ballast. Three-wire ballasts use a switched hot, a dimmed hot, and a neutral wire. The dimmed hot acts as the control signal to the ballast to adjust the output. Four-wire ballasts use a switched hot and neutral to deliver undimmed power to the ballast, plus two additional wires delivering a low voltage control signal to the ballast.

Occupancy and Vacancy Sensors

Occupancy sensors and *vacancy sensors* combine motion detection and an on/off switch to turn lights on only when people are present (Figure 12.7). A built-in, adjustable timer turns the lights off a set amount of time after the last detected motion. The sensitivity and range of most sensors can be adjusted to each space. This adjustment process, called "*commissioning*," is critical to the successful installation and operation of occupancy sensors.

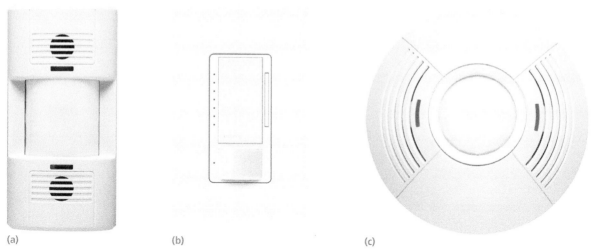

(a)   (b)   (c)

Figure 12.7 (a) Wall Mounted Occupancy Sensor, (b) Switch with Built-In Occupancy Sensor, (c) Ceiling Mounted Occupancy Sensor. *Courtesy of Lutron Electronics Company, Inc.*

There are two technologies used in occupancy sensors, and many sensors employ both. The first technology is passive infrared (PIR). PIR sensors respond to changes in background heat at a wavelength emitted by humans. They operate on line of site, meaning that they can't see around corners or over obstructions such as bathroom stalls. However, the line of sight operation allows the sensor to provide more specific coverage than the second technology, ultrasonic sensors.

Ultrasonic sensors operate by emitting high frequency sound waves that can't be heard by humans. These waves bound off of the objects and surfaces of a room and are measured to establish the baseline for the empty space. When changes or shifts in the measured frequency are detected, the ultrasonic sensor turns on the lights.

To minimize false triggering, the two technologies are frequently combined. Both sensors must be activated to turn the lights on, while only one sensor must be activated to keep the lights on. Some sensors will flash the lights several minutes before turning the lights off to alert occupants who are motionless and are not detected. Most sensors installed at light switch height also have a push-button switch to manually turn the lights on and off.

Increasingly, energy conservation codes require occupancy sensors in spaces such as storerooms and bathrooms to prevent lights from being left on all day. Occupancy sensors can be mounted at light switch level, high on a wall, on the ceiling, in workstations, and outdoors.

Intermediate Controls

Once a project's lighting control requirements become too complex for stand-alone switches, dimmers, and sensors, we begin to think about complete systems. Control devices, control software, dimmers, relays, sensors, and input from devices outside of the lighting system are all components that may become part of a dimming and control system.

The first step in determining what kind of controls to use is to decide which fixtures will operate together. It is important to remember that most dimmers are designed for a specific type of load: line voltage incandescent, low voltage incandescent, compact and linear fluorescent, or LED. This may affect fixture selection and the grouping of fixtures by design intent, commonly called *control zones*. The second step is to create a dimming schedule or zone schedule to consolidate the basic information into a single table. The conference room from Chapter 11 would have the following dimming schedule.

■ *control zones*
A group of luminaires performing the same task and controlled in unison.

Conference Room Dimming Schedule						
Zone Number	Purpose	Fixture Type	Fixture Qty.	Fixture Load	Total Load	Dimmer Type
1	Wall Wash, Whiteboard Wall	WM1	6	50W	300W	ELV
2	Wall Wash, Pinup Wall	WM1	5	50W	250W	ELV
3	Pendant	PF1	1	56W	56W	Relay
4	Sconces	QF1	2	28W	56W	3-Wire Fluorescent
5	Circulation	DC1	4	22W	88W	3-Wire Fluorescent

Dimming Systems

Moderately sized dimming systems provide several advantages over a group of individual switches and dimmers. First, they combine multiple dimmers (usually up to 12) into a single wall mounted panel. The dimmers can be individually configured to dim almost any load (such as line voltage, low voltage, fluorescent, LED), so they don't limit the design. This also leads to the second advantage, reduced wall clutter. In combining multiple dimmers behind a single faceplate, dimming systems present a smaller, cleaner appearance. This may be especially important if the controls are visible to the room's occupants (Figure 12.8).

Third, switch and dimmer settings recorded in an internal memory (called presets or scenes) eliminate guesswork by the users. They simply press a preset button, and the dimmers (and, therefore, the lights) change to their recorded levels. Most manufacturers will engrave or otherwise label each of the buttons so that the operation of the system is clear to the users; they simply press the button with the label for the light setting that they desire. Four or five presets are common, but some systems allow for many more.

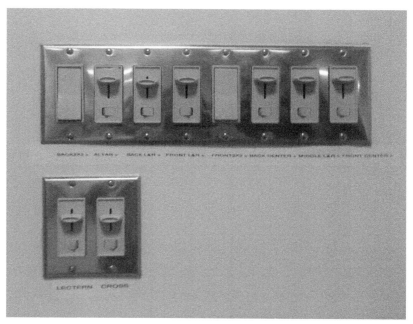

Figure 12.8 Perhaps a Small Dimming System Instead?

Finally, larger spaces can have control stations at each entry point, or anywhere else they are needed, and the presets available can be specific to each control station. These remote stations, which contain communication electronics but no dimmers, communicate with the main panel via low voltage wiring or radio to form a small control system. The manufacturer can also label buttons on the remote control stations (Figure 12.9).

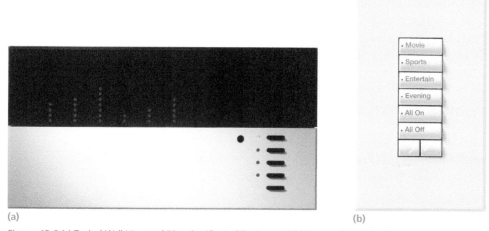

(a)   (b)

Figure 12.9 (a) Typical Wall Mounted Dimming/Control System and (b) Remote Preset Station.
Courtesy of Lutron Electronics Company, Inc.

Photocells

Photocells are another energy-saving component that can be connected to a dimming and control system. Photocells sense the ambient light in a space, both daylight and electric light. That information can be used to dim or turn off electric lights when they are not needed. *Daylight harvesting* is the term used to describe the use of photocells to adjust the electric lighting in response to daylight entering through windows or skylights. A simple daylight harvesting system will dim or turn off a light fixture or group of fixtures. Photocells can also be connected to more complex dimming and control systems that are programmed with more sophisticated responses to information from photocells and occupancy sensors.

Large-Scale Control Systems

When a space requires more than 10 or 12 dimmers, or when the designer wants to control multiple spaces with a single system, larger control systems are indicated. These systems can control groups of fixtures across many rooms, the entire floor of a building, or even multiple floors. These systems typically have expanded capabilities that may include: dimming light fixtures; turning light fixtures on or off; raising or lowering window blinds or opening and closing curtains; time-of-day and day-of-week programming; and responding to input from other systems, such as building energy management and audio/ video systems.

Centralized Systems

Centralized systems place all of the dimmers and relays (an electrically operated switch) in a single housing or multiple, connected housings. Typically, the control system processor is built into, or adjacent to, the dimming hardware. The control stations (push-buttons, sliders, and/or touchscreens) do not directly control power sent to the lighting fixtures. They send a signal to the control system processor, which then sends instructions to the dimmers/relays. This type of system usually has less data wiring than distributed systems (discussed next), and it consolidates the control system hardware in a single location.

As an example of when such a system is appropriate, the dimming system used in the church case study in Chapter 2 is a centralized system. A single cabinet (similar to the one shown in Figure 12.10) houses 48 dimmers and *relays*. The control system is housed in a cabinet adjacent to the dimmers. The dimming cabinet holds three types of dimmers: for incandescent loads (pendant fixtures), electronic low voltage loads (perimeter white LED uplights), and CFL loads (downlights at entries). The cabinet also holds relays that turn on the LED fixtures illuminating the sanctuary. One touch screen is programmed with about a dozen presets Two push-button stations (one near the front door and one in the organ loft) trigger certain light settings in the touch screen. When a button is pressed, the control system sends appropriate instructions to the dimmers, and also sends data to control

■ *photocells*
A light-sensing device used to control luminaires and dimmers in response to detected light levels.

■ *daylight harvesting*
An energy-saving technique in which a dimming system responds to a photocell by reducing light output when daylight is present.

■ *relay*
An electrically controlled switch.

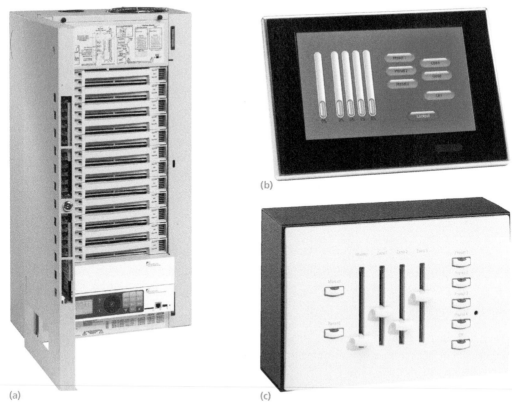

(a)

(b)

(c)

Figure 12.10 (a) Centralized Dimming System, (b) Touch Screen Control Station, and (c) Push-Button/ Slider Control Station.
Courtesy of Electronic Theatre Controls.

the brightness and color of the LEDs illuminating the sanctuary. Finally, the control system has a built-in clock that is programmed to turn lights on each morning, change the light levels at sunset, and turn the lights off at the end of each day.

Distributed Systems

Distributed systems spread the dimming hardware, and sometimes the control processing, over two or more locations. Distributed systems can take several forms, depending on the size of the space being controlled and the lamp technology that is used. Various manufacturers produce variations on each of these forms.

The simplest distributed system networks two or more of the dimming panels shown in Figure 12.9. Once networked, each preset can include dimmer settings from both of the dimming panels.

For example, let's assume there is a hotel ballroom that requires 16 dimmers to control the downlights, chandeliers, and sconces. Let's also assume that there are two employee-only entrances, and four entrances for the public. The hotel's owners want employees to be able to turn on or adjust the lights from both of their entrances. We may decide to place one dimming panel, as shown in Figure 12.9, with eight dimmers each, at the two entrances and link them together. The system has dimming and control equipment in two locations. Since the two locations are linked, pressing any of the presets on either panel triggers both sets of dimmers to produce the desired light setting.

The second type of distributed system centralizes the controls but distributes the dimmers, similar to those shown in Figure 12.10, across the building. The possible advantage of this system over a centralized system is that installation costs may be lower because of shorter runs of wiring between the dimmers and the lighting fixtures. Like centralized systems, these distributed systems can respond to time of day, photocell, occupancy sensor, control station, and other inputs.

The third type of distributed system currently involves only fluorescent lamps, and uses a control protocol called digital addressable lighting interface (DALI). A *DALI* system delivers undimmed power and a control signal to each ballast. Each ballast has a built-in memory holding its unique address and the brightness levels for various presets. The DALI control system can respond to time of day, photocell, occupancy sensor, and control station preset inputs, and then instructs the ballasts to dim to the corresponding preset level.

■ *dali*
A communications protocol in which each luminaire has a distinct address and can communicate with the lighting controller.

Control Protocols

Dimmers, dimming ballasts, and dimming power supplies can be controlled by several different types of devices and by several different protocols. Again, we don't need to get too detailed, but it is important to be familiar with the most common protocols and to know that the controller and the device being controlled must use the same protocol. Some systems can use multiple protocols at once.

0–10V Direct Current

One method of controlling dimming ballasts and dimming LED drivers is with a low voltage direct current (DC) control signal. Devices using 0–10V DC require four wires, two delivering line voltage power and two delivering the DC control voltage. When the control signal is at 10 volts, the ballast or driver is producing the maximum designed light output. When the control signal is at 0 volts, the light source is off.

Digital Addressable Lighting Interface

Digital addressable lighting interface (DALI) is a European standard for controlling fluorescent fixtures that is becoming more common in North America. In a DALI network the switching or dimming hardware is built into the fixture as a DALI enabled ballast. Two wires deliver line voltage power to the ballast, and two additional wires deliver a digital signal.

A DALI system can assign a unique address to every ballast in a building, and control each one individually. Fixtures can also be grouped into control zones which can be reconfigured without any adjustments to the wiring. There is no practical upper limit to the number of devices a DALI system can control.

Every DALI ballast has built-in solid-state memory to record its settings. When the DALI ballast receives a signal, it acts on information contained in its memory. DALI is a two-way protocol. New ballasts can broadcast their presence so that they can be added to the network. Controllers can ask for information and ballasts can broadcast replies.

Digital Multiplex Lighting and Remote Device Management

Digital multiplex lighting (DMX or DMX512) was originally developed in 1986 as a theatre industry standard for control consoles to communicate with dimmers. It is a robust protocol that has also been adopted by many LED fixture manufacturers as the primary means of controlling multicolored LED fixtures.

DMX sends a continuous stream of data for 512 devices or parameters. Each stream of 512 addresses is referred to as a universe. Multiple devices can have the same data address. For example, we may want a row of RGB LED fixtures to respond as one, in which case we would give them all the same address. Some devices require multiple addresses. For example, an RGB LED fixture usually requires three addresses to individually control the red, green, and blue LEDs. In this case we might set the addresses for the row of fixtures to 1, 2, and 3.

DMX is unidirectional. The controller sends out the information and the receiving device is expected to act according to that information. However, because it is one way, the controller cannot know when new devices are connected or when a connected device is not responding properly. In large systems, this can make troubleshooting difficult. The solution is remote device management (RDM).

RDM is a bidirectional extension of DMX512. Like DALI, it enables a device connected to a network to broadcast its presence, the parameters that are available to control, and any faults that are detected. It also enables the controller to discover new devices, configure them, and monitor their performance.

DMX and RDM are continuous streaming protocols. Only the controller has onboard memory to store information about light levels or device actions. The controller sends information over and over, and changes to the stream of information are received and acted upon by the various devices.

Other Protocols

RS232 is a data communications standard used by various types of electronic equipment. It is commonly used as the communication protocol between two systems, such as an AV system and a lighting system. Such a setup would allow the operator of the AV system to turn on, dim, and turn off the lighting without touching the lighting controls. Building management systems (BMS) such as building automation and control network (BACnet) may operate independently of the lighting system and use RS232 to send instructions to the lighting control system.

Some control systems can connect to a computer network over Ethernet. This can allow users to control their lighting via software on their computers, or allow technicians to connect to the lighting system for programming, diagnostics, and updating.

Other protocols may be included in a lighting control system, or may communicate with a lighting control system. For example, universal serial bus (USB) is a common means of connecting external devices to a lighting network to update software or save backup copies of the data.

Control System Features

Many control systems have advanced programming features. The advanced programming interface might be integral to the control system's processor and hardware, or it may be set up on a PC and then uploaded into the control system's memory.

Time of Day Events

Control systems can use an onboard clock to adjust the lighting at the same time every day, for instance, the system can turn a store's lights on at 8 a.m. and off again at 11 p.m. Most systems can hold many such events in memory.

Calendar Events

Many control systems have a built-in calendar in addition to their clock. This allows the designer or users to schedule either unique or recurring events based on day of the week or day of the month. For example, the aforementioned store may have different hours on Saturday and Sunday. If so, one calendar event would turn the lights on and off Mondays through Fridays, a second calendar event would be set up for Saturdays, and a third one would be set up for Sundays.

Astronomical Time Clock Events

When a control system has an *astronomical time clock*, the date and the building's latitude and longitude are entered during system commissioning. The controller can then calculate the time of sunrise and sunset for every day of the year. This allows the controller to execute changes to the lights based on proximity to sunrise and sunset (for instance, adjusting brightness to store windows just before sunset) without the need to reprogram the system with new times throughout the year.

■ *astronomical time clock*
A device that turns a load on or off based on astronomical events such as sunset or sunrise, accounting for geographic location and day of the year.

Control of External Devices

More complex control systems can send information, or at least simple signals, to external devices or systems. For example, in daylight harvesting it is common for the lighting system to also control motorized window blinds so that when the daylight is too bright the lighting system not only turns off the electric lights, but it also lowers the blinds to block out the excess daylight.

Input from External Devices

We've already mentioned occupancy sensors and photocells as stand-alone devices that connect to a single lighting circuit. They can also be integrated into larger control systems. Automated building systems and AV systems can send instructions to the lighting system. Some control systems can connect, via Ethernet, to local computer networks or the Internet. These features allow designers or building operators to see what is happening to the system and make changes remotely.

Documenting Controls

Switching and dimming must be shown on drawings for the contractor. In some instances, such as a fast-food restaurant, there is no dimming and the lights turn on at the beginning of the day and off at the end of the day. Such a project has no need for what most of us would call a control system, and most lighting designers would leave the selection and documentation of the on/off controls to the project's electrical engineer. However, when the lighting design includes decisions about the grouping of fixtures for switching or dimming, and the lighting designer is responsible for determining the actions of the system, the lighting designer will usually have to create the documentation as well. Simple controls may be shown on the lighting plan. Complicated systems may require separate drawings to show the routing of power and/or data to assure that the system is properly installed and connected.

Switching

A simple switching scheme can be shown on the RCP by drawing arcs that connect luminaires to the appropriate switch or wall box dimmer, as shown in Figure 12.11. Here we see three switches. The first switch controls the wall washers and recessed downlights. The second switch controls the central pendant fixture. The third switch controls the wall sconces. Note that these arcs do not instruct the EC on how to wire the room. The only indicate which luminaires should operate together. It is up to the EC to determine the best routing of the wire connecting the luminaires.

Dimming

In more complicated systems, or where the dimmers are located in another room, it may not make sense to visually show the connections. In this case, a good approach is to show the number of the dimmer or relay that controls each fixture adjacent to that fixture's symbol. See Figure 12.12.

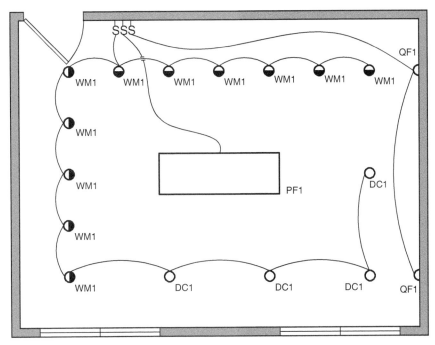

Figure 12.11 Switching Layout.

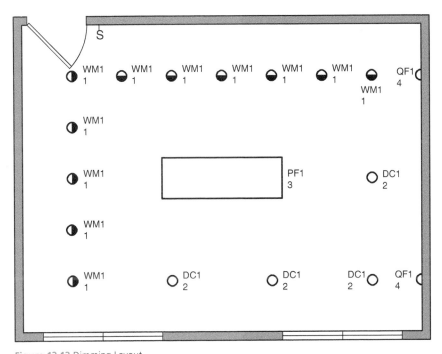

Figure 12.12 Dimming Layout.

Commissioning Control Systems

In order for a lighting control system to operate properly, thereby providing maximum energy savings, it must be commissioned. Commissioning means that the system is inspected for proper connections and operation, all sensors are properly calibrated, and all variables (such as duration of inactivity before an occupancy sensor turns off the lights) are properly set. Most systems will need periodic recommissioning.

The commissioning process begins with the design process. Requirements for the lighting control system are developed during the schematic design phase by the designer based on input from the owner. These requirements form the basis for selecting the appropriate control system. The requirements are documented and regularly updated throughout the design and construction process. The final requirements are submitted to the commissioning team to guide them in their work.

On small projects or systems, the commissioning agent is often someone who is trained and certified by the control system manufacturer. That person will inspect the installation and arrange for corrections by the electrical contractor, if any are required. Once the system is free of errors, input from the owner, designer, and other concerned parties will guide the setup, calibration, and programming of the control system.

On large projects or complicated systems, the owner may engage a commissioning agent as a supplement to the project's design team. In this scenario, the commissioning agent may be responsible for commissioning all of the building's systems (HVAC, lighting, etc.). This commissioning agent works directly for the owner, and takes a leading role in commissioning the building's systems. As a third party not connected to the design team or the equipment manufacturers, the commissioning agent develops a comprehensive commissioning plan based on input from the owner and the designers, may review design documentation and contractor submittals, and supervises the commissioning technicians. The commissioning agent also may be involved in writing operations manuals, and in training the building operations and maintenance staff.

In either case, the requirements for system commissioning are set by the designer in the system commissioning specification.

Online Resources

Advanced Lighting Guide, www.algonline.org

DALI, www.dali-ag.org

Lighting Controls Association, www.lightingcontrolsassociation.org

Lightsearch, www.lightsearch.com

National Lighting Product Information Program at the Lighting Research Center, www.lrc.rpi.edu

Dimming Ballast Manufacturers

GE Lighting, www.gelighting.com

Lutron, www.lutron.com

Osram Sylvania, www.sylvania.com

Philips Advance, www.usa.lighting.philips.com

Universal Lighting Technologies, www.unvlt.com

Designing with Light Resources

Wiley's companion site to *Designing with Light*, www.wiley.com/go/designingwithlight

Author's companion site to *Designing with Light*, www.designinglight.com

References

DiLaura, David, et al., *The Lighting Handbook, Tenth Edition,* New York: Illuminating Engineering Society, 2011.

IES Controls Protocol Committee, *TM-23-11 Lighting Control Protocols*, New York: Illuminating Engineering Society, 2011.

Meshbert, Gary, and Craig DiLouie, "Estimating Energy Savings from Controls," *Lighting Design + Application*, August 2013, 18–22.

NEMA Lighting Systems Division, *LSD 23-2010*. Rosslyn, VA: National Electrical Manufacturers Association, 2010.

NEMA Lighting Systems Division, *LSD 64-2012 Lighting Controls Terminology*, Rosslyn, VA: National Electrical Manufacturers Association, 2012.

Williams, Alison, et al., "Lighting Controls in Commercial Buildings," *Leukos*, 8(3): 161–180.

CHAPTER 13

Photometrics and Calculations

"To measure is to know."

Lord William Thomson Kelvin

Now that we've covered the technical issues of lamps, fixtures, layouts and controls, and the artistic issues of design, there is one big question that is still unanswered. How much light is required? Once we know the amount of light required, the obvious follow-on question is, "How do we calculate the amount of light we're providing?" The answers ripple backward through everything we've covered so far. Higher light levels will require higher wattages and/or more efficient light sources and/or more fixtures, so the answers are important. Before we answer the question of how much light we should provide, let's cover some basic vocabulary.

Please note that while I've placed calculations at this point in the book, it does not mean that lighting designers wait until after they've created an RCP to think about this topic. Thinking about brightness and distribution is part of designing the overall look and feel of a space. It's also critical to understand and plan for the illuminance requirements of important visual tasks.

Terms Describing Brightness

If we measure a box, the height, width, and length would all be expressed in the same units. Unfortunately, with light that is not the case. All measurements of brightness are not expressed in the same units, nor is the vocabulary used to describe quantities of light the same. The general words we use to describe light at various points in its travel are the following:

Luminance is light emitted from a light source. Light sources are luminous.

Illuminance is light landing on a surface, which is also described as light incident upon a surface. Surfaces are illuminated.

Reflectance is light bouncing off of a surface. All surfaces are reflective to some degree.

■ *luminance*
The brightness of a light source.
■ *illuminance*
The light incident on a surface.
■ *reflectance*
The incident light bouncing off of a surface.

Units for Measuring Light

The units of measurement for luminance, illuminance, and reflectance are specific to the measurement being made. Some are the same in both the English and metric systems, while others are not.

Luminance

■ *lumen*
A unit of light flow or luminous flux, used to describe the total light output of a lamp.

■ *candela*
Unit of luminous intensity of a light source in a specific direction.

■ *candlepower*
An obsolete measure of luminous intensity of a light source in a specific direction.

■ *foot candle*
The English unit of measurement of the illuminance on a surface.

A *lumen* (lm) is the unit used to measure a lamp's total visible light output in all directions. This number is used to describe the light output of omnidirectional lamps and is supplied by the lamp manufacturer.

A *candela* (cd) is the intensity of a light source in one direction. This number is used to describe the light output of directional lamps and of luminaires, and is supplied by the lamp manufacture and luminaire manufacturer, respectively. Some manufacturers use *candlepower* (cp) instead of candelas, although it is an obsolete term. For our purposes they are interchangeable. A light source with a luminance of 1 lm emits 12.57 cd.

Illuminance

The *foot candle* (fc) is the measurement of illumination (the density of light arriving an a surface) in the English system. A foot candle is the amount of light landing on a one square foot surface that is one foot away from a source of 1 lm (Figure 13.1).

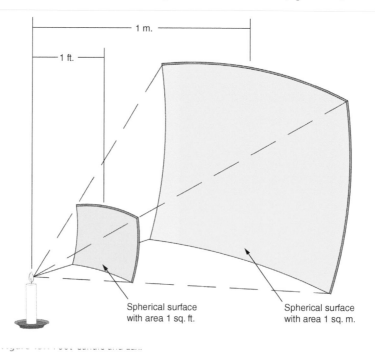

Spherical surface with area 1 sq. ft.

Spherical surface with area 1 sq. m.

The *lux* (lx) is the measurement of illumination in the International System of Units (SI). A lux is the amount of light landing on a one square meter surface that is one meter away from a light source of 1 lm (Figure 13.1).

■ *lux*
The International System of Units (SI) unit of measure for illuminance of a surface.

The definition of both foot candle and lux requires that the light be evenly distributed. One way of imagining a foot candle is to place a candle in the center of a sphere that is one foot in diameter. The amount of light falling on a one square foot section of the sphere is 1 fc. Substitute one meter for one foot and the amount of light is 1 lx:

$$1\ lx = .09\ fc \text{ and } 1\ fc = 10.76\ lx$$

This is frequently rounded off to 1 lx = .1 fc and 1 fc = 10 lx to simplify conversion.

Reflectance

A *foot-lambert* (fL) is the measurement of the luminosity of a surface. It applies to light reflecting off of a surface and to a luminous surface such as a luminous ceiling or an OLED panel. It is equal to $1/\pi$ candela per square foot.

■ *foot-lambert*
The English unit of luminance.

A *candela per square meter* (cd/m^2) is the measurement of luminance in the SI system:

■ *candela per square meter*
The SI unit of luminance.

$$1\ fL = 3.426\ cd/m^2 \text{ and } 1\ cd/m^2 = .2919\ fL$$

How Much Light Is Required?

The quality of our vision depends, in part, on the amount of light entering the eye and striking the retina. In an ideal world we would know the reflective value (which is expressed as a percentage) of every object brought into a room. That knowledge would allow us to adjust the illuminance of the surfaces by changing the luminosity of the light sources. This would give us control over the amount of light entering the eye and allow us to adjust it as required for each task.

In practice, of course, this is not possible. Our first concern in establishing appropriate light levels, then, is not with the reflective value of specific objects (in most applications) but with the illuminance of surfaces of average reflectance.

There has been a great deal of research on this subject, and research is ongoing. Guidance on illumination levels for various space types or various activities is plentiful. It is important to remember, however, that guidance is not instruction. We must consider the recommended illuminance with respect to the users, the activities, and the over-all desired ambience. We are then free to adjust the project's target illuminance, if appropriate.

There are several places we can turn to for typical illumination levels that will serve as a starting point. First, *The Lighting Handbook,* published by the Illuminating Engineering

Society (IES), provides general light level recommendations for a wide range of applications and activities.

Second, the IES also publishes Recommended Practices (RP) and Design Guides (DG) for applications as diverse as educational facilities, senior living, and roadways. These booklets are not checklists, but guides and reminders so that you don't overlook an important consideration in your design. They contain information, among other things, about appropriate light levels for the visual tasks performed in each application.

Third, we can perform mock-ups either in the studio or in another location. Mock-ups may be simple, such as using foam core to test the dimensions of a cove or soffit. They may also be complicated, such as mocking up an entire room or floor to test a complete lighting system.

Fourth, we can take real world light measurements and compare the measured light levels with our evaluation of the lighting design to develop a target brightness level.

Finally, we can rely on our professional experience and knowledge (once we have enough).

Illuminance Calculations

Once we've determined the target illuminance, selected lamps and luminaires, and developed a preliminary RCP, it's time to test our design against our illuminance goals. Some calculations can be quickly confirmed on a piece of scratch paper or a calculator. Others may make use of a manufacturer's online calculator or a spreadsheet. The most complex calculations require dedicated software or plug-ins to CAD software.

Point Method

The point method (or the point-to-point method) allows us to quickly calculate the amount of light from a single source landing on a specific point. The point method begins with the inverse square law. We all understand that as the distance increases the same amount of light is spread over a larger surface area, resulting in lower illumination. The inverse square law states that when the distance between a phenomenon and an object doubles, the impact is reduced by the inverse of the square ($1/2^2$, or 1/4) not 1/2 as you might expect (Figure 13.2). This is true for light reaching a surface, sound reaching your ear, radio waves reaching your radio, etc.

When using the point method, the light source does not need to be, literally, a single point in space, but it does need to be small enough to act as a point when compared to the target. In practical terms this means that the greatest measurement of the light source must be a minimum of 1/5 the distance between the light source and the target (this is referred to as the 1/5th rule). A luminaire with a 6" diameter aperture, then, would have to be at least 30" above from the target. A 2' x 4' fluorescent has a diagonal measurement of about 4'-5", and would have to be slightly more than 22'-0" above the target. A good rule of thumb is that the point method shouldn't be used with luminaires that have an aperture greater than 12".

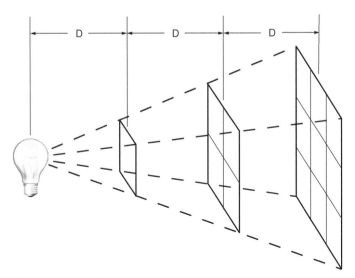

Figure 13.2 Inverse Square Law.

The point method formula is used when light is evenly distributed, which means that the light strikes the surface at a right angle. This occurrence is so common in our calculations (imagine a ceiling luminaire over a desk) that we actually refer to it as "normal" (Figure 13.3). We also define the angle of light exiting a luminaire straight down as 0°, which is also called the *nadir*.

■ *nadir*
A reference direction directly below a luminaire.

"Normal" ray of light strikes surface at 90°

Figure 13.3 Light Normal to Surface.

Assuming the calculation we're making meets these conditions, the Point Method formula is:

$$E = \frac{I}{D^2}$$

E = Intensity of light (illumination) falling on the surface measured in fc or lx.

I = Intensity of the lamp or luminaire, measured in cp or cd, in the direction of interest.

D = Distance between the light source and the point of calculation, measured in feet (fc) or meters (lx).

E is what the formula is calculating. *D* is easy to measure, but where do we find *I*? It depends on the luminaire we're using. If the luminaire is using a directional lamp, then the lamp is controlling the beam, so we go to the lamp manufacturer. We assume that we're calculating the brightness at the center of the beam focused straight down onto the target, so *I* is found under the column called MBCP for Middle Beam Candle Power, or CBCP for Center Beam Candle Power (Figure 13.4).

■ ***candlepower distribution curve***
A curve, plotted on polar coordinates, illustrating the distribution of light from a lamp or luminaire.

If the luminaire is using an omnidirectional lamp then the luminaire, through the reflector and lens, is controlling the distribution and the center beam brightness. Therefore, we go to the luminaire's cut sheet and look at the candelas table or the ***candlepower distribution curve*** (Figure 13.5).

Watts	Bulb	Base	Product Number	Symbols, Footnotes	Ordering Code	Volts	Pkg. Qty.‡	Description	Class Filament	MOL (In.)	Rated Avg. Life (Hrs.)(93)	Approx. MBCP*	Lumens	Life Years (446)	Energy Cost (445)	Color Temp. (K)
Energy Advantage IR Plus (IRC+) Halogen PAR38																
39	PAR38	Med.Skt.	23844-4	$	39PAR38/IRC+/SP10	120	12	Spot 10°	C, CC-8	$5\frac{5}{16}$	4400	11,000	680	4.0	$4.70	2800
			23845-1	$	39PAR38/IRC+/FL25	120	12	Flood 25°	C, CC-8	$5\frac{5}{16}$	4400	2500	680	4.0	$4.70	2800
50	PAR38	Med.Skt.	14505-2	$ Ⓔ (104)	50PAR38/IRC+/SP10	120	12	Spot 10°	C, CC-8	$5\frac{5}{16}$	4400	15,500	950	4.0	$6.02	2760
	Dioptic Reflector		14506-0	$ Ⓔ (104)	50PAR38/IRC+/FL25	120	12	Flood 25°	C, CC-8	$5\frac{5}{16}$	4400	4000	950	4.0	$6.02	2760
55	PAR38	Med.Skt.	23847-7	$ Ⓔ (104)	55PAR38/IRC+/SP10	120	12	Spot 10°	C, CC-8	$5\frac{5}{16}$	4400	16,500	1100	4.0	$6.62	2700
			23865-9	$ Ⓔ (104)	55PAR38/IRC+/FL25	120	12	Flood 25°	C, CC-8	$5\frac{5}{16}$	4400	4100	1100	4.0	$6.62	2700
			23849-3	$ Ⓔ (104)	55PAR38/IRC+/WFL40	120	12	Wide Flood 40°	C, CC-8	$5\frac{5}{16}$	4400	1800	1100	4.0	$6.62	2700
70	PAR38	Med.Skt.	13861-0	$ Ⓔ (104)	70PAR38/IRC+/SP10	120	12	Spot 10°	C, CC-8	$5\frac{5}{16}$	4400	17,800	1500	4.0	$8.43	2860
			13862-8	$ Ⓔ (104)	70PAR38/IRC+/FL25	120	12	Flood 25°	C, CC-8	$5\frac{5}{16}$	4400	6170	1500	4.0	$8.43	2860
			13863-6	$ Ⓔ (104)	70PAR38/IRC+/WFL40	120	12	Wide Flood 40°	C, CC-8	$5\frac{5}{16}$	4400	2320	1500	4.0	$8.43	2860
83	PAR38	Med.Skt.	23850-1	$ Ⓔ (104)	83PAR38/IRC+/SP10	120	12	Spot 10°	C, CC-8	$5\frac{5}{16}$	4400	25,000	1750	4.0	$10.00	2730
	Dioptic		23851-9	$ Ⓔ (104)	83PAR38/IRC+FL25	120	12	Flood 25°	C, CC-8	$5\frac{5}{16}$	4400	7000	1750	4.0	$10.00	2730
	Reflector		23852-7	$ Ⓔ (104)	83PAR38/IRC+/WFL40	120	12	Wide Flood 40°	C, CC-8	$5\frac{5}{16}$	4400	3000	1750	4.0	$10.00	2730
100	PAR38	Med.Skt.	13876-8	$ Ⓔ (104)	100PAR38/IRC+/SP10	120	12	Spot 10°	C, CC-8	$5\frac{5}{16}$	4400	26,400	2150	4.0	$12.05	2830
	Dioptic		13877-6	$ Ⓔ (104)	100PAR38/IRC+/FL25	120	12	Flood 25°	C, CC-8	$5\frac{5}{16}$	4400	8500	2150	4.0	$12.05	2830
	Reflector		13878-4	$ Ⓔ (104)	100PAR38/IRC+/WFL40	120	12	Wide Flood 40°	C, CC-8	$5\frac{5}{16}$	4400	3500	2150	4.0	$12.05	2830

Figure 13.4 Typical Catalog Page for a PAR Lamp.
Courtesy of Philips Lighting Company.

Candelas

Vertical Angle	Candelas
0	780
5	805
10	785
15	710
20	648
25	567
30	479
35	408
40	295
45	84
50	15
55	4
60	0
65	0
70	0
75	0
80	0
85	0
90	0

Candlepower Distribution

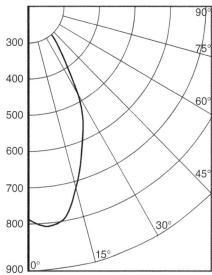

Figure 13.5 Typical Candelas Table (Left) and Candlepower Distribution Curve (Right).
Courtesy of Edison Price Lighting, Inc.

The first variation on the point method is when the illuminated surface is not horizontal and therefore the angle of incidence is not perpendicular to the surface. Remember that part of the definition of a foot-candle is that the light is evenly distributed. When light strikes a surface at any angle other than perpendicular, this it is no longer the case. There is a correction factor we must apply to get an accurate result. To calculate the correction factor we need to know the angle of incidence measured from normal (Figure 13.6).

The correction factor used to account for the asymmetrical distribution of light is the cosine of the angle of incidence measured from surface normal. The new formula looks like this:

$$E = \frac{I \cos X}{D^2}$$

E = Illuminance in fc or lx

I = Intensity in cd or cp

D = Distance in ft or m

X = Angle (between incident light and surface normal)

There is one other scenario we may encounter with the point method: The light isn't striking the target at a perpendicular angle *and* the ray of light in question isn't at the center of the beam (Figure 13.7).

How do we read the candelas table and the candlepower distribution curve? The candelas table is the easiest. If the luminaire is directly over the target then *I* is the candelas output at the vertical angle of 0° (straight down). If the target is at an angle other than 0°, simply read down the vertical angle column to the correct angle and read across to find the candela output at that angle.

Figure 13.A Section of a Luminaire with a Polar Graph.

The candlepower distribution curve is a bit more complicated, but not by much. The curve shown in Figure 13.5 is one quarter of a polar graph, and is read like this: Imagine that you are looking at a section through a luminaire that is centered on the graph, as in Figure 13.A. The lines radiating from center mark the angles at which light is emitted. The concentric circles represent candlepower, with larger numbers at the outer circles and smaller numbers at the inner circles.

Figure 13.B Figure 13.A with Candelas Table Information Plotted on the Graph.

Figure 13.B shows the information from the candelas table from Figure 13.5 plotted onto the polar graph and connected by a curve. Since there is no light emitted above 90°, there's no need to show that half of the graph (although luminaires that emit light above 90° will show the upper half of the graph). Since the light is symmetrical about the centerline of the luminaire, there's no need to show both of the lower halves. In this case, what we're left with is the lower right quadrant as shown in Figure 13.5.

Some luminaires do not have symmetric distributions. In those cases, manufacturers usually use a dashed line to represent the distribution at 90° to the first plane, as shown in Figure 13.C.

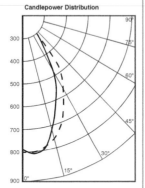

Candlepower Distribution

Figure 13.C Candlepower Distribution Curve for a Fixture with an Asymmetrical Distribution.
Adapted from Edison Price Lighting, Inc.

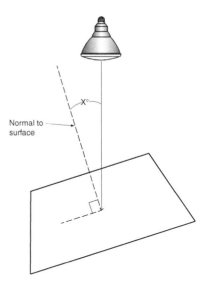

Figure 13.6 Measuring Angle of Incidence Relative to Normal.

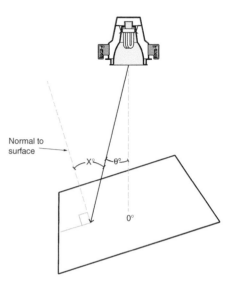

Figure 13.7 Light Exiting a Luminaire at an Angle Other than 0° and Striking a Surface at an Angle Other than 90°.

In this case we still apply the cosine of the angle of incidence (cos X), but I is no longer the center beam brightness. Instead, we have to find the intensity of the light emitted at the angle in the direction of the calculation point (I_θ), which we can do by consulting the candela table or the candlepower distribution curve.

$$E = \frac{I_\theta \cos X}{D^2}$$

E = Illuminance in fc or lx

I_θ = Intensity of luminaire (in the direction of the calculation point) in cd or cp

D = Distance in ft (fc) or m (lux)

X = Angle (between incident light ray and surface normal)

Lumen Method

When we want to calculate the average amount of light in an entire room, the point method is too cumbersome. Instead we use the lumen method. The lumen method has some advantages and some disadvantages over the point method. The advantage is that the lumen method not only calculates the average illuminance across the entire plan of the room, it also calculates the average illuminance across the life of the lighting system by including factors that affect the system at the outset and over time. This is referred to as maintained illuminance. The disadvantage is that the lumen method does not tell us the amount of light landing at any single point. Also, it can only be used to calculate the illuminance on horizontal planes such as the floor or work plane.

We begin by calculating the average amount of light generated per square foot:

$$E = \frac{L \times N}{A}$$

E = Average illumination in fc or lx

L = Lumen output of the lamp used

N = Number of lamps used

A = Area of the space in square feet for fc, square meters for lux

This gives us the lumens per square foot, but lumens aren't foot-candles. What's missing is distance since lumens measure light at the lamp. Other considerations that are missing include fixture efficiency (how much light exits the fixture), room surface reflectance and absorption, room size and shape, etc. All of these measurements are combined into a correction factor called the ***coefficient of utilization*** (CU).

■ *coefficient of utilization*
The fraction of lamp lumens that reach the work plane directly from the source and from inter-reflections.

COEFFICIENTS OF UTILIZATION – ZONAL CAVITY METHOD

Effective Floor Cavity Reflectance 20%

Ceiling Reflectance (%)	80				70				50			30			10			0
Wall Reflectance (%)	70	50	30	10	70	50	30	10	50	30	10	50	30	10	50	30	10	0
Room Cavity Ratio																		
0	77	77	77	77	76	76	76	76	72	72	72	69	69	69	66	66	66	65
1	74	72	71	70	73	71	70	68	68	67	66	66	65	64	64	63	63	61
2	71	68	66	64	70	67	65	63	65	63	62	63	61	60	61	60	59	58
3	68	64	61	59	66	63	60	58	61	59	57	60	58	56	58	57	55	54
4	65	60	57	54	63	59	56	54	58	55	53	57	55	53	56	54	52	51
5	61	56	53	50	60	56	53	50	55	52	50	54	51	49	53	50	49	48
6	59	53	49	47	58	53	49	47	52	49	46	51	48	46	50	48	46	45
7	55	50	46	43	55	49	46	43	48	45	43	48	45	43	47	45	43	42
8	53	47	43	40	52	46	43	40	46	42	40	45	42	40	44	42	40	39
9	50	44	40	37	49	43	40	37	43	39	37	42	39	37	42	39	37	36
10	47	41	37	35	46	41	37	35	40	37	35	40	37	34	39	36	34	34

Figure 13.8 Typical Coefficients of Utilization Table.
Courtesy of Edison Price Lighting, Inc.

The CU is specific to each luminaire and is found on the cut sheet. Let's take a look at a typical CU table (Figure 13.8). To determine the CU we need to know a few things about the room. As you can see, the top row asks us for the ceiling reflectance (measured as a percentage). That is, what percentage of the light that strikes the ceiling is reflected? This information can be obtained from the acoustic tile manufacturer, the paint manufacturer, or the IES *Lighting Handbook* (for wood or other materials).

The next row down asks for the wall reflectance. Wall reflectance information is supplied by the paint manufacturer or the IES *Lighting Handbook* (for wood or other materials).

The lumen method assumes that 20 percent of light passing the work plane will re-enter the upper part of the room, so we don't need to collect information about the floor reflectance.

■ *room cavity ratio*
A ratio of room dimensions used to quantify how light will interact with room surfaces.

The next piece of information we need is the *room cavity ratio* (RCR). The formula to calculate the RCR is:

$$RCR = \frac{5h(L+W)}{L \times W}$$

h = Room cavity height

L = Room length

W = Room width

Length and width are obvious, but what's the room cavity height? We can divide a room into as many as three layers. The room cavity is the space between the bottom of the lighting fixtures and the plane where the calculation is being made (Figure 13.9). In many

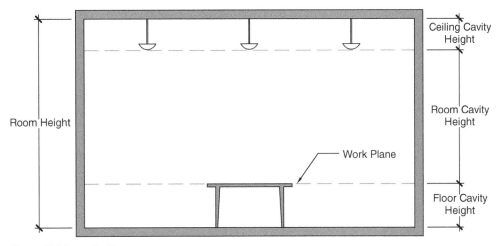

Figure 13.9 Room Cavities.

office spaces the room cavity height is as shown in Figure 13.9. If an office is illuminated with recessed luminaires, the room cavity height would be the distance between the work plane and the ceiling, and there would be no ceiling cavity. If the calculation was being made for the floor, as with an atrium, the room cavity height would extend to the floor and there would be no floor cavity.

Once we calculate the RCR, we can start at the top of the CU table and read down from ceiling reflectance to wall reflectance to RCR. It's important to remember that the CU is always a decimal value (less than 1) because not all manufacturers put a decimal in front of each CU value. There's a huge difference between a CU of 65 and a CU of .65!

Once we have the CU, we're back to this:

$$E = \frac{L \times N \times CU}{A}$$

The formula at this point assumes a perfect world. It doesn't make allowances for decreased efficiency of the lighting system over time as the luminaires and the room age. This is important because we're less concerned with the amount of light delivered on the first day than we are with the average amount of light delivered over time, which is called *maintained illuminance*. Once again, there is a correction factor that we can include in our calculation, or actually a number of *light loss factors* (LLFs) to account for this degradation.

LLFs are divided into two groups. First, there are recoverable light loss factors. These factors reduce the amount of light delivered to the work plane over time, but can be recovered through normal maintenance. The most significant recoverable light loss factors are as follows:

■ *maintained illuminance*
The calculated light levels of a space after factoring in light loss factors.

■ *light loss factors*
Factors that account for a lighting system's operation at less than initial conditions.

<u>Lamp lumen depreciation factor (LLD).</u> The lumen output of all lamps gradually decreases over the lamp's life. LLD is a percentage of the lamp's *initial lumens*. It is calculated by dividing the mean lumens by the initial lumens. This information is available from lamp manufacturers for each of their lamps. Typical values are shown in the Table 13.1.

Table 13.1 Typical Lamp Lumen Depreciation Values

Lamp Type	Typical Lamp Lumen Depreciation
Standard Incandescent	.92
Halogen	.95
T5 Linear Fluorescent	.95–.97
T8 Linear Fluorescent	.92–.95
Compact Fluorescent	.85–.90
Quartz Metal Halide	.65–.80
Ceramic Metal Halide	.80–.90

Note: The rapid advances in LED and OLED technology make it impossible to provide typical LLD values. Consult current manufacturer's Web sites for information on specific products.

<u>Luminaire dirt depreciation factor (LDD).</u> When dirt accumulates on fixture surfaces and lamps, the light output of the fixture is reduced because the dirty surfaces are less effective as reflectors or refractors. The LDD is calculated by first looking at the type of luminaire and the amount of airborne dirt in the space, as shown in Table 13.2.

Table 13.2 Combinations of CIE Classifications and Environments (except Industrial)

Environment	Luminaire Ventilation	CIE Classification				
		Direct	Semi-Direct	General Diffuse	Semi-Indirect	Indirect
Clean	Open/Unventilated	W	W	W	X	X
	All Other	W	W	W	X	X
Moderate	Open/Unventilated	XY	XY	XY	X	X
	All Other	X	X	X	Y	Y
Dirty	Open/Unventilated	Z	Z	Z	Z	Z
	All Other	Y	Y	Y	Y	Y

With permission from the *Lighting Handbook, 10th Ed.,* published by the Illuminating Engineering Society.

Open/Unventilated luminaires are those with no path for the free and steady movement of air through the luminaire.

Clean refers to retail, office, and other spaces using air filtration that is generally part of HVAC systems.

Moderate refers to spaces such as light industrial, spaces that use upon windows for ventilation, and spaces that do not have air filtration.

Dirty refers to spaces where normal activity produces a significant amount of airborne dirt.

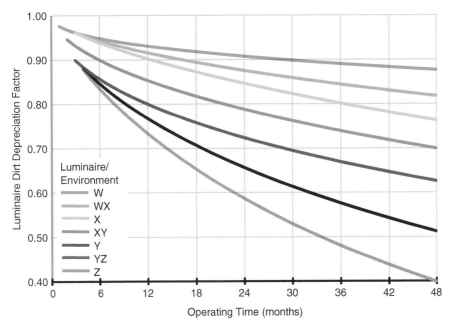

Figure 13.10 Luminaire Dirt Depreciation Factors.
With permission from the Lighting Handbook, 10th Ed., *published by the Illuminating Engineering Society.*

After determining the letter for the category of dirt depreciation, find the LLD in Figure 13.10.

Lamp burnout factor (LBO). Burned out lamps cause a loss of illumination. If lamps are not promptly replaced, the result is a persistent reduction in maintained illuminance. The lamp burnout factor is the percentage of the number of lamps remaining lighted to the total for the maximum number of burnouts permitted:

$$E = \frac{L \times N \times CU \times LLD \times LDD \times LBO}{A}$$

Next, there are nonrecoverable light loss factors. These factors reduce the amount of light delivered to the work plane and that cannot be recovered or changed, and include the following:

Voltage to luminaire factor (VF). If the voltage to the luminaire is higher or lower than the standard voltage, the light output will increase or decrease. The change is greatest for incandescent lamps, but is seen in all lamps. If there are concerns about the voltage that may be delivered to the luminaires, consult the project's electrical engineer.

Ballast factor (BF). The lumen output of a lamp is dependent on the ballast used to drive the lamp. Some ballasts overdrive or underdrive a lamp, causing the lamp output to differ from the rated output. The lamps used also affect light output. For example, the ballast factor for a standard lamp is not the same when an energy saving lamp is used. Ballast factors for every ballast are available from their manufacturers.

■ *ballast factor*
The percentage of the rated lamp lumens that will be produced by a lamp-ballast combination.

I'm going to mention one other light loss factor, and I'm going to call it the reflector factor (RF). It's usually not included in the lumen method, but at times it should be. When manufacturers are calculating the CU of a luminaire, they're using the standard clear specular reflector that they offer. Many manufacturers offer reflectors with semi-specular finishes and in colors other than clear (as discussed in Chapter 9). If we select one of these other reflectors, we must understand that it is probably not as efficient as the standard clear specular reflector, and we have to include the correction factor for that reflector (see Figure 9.22):

$$E = \frac{L \times N \times CU \times LLD \times LDD \times RSDD \times VF \times BF \times RF}{A}$$

Or, we can combine all of the light loss factors (LLF) to get:

$$E = \frac{L \times N \times CU \times LLF}{A}$$

Finally, if we know the desired light level (E) and the lamp/fixture combination we plan to use (therefore L and N), we can calculate the number of luminaires (F) required by rearranging the formula to read:

$$F = \frac{A \times E}{L \times P \times CU \times LLF}$$

P = Number of lamps per luminaire

The accompanying worksheet can be used to help calculate the average maintained illumination.

Software for Calculations

Often, we require greater detail or a wider range of information about illuminance than can be calculated with the point or lumen methods. For instance, we may want to know the illuminance levels on a vertical surface such as a whiteboard or bookcase. Or, we may want to see the brightest and dimmest values on the work plane and their locations. In cases like these we turn to specialized computer software, either as a stand-alone program or as a CAD plug-in.

There are several stand-alone programs for illuminance calculations. All of them allow us to calculate the amount of light landing on any surface or plane. The programs vary in capabilities, but the setup is similar. The first step is to create a 3-D model of the room, either by importing a 3-D CAD file, tracing an imported 2-D CAD file, or using a room builder tool to enter the size of the room. The second step is to assign reflective values and/or colors to the room surfaces, and to populate the room with furniture, plants, artwork, doors, and windows. Each of these elements can be selected from the software's built-in object library or imported as a 3-D CAD object.

Average Maintained Illumination Calculation Worksheet—Lumen Method ✳

1. Room name:_____

2. Design illuminance level:_____

3. Luminaire manufacturer & catalog number:_____

4. Lamps: type, color, lumen rating:_____

5. Lamps per luminaire:_____

6. Total lumens per luminaire:_____

7. Fill in sketch:_____

Reflectance	Room Cavity Ht.	Room Size
Ceiling _____	Ceiling _____	L _____
Wall _____	Wall _____	W _____
Floor _____	Floor _____	Area _____

8. Determine Room Cavity Ratio:

$$RCR = \frac{5 \times \text{Room Cavity Height} \times (L + W)}{L \times W} =$$

9. CU from luminaire cut sheet: _____

10. Determine light loss factors:

Nonrecoverable	Recoverable
Voltage Factor _____	LDD _____
Ballast Factor _____	LLD _____
Thermal Factor _____	RSDD _____
Reflector Factor _____	

Product of All Light Loss Factors _____

11. Calculate maintained illuminance level achieved:

$$\frac{\text{Lamp Lumens} \times \text{Lamps} \times \text{Lumiaires} \times CU \times LLF}{\text{Area}} =$$

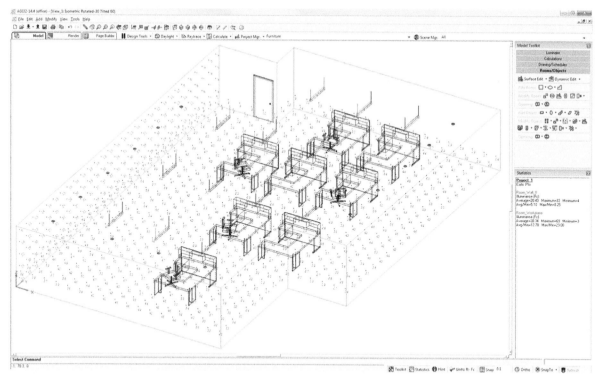

Figure 13.11 Wireframe View with Calculation Overlay.
Courtesy of Lighting Analysts.

The next step is to add the luminaires. You may have noticed a link to .IES files or photometric files on manufacturers Web sites. The .IES file is a data file containing information on the optical performance of a lamp or luminaire that is used for these calculations (see sidebar for more information). To add a luminaire we download the appropriate .IES file, import it into the calculation software, and place instances of the luminaire in the 3-D room. Some software packages allow for plug-ins that make the entire product line of a manufacturer available from within the software rather than downloading individual .IES files.

The final step before running the calculation software is to select one or more planes or objects and attach a calculation grid. Grids can generally be attached to any surface or set at any elevation, such as the work plane. Once the calculation is complete, we can view the room in a number of ways. Figure 13.11 shows a wireframe view with calculation results. Figure 13.12 shows the room with solids and colors, with the calculation results overlaid on the room.

Some software packages can also make calculations for daylight through windows and skylights. These require the additional information of the building's latitude and longitude, its orientation relative to north/south, and accurate placement of the windows and skylights within the model.

Well-made building information modeling (BIM) models already contain information about the room and object geometry, colors, reflectances, etc. The only information

Figure 13.12 Solid View with Calculation Overlay.
Courtesy of Lighting Analysts.

missing is the .IES file for the luminaires and the calculation resources. Many BIM software packages include a global lighting tool, but that is of little use to lighting designers. At least one plug-in is on the market (for Autodesk's Revit), and we should expect to see more become available as the design industry moves from 2-D drawings toward 3-D models.

Online Resources

Illuminance Calculation Software

AGI32 (Windows), www.agi32.com

DiaLUX (English) (Windows), www.dial.de/DIAL/en/home.html

Let There Be Light (Mac), www.ltblight.com

Radiance (Unix), www.radsite.lbl.gov

Relux (Windows), www.relux.biz

Visual (Windows), www.visual-3d.com

Understanding Photometric Files

Before software can perform a calculation, it needs the appropriate data. Data for the performance of a lamp or luminaire is compiled in a file with either an .ies file extension (used in North America and available in Europe), or .ldt (also known as Eulumdat), which is the standard in Europe. They're quite similar, so most of what we're about to see regarding .IES files applies to .ldt files.

Once you've downloaded an .IES file, there's no reason to look at it or attempt to modify it. If the file is properly formatted, the calculation software will import the data without any problems. However, if you're curious, you can open the file with a simple text reader such as WordPad in Windows or TextEdit in OSX. If you do, here's a sample of what you'll see:

IESNA91

[DATE] 07/20/95

[TEST] ITL43983

[MANUFAC] EDISON PRICE LIGHTING

[LUMCAT] DUPLUX/6

[LUMINAIRE] FABRICATED METAL FRAMEWORK, SPUN SPECULAR ALUMINUM REFLECTOR,

[MORE] OPEN BOTTOM.

[LAMP] ONE 18-WATT DOUBLE TWIN TUBE COMPACT FLUORESCENT, OSRAM DULUX/D

[MORE] 18W/27K, HORIZONTAL POSITION.

[BALLAST] KEYSTONE M18QPFP

[MOUNTING] RECESSED

[OTHER] THE 0 DEGREE PLANE IS OPPOSITE THE SOCKET.

[OTHER] TOTAL INPUT WATTS= 27.1 AT 120.0 VOLTS

TILT=NONE

1 1250 1 19 5 1 1 -0.5104 0 0

1 1 27.1

0 5 10 15 20 25 30 35 40 45 50 55 60 65 70 75 80 85 90

0 45 90 135 180

271 273 279 291 319 350 326 249 183 128 84 72 0 0 0 0 0 0 0

271 281 284 290 296 327 311 290 250 162 109 64 0 0 0 0 0 0 0

271 283 285 301 273 303 322 307 275 187 135 38 0 0 0 0 0 0 0

271 283 285 292 306 335 318 291 259 175 126 37 0 0 0 0 0 0 0

271 281 291 298 316 342 326 258 203 140 117 37 0 0 0 0 0 0 0

(Adapted from Edison Price Lighting, Inc.)

What does all of this information mean? The first line identifies the test method (the original test method was developed in 1986, and there have been revisions in 1991 and 1995).

The next group of lines is self-explanatory. They contain information about the luminaire manufacturer, the lamp used, etc.

The first row of numbers is information about the lamp to luminaire geometry.

The next two rows of numbers contain information about the number of angles and multiplying factors.

The third row of numbers lists the vertical angles that were measured.

The fourth row of numbers lists the horizontal angles that were measured.

The next row (beginning with 271 273) lists the candela values for all vertical angles at first horizontal angle (0°). The next row of numbers lists the candela values for all vertical angles at second horizontal angle (45°), etc.

BIM Calculation Plug-In

ElumTools (Autodesk Revit), www.ElumTools.com

Daylight Simulation Software

Daysim Daylight simulation plug-in for Ecotect, Rhonoceros and SketchUp (Windows), www.daysim.ning.com

.IES Files of Bare Lamps

.IES files of GE lamps are available at, www.gelighting.com/LightingWeb/na/resources/tools/lamp-and-ballast/

.IES files of Philips lamps are available at, www.usa.lighting.philips.com/connect/tools_literature/more_literature.wpd

.IES files of Sylvania lamps are available at, www.sylvania.com/en-us/tools-and-resources/Pages/product-literature.aspx

IES File Viewer

IESviewer (Windows), www.photometricviewer.com

Designing with Light Resources

Wiley's companion site to *Designing with Light*, www.wiley.com/go/designingwithlight

Author's companion site to *Designing with Light,* www.designinglight.com

References

DiLaura, David, et al., *The Lighting Handbook, Tenth Edition,* New York: Illuminating Engineering Society, 2011.

Egan, M. David, *Concepts in Architectural Lighting*, New York: McGraw-Hill, 1983.

IES Computer Committee Subcommittee on Photometry, *LM-63-02 IESNA Standard File Format for the Electronic Transfer of Photometric Data and Related Information.* New York: Illuminating Engineering Society, 2002.

IES Nomenclature Committee, *RP-16-05 Nomenclature and Definitions for Illuminating Engineering*, New York: Illuminating Engineering Society, 2005.

Steffy, Gary, *Architectural Lighting Design, Third Edition,* Hoboken, NJ: John Wiley & Sons, 2008.

CHAPTER 14

Building and Energy Codes

"If a builder build a house for some one, and does not construct it properly, and the house which he built fall in and kill its owner, then that builder shall be put to death."

Code of Hammurabi, circa 1772 B.C.

A lighting design is deeply rooted in the needs of the users, and it supports and enhances the architecture and interior design. That, however, is only part of the designer's efforts. We also have the responsibility to ensure that our designs comply with laws (also called codes) that set requirements for what the design can or can't and must or mustn't do. These codes make sure that the electrical system is safe, that the electrical system doesn't use power indiscriminately, and that able-bodied and disabled people can use the building with equal ease.

Model Codes

Most codes are not invented whole by the state or city that adopts them. There are several organizations that create and maintain model codes. These model codes typically form the basis of any municipality, city, or state code. Each locality adopts a code that best meets their needs, and makes additions, deletions, and/or alterations, as they deem appropriate. The result can be confusing to the uninitiated. For example, the National Electric Code (NEC) isn't actually the electric code for the nation. It is a model code created by the National Fire Protection Association (NFPA) that localities nationwide can choose to adopt, in whole or in part, as their own electrical code.

The advantage of model codes is that a group of experts who may be spread across the country or the world can create detailed codes that are beyond the expertise of most city and state employees and inspectors. Model codes are updated on a regular cycle, typically every three years. After an updated model is issued, it may or may not be immediately adopted by any given locality. Many states are two or three years "behind" the code revision process because it takes them that long to review the new version, consider making changes, and then wait for it to be adopted by the legislature.

Once adopted, a model code has the force of law, making compliance mandatory. Lighting design is not a licensed profession, so we don't certify (also called stamp, or sign and seal) that our work complies with the applicable codes. That responsibility falls to the licensed professionals—in our case, to the architect and/or electrical engineer. However, it would be unprofessional of us to ignore code requirements just because we don't stamp the drawings. At a minimum, we have to understand those codes that apply to lighting equipment and dimming systems and work within their limitations and requirements.

The code that applies to a project is usually the one that is in effect when construction documents are first filed with the city, county, or state. Confusion can arise if the designers assume that building codes based on the same model are, in fact, the same. Since model codes can be adopted with any number of changes, it's important that designers always check for changes to the model code in each locality for each project.

Programs differ from codes in that they are voluntary. Many utility companies have rebate programs for building owners, designers, and/or contractors that offer refunds or payment when construction or renovations meet certain energy efficiency requirements. Other organizations, such as United States Green Building Council (USGBC), have established voluntary programs that address other aspects of buildings, such as construction and maintenance. Voluntary green building programs are often seen as sustainability issues, and are covered in more detail in Chapter 15.

Model Building Codes

Building codes set the minimum requirements for designing and constructing safe, efficient buildings. They are comprehensive in addressing types of occupancy, types of construction, fire resistance and protection, all building systems (structure, plumbing, mechanical, electrical etc.), and safeguards during construction.

International Building Code

The International Building Code (IBC) was developed, and is maintained, by the International Code Council (ICC). The International Code Council develops model codes and standards used in the design and construction process to construct safe and resilient structures.

The IBC is the model code adopted by most state and local governments in the U.S., and is also used abroad. The code covers use and occupancy of buildings, special requirements, height and area limitations, fire resistance and protection, evacuation, access for persons with disabilities, building systems, structural components, and other aspects of building design.

The sections related to lighting set requirements for daylight via windows, and minimum illuminance levels in rooms, stairways, and egress paths.

International Green Construction Code

The International Green Construction Code (IgCC) was developed by the American Institute of Architects (AIA), ASHRAE (American Society of Heating, Refrigerating and

Air-Conditioning Engineers), USGBC, and IES, and is maintained by the ICC. It is the first model code (as opposed to a voluntary program) that addresses sustainability from design and construction through occupancy. As such, it is similar to the older and more familiar LEED program, but is written as a model code, not a voluntary program.

National Electric Code

The National Electric Code, also referred to as the NEC or NFPA 70, was developed and is maintained by the National Fire Prevention Association (NFPA). The mission of the NFPA is to reduce the worldwide risk of fire and other hazards by developing codes and standards, research, training, and education.

The NEC covers the requirements for safe electrical installation of wiring and equipment. It covers conductors of electricity, signaling and communication conductors, optical fibers, equipment, and raceways.

Model Lighting Ordinance

Developed by the International Dark-Sky Association and the IES, the Model Lighting Ordinance (MLO) is intended to help municipalities develop outdoor lighting standards that address light pollution by reducing glare, *light trespass*, and *skyglow*. The MLO includes use and occupancy criteria for five lighting zones, and identifies appropriate lighting levels for each zone.

Standards for Accessible Design

The Americans with Disabilities Act (ADA) includes requirements that newly designed and constructed, or altered, state and local government facilities, public accommodations, and commercial facilities be readily accessible to, and usable by, individuals with disabilities. These requirements are contained in the *Standards for Accessible Design*, which is available online or can be downloaded as a PDF. Some of the standards relate to lighting design. For example, the mounting height of wall sconces and the distance they project from the face of the wall are addressed.

Model Energy Codes

Building energy codes and standards set requirements for the energy efficient design for new construction and renovations of existing buildings. For lighting designers, energy conservation codes set the maximum allowable electrical load for the lighting as determined by building or space type. They also set requirements for energy conserving devices, such as occupancy sensors and timers, to further reduce energy consumption by the lighting system. For more information on the development of energy codes, visit www.EnergyCodes.gov

ANSI/ASHRAE/IESNA Standard 90.1 Energy Standard for Buildings Except Low-Rise Residential Buildings

ASHRAE and the IES jointly created and maintain Standard 90.1 under an American National Standards Institute (ANSI) approved process. This model code is commonly

■ light trespass
Light from one property falling onto an adjacent property.

■ skyglow
Light that is emitted upward by luminaires and scattered in the atmosphere, producing a luminous background in the sky which reduces one's ability to view the stars.

referred to as ASHRAE/IESNA 90.1 or ASHRAE 90.1. The standard sets minimum energy efficiency requirements for building envelopes, and for equipment used for heating, ventilation, cooling, heating water, electric motors, and lighting. The section on lighting contains lighting power allowances by building type and by space type. Since the NEC addresses safe installation and ASHRAE 90.1 addresses energy efficiency, they can be adopted to complement each other.

The U.S. Department of Energy evaluates each new edition of ASHRAE 90.1 to determine if it will improve the efficiency of commercial buildings. If so, states are required by the Energy Policy Act of 1992 (EPAct 1992) to certify that their building energy codes or standards meet or exceed the requirements of the new version within two years. As of this writing each state's energy code for commercial buildings must meet or exceed ASHRAE 90.1-2010.

■ *lighting power density*
A calculation of the watts per square foot of power used by, or allocated to, lighting.

For lighting designers, energy conservation codes work by limiting the amount of power that can be consumed by the lighting system based on the activities occurring in the building. This *lighting power density* (LPD) is used to calculate a power allowance, measured in watts, for the floor area of the building or room type. It is below 1W per square foot for most buildings. There are two methods that can be applied: the building area method or the space-by-space method.

The building area method calculates the lighting power allowance by assigning a maximum number of watts per square foot to the building area based on the building type, and multiplying the LPD by the building's total area. The lighting designer is free to use any lamp technology, any number of fixtures, and any lighting methods or techniques as long as the total wattage does not exceed the building's total calculated lighting power allowance.

The space-by-space method calculates the lighting power allowance by assigning a maximum number of watts per room area based on the room type, and multiplying the LPD by the room's area. The power allowance for every room is added together to determine the total lighting power allowance for the building. This method takes longer to calculate, but may result in a higher overall power allowance. The lighting designer is free to use any lamp technology, any number of fixtures, and any lighting methods or techniques as long as the total wattage does not exceed the total lighting power allowance.

Standard 90.1 also sets LPDs for exterior lighting based on the building type and the location (rural vs. urban), and requirements for lighting controls including automatic shut-off, occupancy sensors, and automatic controls for spaces with significant daylight.

ASHRAE/USGBC/IES Standard 189.1 Standard for the Design of High-Performance Green Buildings Except Low-Rise Residential Buildings

Developed and maintained jointly by ASHRAE, IES, and the USGBC, Standard 189.1 covers all aspects of green design and construction, from energy use to recycling. The standard addresses site sustainability, water use efficiency, energy efficiency, indoor environmental quality, and the building's impact on the atmosphere, materials, and resources. Like the IgCC, it is written as a model code, not a voluntary program.

International Energy Conservation Code

The International Energy Conservation Code (IECC) is an alternative to ASHRAE 90.1 that was developed and is maintained by the International Code Council. The IECC covers both residential and commercial construction, and sets minimum energy efficiency requirements for building envelopes, and for equipment used for heating, ventilation, cooling, heating water, and lighting. The section on lighting contains lighting power allowances by space type and control requirements that are similar to Standard 90.1.

The same laws that require the U.S. Department of Energy to use ASHRAE 90.1 as a baseline energy efficiency code for commercial buildings require the use of the IECC as the baseline energy efficiency code for residential buildings. As of this writing each state's energy code for residential buildings must meet or exceed IECC-2012.

California Title 24

The state of California has led the way in developing energy efficiency codes. California's Title 24 (which refers to the section of the California Code of Regulations) Energy Efficiency Standards for Residential and Nonresidential Buildings was first established in 1978. Obviously, Title 24 only applies to projects in California. Knowledge of Title 24 and its ongoing development is useful, however, because many of its provisions are later adopted by other states and by model codes.

Verifying Energy Code Compliance

As we've discussed, energy conservation codes set limits for maximum energy usage for electrical devices. For lighting, this typically appears as a maximum number of watts per square foot (W/ft^2) or watts per square meter (W/m^2) based on the building or space's usage type. Since the law requires compliance with these codes, a licensed professional must certify that the project is within the limits of the code. In the case of lighting design, the certified professional is usually the electrical engineer, who expects the lighting designer to create a code compliant design. A state or building official is usually the person responsible for verifying code compliance. Verification may include one or more of the following:

- Review of building plans
- Review of equipment cut sheets and specifications
- Review of calculations related to code compliance
- Inspection of the building during construction
- Inspection of the installed systems and testing of system functionality

Helpful Software

Compliance with energy codes is not enough. Building code officials want to see documentation and calculations proving compliance. The U.S. Department of Energy has developed two free software packages for this purpose. Both are available for PC and Apple computers. Both are also available as Web-based tools.

COMcheck is used for commercial and high-rise residential energy code compliance. It incorporates the requirements for most energy codes. At the beginning of a project the user selects the appropriate code and inputs the relevant information. COMcheck then creates the appropriate forms and checklists, and reports whether the project has passed or not. REScheck is similar to COMcheck, but is for residential construction.

Online Resources

Advanced Energy Design Guides Free Downloads, www.ashrae.org

Americans with Disabilities Act, www.ada.gov

ASHRAE, www.ashrae.org

California Title 24, www.energy.ca.gov/title24/

Canadian Green Building Council (CaGBC), www.cagbc.org

COMcheck, www.energycodes.gov/comcheck/

International Code Council, www.iccsafe.org

International Dark Sky Association, www.darksky.org

National Fire Prevention Association, www.nfpa.org

Online Code Environment & Advocacy Network, www.energycodesocean.org

REScheck, www.energycodes.gov/rescheck/

U.S. Department of Energy's Building Energy Codes Program, www.energycodes.gov

Online seminars, and product and legislative updates:

GELighting, www.gelighting.com/LightingWeb/na/resources/legislation/overview/index.jsp

Osram Sylvania, www.sylvania.com/en-us/sustainability/regulations-legislation/Pages/default.aspx

Philips Lighting, www.usa.lighting.philips.com/lightcommunity/trends/legislation/

Designing with Light Resources

Wiley's companion site to *Designing with Light*, www.wiley.com/go/designingwithlight

Author's companion site to *Designing with Light,* www.designinglight.com

References

2009 International Building Code, Washington, DC: International Code Council, Inc., 2009.

2009 International Energy Conservation Code, Washington, DC: International Code Council, Inc., 2009.

ASHRAE Standing Standard Project Committee 90.1, *ANSI/ASHRAE/IESNA Standard 90.1-2010 Energy Standard for Buildings Except Low-Rise Residential Buildings*, Atlanta: American Society of Heating, Refrigeration and Air-Conditioning Engineers, Inc., 2004.

ASHRAE Journal's Guide to Standard 189.1, Atlanta: American Society of Heating, Refrigeration and Air-Conditioning Engineers, Inc., June 2010.

"Building Energy Codes Program Compliance," U.S. Department of Energy, accessed August 15, 2012, www.energycodes.gov/compliance.

California Energy Commission, *2008 Building Energy Efficiency Standards*, California Energy Commission, 2008.

Department of Justice, *2010 ADA Standards for Accessible Design*, Washington, DC: Department of Justice, 2010.

DiLaura, David, et al., *The Lighting Handbook*, *Tenth Edition*, New York: Illuminating Engineering Society, 2011.

International Dark Sky and Illuminating Engineering Society MLO Task Force, *Model Lighting Ordinance*, Tuscon, AZ: International Dark Sky Association, 2011.

"International Green Construction Code," International Code Council, Inc., accessed August 15, 2012, www.iccsafe.org/cs/IGCC/Pages/default.aspx.

"Lighting Development, Adoption and Compliance Guide," U.S. Department of Energy Building Technologies Program, 2012.

National Electric Code Committee, *NFPA70 National Electric Code, 2008 Edition*, Quincy, MA: National Fire Prevention Association, 2007.

CHAPTER 15

Sustainability

"We do not inherit the earth from our ancestors, we borrow it from our children."

Native American Proverb

Lighting accounts for over 10 percent of all residential electricity consumption and nearly 20 percent of all commercial electricity consumption. Electric lighting consumes twice as much power than any other single use. Clearly lighting is a prime candidate to help reduce consumption, and the resulting environmental impact, through energy efficiency. Lighting in offices uses more than twice as much electricity as lighting in any other type of building, making offices an especially attractive target for lighting energy use reduction.

With the impact of climate change on society and ecosystems, responsible lighting design includes conserving resources, both the planet's and the client's. A lighting designer conserves a client's resources in several ways: first, by selecting fixtures whose price is in line with their performance and life expectancy; second, by selecting fixtures with higher efficiencies rather than similar, less efficient fixtures; and third, by analyzing the costs for the several lamp/fixture combinations under consideration. In some cases, the increased cost of a longer life lamp is offset by reduced labor to replace the lamp. In other cases, the increased cost of a more efficient lamp is offset by reduced electricity consumption.

Voluntary Energy Programs

Codes, once adopted, are legal requirements. There are also a variety of voluntary programs related to green construction and energy conservation that owners may ask the design and construction team to integrate into the project's goals.

Leadership in Energy and Environmental Design

Leadership in Energy and Environmental Design (LEED) is a voluntary program established by the U.S. Green Building Council (USGBC), a not-for-profit organization committed to sustainability in the built environment. LEED is a suite of rating systems covering a range of building types, existing building operations and maintenance, and neighborhood development. Each rating system has a set of prerequisites and awards points in several categories. Buildings that meet requirements are allotted points which, depending on the score, certify buildings as Certified, Certified Silver, Certified Gold, or Certified Platinum. Once certified, owners and operators must monitor and record the building's performance, and submit the data for periodic recertification. In Canada LEED is administered by the Canadian Green Building Council (CaGBC).

There are seven "impact categories" that make up the main framework of the current version, LEED v4.

- Reverse contribution to global climate change
- Enhance individual human health and well-being
- Protect and restore water resources
- Protect, enhance, and restore biodiversity and ecosystem services
- Promote sustainable and regenerative material resources cycles
- Build a greener economy
- Enhance social equity, environmental justice, and community quality of life

Lighting design can contribute to earning points in several categories. For example, points can be earned by designing a lighting system that uses less power than the baseline building, by specifying luminaires that have at least 10 percent recycled content, by specifying luminaires that are manufactured within the region of the building (generally 500 miles [800 kilometers] or less), by providing a high level of lighting system control, and by providing adequate daylight in regularly occupied spaces.

Green Globes

An alternative to LEED, Green Globes was developed and is administered in Canada by the Canadian Standards Association, and is administered in the U.S. by the Green Building Initiative (GBI). Green Globes uses an online assessment and rating tool to assess a project, and assigns points based on seven criteria:

- Energy
- Water
- Resources
- Emissions
- Indoor environment
- Project management
- Site

Once the online questionnaire has been completed, a report is automatically generated which provides ratings, a list of achievements, and recommendations to improve the green rating of building. Green Globes projects must earn 35 percent or more of the

1,000 points possible. Depending on the number of points earned, projects are certified for one, two, three, or four Green Globes. The certification process uses third-party evaluators to review design documentation and conduct on-site audits.

Like LEED, points are earned for the use of energy efficient luminaires, lamps, and ballasts; the inclusion of lighting controls; and the provision of daylight and views. Like LEED, building owners and operators also use Green Globes on an ongoing basis to assess performance.

Energy Star

Energy Star is a program of the U.S. Environmental Protection Agency. Energy Star programs cover products, homes, and commercial buildings. Lamps and light fixtures can earn Energy Star labels by complying with their respective program requirements. Energy Star programs exist for both LED and CFL lamps.

Energy Star LED lamps must meet criteria including:

- Correlated color temperature of 2,700K, 3,000K, 3,500K, or 4,000K
- CRI ≥ 80
- Packaging mention if dimmable
- Minimum three-year warranty

Energy Star CFL lamps must meet criteria including:

- Production of 80 percent of initial lumens at 40 percent of rated life
- A minimum rated life of 6,000 hours
- CRI ≥ 80
- Ability to start in less than one second, and reach full output in less than three minutes

New homes can earn an Energy Star label by complying with one of two paths. The first is the National Performance Path, which uses a free, online calculator to model the home's energy use to confirm that it meets a target score. The second is the National Prescriptive Path, which has builders use a set of construction specifications that meet the program's requirements.

Commercial buildings can earn an Energy Star labels by setting an energy target for the building using a free, online calculator; determining that the designed building meets or exceeds the energy target and, finally, verifying the building's actual energy performance through a third party audit of the completed building.

ICC 700 National Green Building Standard

The National Green Building Standard (NGBS) was developed by the National Association of Home Builders (NAHB) and the International Codes Council (ICC), and is for home construction, remodeling and additions (including multifamily buildings), hotels and dormitories, and residential land developments. To comply with the NGBS, a builder must incorporate a minimum number of features in the following areas:

- Lot design, preparation, and development
- Resource efficiency
- Energy efficiency
- Water efficiency
- Indoor environmental quality
- Operation, maintenance, and building owner education

The certification process uses third-party assessors, who are trained and approved by the NAHB Research Center, to review design documentation and conduct on-site evaluations.

Life-Cycle Cost Analysis

When we are evaluating two or more comparable lighting systems, there are many factors to consider. Lighting quality is the most obvious factor, but others include benefit relative to cost, maintenance requirements, energy consumption, and the project's budget. We can evaluate the financial implications of the systems by performing a *life-cycle cost analysis* to determine the total cost of ownership for the client.

life-cycle cost analysis
The total costs associated with purchasing, operating, and maintaining a system over the life of that system.

There are two categories of costs to consider, along with possible offsets. The first category is initial cost. The initial cost of a lighting system includes the purchase price of the fixtures, lamps and controls, along with the labor and materials required to install the system. The second category is the annual costs, which include energy charges, maintenance (including lamps, ballasts, transformers, and labor), cleaning costs and lamp disposal costs (for fluorescent and HID lamps, if applicable). Annual costs may also include the air-conditioning costs associated with the heat generated by the lighting system. The possible offsets to those expenses are utility rebates and tax credits.

There are two methods of calculating life-cycle costs. The simple method ignores inflation and therefore treats all dollars the same. The complex method includes the affect inflation has on costs and translates that into the value of today's dollars (called present value). This chapter includes a Simple Life-Cycle Cost Analysis Worksheet on the next page as well as a spreadsheet on Wiley's web site.

Keep in mind that any financial calculation of this kind assumes that the two systems provide the same quality of light. Lighting systems that do not are not as easy to compare financially, because the analysis will not include the real, but less easily measured, effects of lighting such as employee efficiency, employee retention, increased sales, guest satisfaction, student performance, etc.

Simple Life Cycle Cost Analysis Worksheet		
Project Name: _____		
System 1: _____		
System 2: _____		

System Information		System 1	System 2
1	Lighting System Life (in years)		
2	Annual Operation (in hours) [1]		Same as System 1
3	Electricity Cost (per kilowatt hour) [2]	$	Same as System 1
4	System Wattage (in kilowatts)		

Initial Costs		System 1	System 2
5	Lighting System Equipment [3]	$	$
6	Lighting System Installation (labor and materials) [4]	$	$
7	HVAC System [5]	$	$
8	**Subtotal**		
9	Subtract utility rebates and/or tax credits	$	$
10	**Total Initial Cost**	$	$

Annual Costs		System 1	System 2
11	Electricity (lines 2 × 3 × 4)	$	$
12	Lamp Replacement	$	$
13	Ballast Replacement	$	$
14	Luminaire Cleaning	$	$
15	HVAC Cooling [6]	$	$
16	**Total Annual Cost**	$	$

		System 1	System 2
17	**Total Cost of Ownership** lines 9 + (1 × 15)	$	$

Notes:

1. Provided by project owner.

2. Provided by utility company or found on recent utility bill.

3. Budget pricing can be obtained from sales representatives.

4. Consult contractor or cost estimator.

5. One ton of cooling is required for every 3.5 kW of lighting. Calculate number of tons required and consult the project's mechanical engineer for costs.

6. Calculated by the mechanical engineer based on system wattage (line 4).

Payback, or Return on Investment

■ *return on investment*
The benefit resulting from
the investment of a resource.

When renovating or replacing the lighting in an existing space, the owner is likely to be concerned with two values: the cost of the renovation/replacement and the *return on investment* (ROI), which is the number of years that will pass before the savings pay for the new installation. As with life-cycle cost analysis, the ROI can be calculated with or without a consideration of inflation. See the Simple Return on Investment Worksheet.

Simple Return on Investment Worksheet		
Project Name: _____		
1	New Lighting System Equipment Cost [1,2]	$
2	Lighting System Installation (labor and materials) [2]	$
3	Utility Rebates and/or Tax Credits	$
4	Total Cost of New Lighting System (Line 1 + 2–3)	$
5	Existing Lighting System Wattage (in kilowatts)	
6	New Lighting System Wattage (in kilowatts)	
7	Kilowatts Saved (Line 5–6)	
8	Annual Operation (in hours) [3]	
9	Kilowatt Hours Saved (Line 7 × 8)	
10	Electricity Cost (per kilowatt hour) [4]	$
11	Annual Savings (Line 9 × 10)	$
12	Payback Period in Years (Line 4 ÷ 11)	$

Notes:

1. Budget pricing can be obtained from sales representatives.

2. Consult contractor or cost estimator.

3. Provided by project owner.

4. Provided by utility company or found on recent utility bill.

Online Resources

ASHRAE Advanced Energy Design Guides, www.ashrae.org

Canadian Green Building Council, www.cagbc.org

Cradle To Cradle Product Innovation Institute, www.c2ccertified.org

Energy Star, www.energystar.gov

Energy Star LED Lamp Criteria, www.energystar.gov/index.cfm?c=iledl.pr_key_product

Energy Star CFL Lamp Criteria, www.energystar.gov/index.cfm?c=cfls.pr_crit_cfls

Green Building Initiative (Green Globes, U.S.), www.thegbi.org

Green Globes (Canada), www.greenglobes.com

National Green Building Program, www.nahbgreen.org

U.S. Energy Information Administration FAQ web page, www.eia.gov/tools/faqs/faq.cfm?id=99&t=3

U.S. Green Building Council, www.usgbc.org

Fluorescent Lamp Recycling

Earth911.com, www.earth911.com

EPA CFL Recycling Web Page, http://epa.gov/cfl/cflrecycling.html#whererecycle

LampRecycle.org, www.lamprecycle.org

Designing with Light Resources

Wiley's companion site to *Designing with Light*, www.wiley.com/go/designingwithlight

Author's companion site to *Designing With Light*, www.designinglight.com

References

"Compact Fluorescent Light Bulbs Key Product Criteria." Energy Star, accessed May 19, 2013, www.energystar.gov/index.cfm?c=cfls.pr_crit_cfls.

DiLaura, David, et al., *The Lighting Handbook, Tenth Edition*, New York: Illuminating Engineering Society, 2011.

"Energy Star Qualified Homes, Version 3 (Rev. 06) National Program Requirements," Energy Star, U.S. Environmental Protection Agency, 2012.

"How Much Electricity Is Used for Lighting in the United States?" U.S. Energy Information Administration, accessed September 29, 2013, www.eia.gov/tools/faqs/how-much-electricity-used-lighting-united-states.

"LED Bulb Key Product Criteria." Energy Star, accessed May 19, 2013, www.energystar.gov/index.cfm?c=iledl.pr_key_product.

"LEED 2009 for New Construction and Major Renovations," Washington D.C.: U.S. Green Building Council, 2009, reaffirmed 2013.

"LEED U.S. Green Building Council," U.S. Green Building Council, accessed August 15, 2012, www.usgbc.org/leed.

CHAPTER 16

Light and Health

"It is the unqualified result of all my experience with the sick that, second only to their need of fresh air, is their need of light; that, after a close room, what hurts them most is a dark room and that it is not only light but direct sunlight they want."

Florence Nightingale, *Notes on Nursing: What It Is and What It Is Not* (1860)

For centuries people have believed that there was a connection between light (notably sunshine) and health. However, the scientific exploration of the relationship between light and health is relatively new, with the first significant research conducted in the 1970s. Some aspects of the relationship between light and health, such as the benefits of views to the outside, are already finding a place in professional design practice. Others, yet to be proven or difficult to implement, may become design considerations in the future.

Biological Rhythms

Many of our bodily functions occur in predictable cycles. For example, *circadian* rhythms, such as sleep, are cycles with a duration of one day. We have an internal clock that keeps these rhythms synchronized and thus regulates wake and sleep, heart rate, blood pressure, body temperature, and more. Our internal clock needs to be synchronized with the outside world, a process called entrainment. How does this happen?

■ *circadian*
Variations with a cycle of approximately 24 hours.

We discussed rods and cones in Chapter 4, but there is a third type of light sensitive cell in the eye called the intrinsically photosensitive retinal ganglion cell (ipRGC). These photoreceptors, which are evenly distributed across the retina, seem to be unrelated to vision. When stimulated by light, they send nonvisual information to the brain's master time clock, the suprachiasmatic nucleus (SCN), which coordinates and regulates all of the body's clocks and hormone production. The ipRGC has a peak response in the blue range between 460 and 480 nanometers (nm). Figure 16.1 shows the circadian sensitivity curve, in addition to those of photopic and scotopic vision.

Circadian rhythms, which are synchronized with day and night, are most strongly affected by information from the ipRGCs. People with inadequate exposure to daylight may lose entrainment of their body clock. There are three hormones that are especially

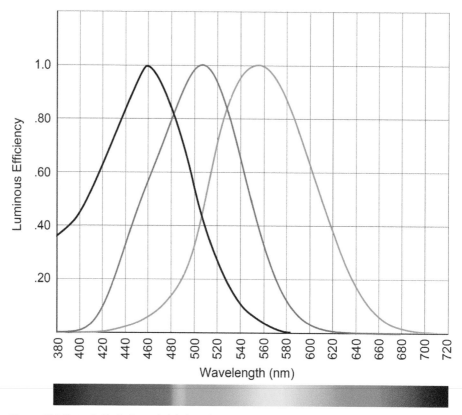

Figure 16.1 Photopic (Red), Scotopic (Blue), and Circadian (Black) Sensitivity Curves.

affected. The first is serotonin, a mood enhancer that gives us several performance peaks throughout the day. Serotonin is also important in the regulation of disorders such as depression and anxiety. The second is melatonin, which makes us feel drowsy and slows our body functions for sleep. The third is cortisol, which is involved in stress management and also in regulation of blood pressure, metabolism of sugar, and the immune system. Clearly, we want to maintain entrainment of our circadian rhythms. Light helps us to do that.

Simple exposure to light, though, is not enough. The exposure time of day, duration, and wavelengths all contribute to proper entrainment. SCN regulation seems to be maintained by high brightness, short wavelength light in the morning (i.e., morning daylight). If appropriate stimulation does not occur, the timing signals for hormone production can become desynchronized. It is known that circadian desynchronization plays a roll in insomnia, mood, depression, reaction time, creativity, and alertness. It is suspected that this desynchronization also plays a roll in cancer, diabetes, dementia, and cardiovascular disease.

Researchers around the world are exploring the use of light in healthcare facilities to support circadian rhythm entrainment to determine if it can speed recovery time. Other researchers are testing lighting systems to see if they can improve sleep in the elderly, and boost the well being of students and workers.

Light Deficiency and Light Therapy

While these issues do not fall within the responsibility of the lighting designer, they are the result of exposure to light and are mentioned here as additional examples of the way light can affect health.

Seasonal Affective Disorder

Seasonal Affective Disorder (SAD) is a kind of depression caused by inadequate or ill-timed exposure to light, especially light with a high blue content. It may also be affected by a lack of light variety that comes with the daytime changes in sunlight. Symptoms tend to build slowly during the late autumn and early winter, and are generally those associated with other forms of depression. With no treatment SAD symptoms usually get better with the lengthening of days and the arrival of spring. However, strong symptoms should be discussed with a doctor. SAD may be treated with talk therapy, antidepressants, and/or light therapy per a doctor's recommendation.

Light therapy may be effective for up to 80 percent of SAD sufferers. Light therapy involves exposure to a very bright light source (2,500 to 10,000 lx) with a high color temperature (over 5,000K) in the morning (usually between 6 and 9 a.m.). Common practice is to sit a few feet away from the light for 30 minutes to 3 hours each morning to mimic the effect of morning daylight. Results are usually seen in less than four weeks. Side effects are minor and may include eyestrain and headache.

Skin Disease

People with some chronic skin diseases, such as psoriasis and eczema, can be treated with ultraviolet B radiation from the sun or a UV-B producing lamp. Brief exposure helps some people, but excessive exposure may make symptoms worse. Patients should consult their doctor before beginning light treatments.

Vitamin D Deficiency

Our skin produces vitamin D when exposed to ultraviolet B radiation in sunlight. Today, many people spend so much time indoors, especially in the winter, that vitamin D deficiency has become common in the developed world. Vitamin D deficiency can lead to rickets (malformation of bones) and is a suspected contributor in several other diseases. The solution to Vitamin D deficiency is a daily supplement. Vitamin D is also found in fatty fish such as catfish, salmon, sardines, and tuna.

Full-Spectrum Lighting

The term full-spectrum lighting was first used in the 1960s by Dr. John Ott to describe electric light sources with visible and ultraviolet spectrum similar to that of natural light. In the years since, many lamp manufacturers have developed premium-priced products advertised as full-spectrum with a variety of claims, including better visibility, better color discrimination, reduction of eye strain, improved mood, and improved productivity.

In marketing full-spectrum sources, manufacturers claim that the source is similar to or the same as daylight. The implication, for those of us who understand the science of light, is that these sources produce a continuous spectrum without significant peaks or valleys in the SPD, that the color temperature or correlated color temperature would be above 5,000K, and that that the CRI would be close to 100. The health and visibility claims have been examined by a number of research institutions, including the National Lighting Product Information Program (NLPIP) at the Lighting Research Center at Rensselaer Polytechnic Institute and the National Research Council Canada. The results of the research indicate that full-spectrum light sources do not provide the claimed benefits.

Harmful Effects of Light

We all know that excessive exposure to sunlight, especially ultraviolet light, can cause sunburn. Some medications can increase the skin's sensitivity to light. Ultraviolet light can also contribute to premature aging of the skin and to the formation of cataracts.

Skin Cancer

Skin cancer has several causes, but we know that UV radiation is one of them. Skin cancer is the most common form of cancer in the U.S., with more then 80,000 cases diagnosed in 2012 alone. Prevention of skin cancer includes simple steps such as avoiding exposure to UV radiation and wearing a broad spectrum (UVA/UVB) sunscreen with an SPF of 15 or higher.

Light and the Aging Eye

As we age, changes occur in the eye, which require us to think differently about spaces that will be occupied by older people. The first notable change is that the older eye simply requires more light for several reasons. Pupil size reduces with age, so less light enters the eye. The second change is that the lens yellows and thickens with age (it also becomes less flexible, resulting in presbyopia or age-related farsightedness), which reduces light transmission. The result is that people in their 60s requires twice as much light as they did at 20. The first consideration in lighting for the aging eye, then, is to increase target illuminance levels by as much as doubling them. Note that this requirement is not taken into consideration in current energy conservation codes (see Chapter 14), but several groups are trying to change that.

The aging eye also has difficulty adapting to changes in brightness, so the second change in our design approach is to reduce lighting contrast from one area to another. High levels of ambient light should be favored over a low ambient light/high task light approach.

Next, as the lens yellows and even becomes cloudy, more light is scattered inside the eye, making older people more sensitive to glare. Lighting designers can help reduce glare by using indirect lighting techniques and well-shielded fixtures.

Finally, the aging eye can contribute to sleep disorders in older people by interfering with biological rhythms. This is at least in part because the yellowed lens of an older person blocks morning blue light which, as we've discussed, is essential to regulating our circadian rhythms.

Online Resources

Advanced Lighting Guide—Health & Performance (subscription required), www.algonline.org

The Light and Health Program at the Lighting Research Center, www.lrc.rpi.edu

National Institutes for Health, www.nih.gov

Designing with Light Resources

Wiley's companion site to *Designing with Light,* www.wiley.com/go/designingwithlight

Author's companion site to *Designing with Light,* www.designinglight.com

References

American Cancer Society, "Cancer Facts & Figures 2012," Atlanta: American Cancer Society, 2012.

Boubekri, Mohamad, *Daylighting, Architecture and Health*, Oxford, UK: Elsevier Ltd., 2012.

DiLaura, David, et al., *The Lighting Handbook, Tenth Edition*, New York: Illuminating Engineering Society, 2011.

Edwards, L., and P. Torcellini, *A Literature Review of the Effects of Natural Light on Building Occupants*, Golden, CO: National Renewable Energy Laboratory, 2002.

"Health Issues: What Is Full Spectrum Lighting and Are There Any Health Benefits?" Osram Sylvania, 2005.

"Impact of Light on Human Beings," Licht.wissen, Issue 19, Fördergemeinschaft Gutes Licht.

Rea, Mark, Lei Deng, and Robert Wolsey, *Lighting Answers: Full-Spectrum Light Sources*. Vol. 7, Issue 5, Rev. 1, 2005.

"Seasonal Affective Disorder," *PubMed Health*, U.S. National Library of Medicine, accessed June 8, 2012, www.ncbi.nlm.nih.gov/pubmedhealth/PMH0002499/.

Turner, P.L., M.A. Mainster, "Circadian Photoreception: Ageing And The Eye's Important Role In Systemic Health," *British Journal of Ophthalmology* 2008: 1439–1444.

APPENDIX I

Lighting Design–Related Professional Organizations

Illuminating Engineering Society (IES)

Founded in 1906, the IES is the recognized technical authority on illumination. Their primary mission is to disseminate information on lighting design to the lighting design community and others through publications, programs, and services. Membership is open to anyone involved in the lighting field: lighting designers, architects, interior designers, government and utility personnel, engineers, contractors, manufacturers, distributors, researchers, and educators.

Through technical committees the IES correlates research, investigations, and discussions to guide lighting professionals via consensus-based lighting recommendations. The results of these committees' work are published in nearly 100 varied technical publications. The IES also works cooperatively with related organizations on a variety of programs and in the production of jointly published documents and standards.

www.ies.org

International Association of Lighting Designers (IALD)

Founded in 1969, the IALD is dedicated solely to the concerns and promotion of independent professional lighting designers. The IALD works to set standards for lighting design excellence by promoting the advancement and recognition of professional lighting designers.

www.iald.org

Designers Lighting Forum (DLF)

The DLF focuses on presenting lighting design and designers through monthly meetings and events tailored to professional designers.

www.dlfny.com (New York City)
www.dlfla.org (Los Angeles)
www.dlf-ne.org (New England)

International Commission on Illumination (CIE)

Founded in 1913, the International Commission on Illumination—also known as the CIE from its French title, the Commission Internationale de l'Eclairage—is devoted to world-wide cooperation and the exchange of information on all matters relating to the science and art of light and lighting, color and vision, photobiology, and image technology.

www.cie.co.at (International)
www.cie-usnc.org (USA)

National Council on Qualifications for the Lighting Professions (NCQLP)

The NCQLP was founded in 1991 to establish a professional credential for lighting designers. Designers who demonstrate they have met minimum requirements in education and experience are eligible to sit for the lighting certification examination that tests a broad base of lighting knowledge. Passing the exam allows designers to use the designation LC (Lighting Certified) after their name.

Since 2005 the U.S. General Services Administration (GSA) has required that "lighting design be performed or supervised by a practitioner credentialed as Lighting Certified (LC) by the National Council on Qualifications for the Lighting Professions (NCQLP)."

www.ncqlp.org

International Dark-Sky Association

The International Dark-Sky Association was founded in 1988, and is dedicated to reducing and/or preventing nighttime light pollution. They work with the IES, state and national governments, and others to promote the Model Lighting Ordinance and dark-sky preserves.

www.darksky.org

APPENDIX II

Lighting-Related Trade Publications

Architectural Lighting

Architectural Lighting Magazine

Architectural Lighting Magazine is a free, monthly publication to members of the lighting design community. Articles focus on design projects, industry news, lighting products, and lighting technology.

www.archlighting.com

Architectural SSL

Architectural SSL is a free, monthly publication to members of the lighting design community. *Architectural SSL* focuses on the development, application, specification and use of solid-state lighting.

www.architecturalssl.com

Leukos, the Journal of the Illuminating Engineering Society

Leukos is a quarterly publication of the IES. It is free for IES members as a benefit of their membership, and is available by subscription to nonmembers. *Leukos* publishes papers on scientific research results, engineering developments, technical aspects of lighting applications, tutorial articles or critical reviews, and brief communications.

http://ies.org/leukos/introduction.cfm

Lighting Design + Application (LD+A)

LD+A is published monthly by the IES. It is free online for IES members as a benefit of their membership, and is available by subscription to nonmembers. Issues include case studies, technology overviews, career development, and legislative issues.

http://ies.org/lda/members_contact.cfm

Mondo ARC

Mondo ARC is an international magazine for architectural, retail, and commercial lighting. It is available as a paid subscription and a free iPad app. Articles cover various building types, light art, technology, and interviews with lighting designers and light artists.
www.mondoarc.com

Professional Lighting Design

Professional Lighting Design is published monthly by the PLDA. Its articles cover design philosophies, historical background information, theoretical topics, professional issues, and the technical aspects of lighting design and applications.
www.via-verlag.com

Theatrical Lighting

Lighting & Sound America

Lighting & Sound America is a monthly publication of PLASA, an entertainment industry trade association. It is available for free as a monthly magazine to qualified professionals, or as an iPhone/iPad app. Articles cover theatre, opera, dance, television, film, event, and "architainment" lighting and sound projects, new equipment, professional practice, and profiles of industry leaders.
www.lightingandsoundamerica.com

Live Design

Live Design content is similar to that of *Lighting & Sound America*.
www.livedesignonline.com

Architecture and Interior Design

Architect

Architect is the magazine of the American Institute of Architects. It is available as a free magazine for qualified professionals and as a free iPad app. Articles cover design, project profiles, practice and business issues, and interviews with industry leaders.
www.architectmagazine.com

Architectural Record

Architectural Record is a monthly magazine covering architecture and interior design. Articles cover commercial and residential architecture, critiques, architectural practice, and interviews with industry leaders.
www.architecturalrecord.com

Building Design + Construction

Building Design + Construction is a free monthly magazine for qualified professionals and a free iPad app. Articles cover most building types, including green design and construction and historic preservation.

www.bdcnetwork.com

Icon

Icon is the magazine of the American Society of Interior Designers. Articles cover commercial and residential work, professional practice, and industry outlooks. It is printed quarterly. Digital editions can be viewed on the Web site.

www.asid.org/icon

Visual Merchandising and Store Design (VMSD)

VMSD showcases the latest store designs and visual presentations, presents merchandising strategies and new products, and reports on industry news and events.

www.vmsd.com

Green Building

Eco-Structure

Eco-Structure is a magazine of the American Institute of Architects. It is available free to members of the design and construction communities. *Eco-Structure* is for architects, builders, interior designers, and others interested in the green building industry. Articles profile green projects, products and practices, as well as industry leaders.

www.ecobuildingpulse.com

Green Building & Design

Green Building & Design is a bimonthly magazine. It is available free to qualified professionals and as an iPad app. Articles cover architecture and design of various building types, real estate and development, green products, and interviews.

www.gbdmagazine.com

Glossary

Accent Light
A directional light used to emphasize an object or draw attention

Accommodation
The ability of the eye to change focus from one distance to another

Adaptation
The ability of the eye to adjust to different illumination levels

Additive Mixing
In light, combining the colored light from two sources on a surface producing the appearance of a third color

Aiming Angle
The angle, measured in degrees, between vertical and the centerline of the beam of light illuminating an object

Ambient Light
The general light in a space; it is the result of light from all light sources plus all inter-reflection.

Ampere
The unit of measurement for electric current; it is the amount of electricity moving past a given point in a circuit during a specific period, also referred to as amp. Amperage is equal to wattage divided by voltage.

Angle of Incidence
The angle between a ray of light striking a surface and a line perpendicular to that surface

Aperture
The opening in a luminaire through which light exits

Apparent Brightness
The perceived brightness of a light source or illuminated object as determined by the brightness range to which the eye has adapted

Apparent Color
The perceived color of an object resulting from the color content of the light source, the object's reflective properties, and the eye's adaptation to the illuminated environment

Arc Tube
A tube made of glass, clear quartz, or ceramic that contains the arc stream in an HID lamp

ASHRAE
Abbreviation for American Society of Heating, Refrigerating and Air-Conditioning Engineers

Astronomical Time Clock
A device that provides a signal to turn a load on or off or adjust power in steps based on the time of day or based on astronomical events such as sunset or sunrise, accounting for geographic location and day of the year.

Baffle
A vertical blade at the aperture of a luminaire used to block light distribution at high angles to prevent glare

Ballast
A device used to operate fluorescent and HID lamps; the ballast provides the necessary starting voltage and regulates the current during operation.

Ballast Factor
The ballast factor (BF) for a specific lamp-ballast combination is the percentage of the rated lamp lumens that will be produced by the combination

Beam Angle
The angle through the center of the beam where the light level has fallen to 50 percent of the beam's maximum brightness (typically at the center of the beam)

Binning
The sorting of LEDs by their color characteristics and electrical requirements

Blackbody Radiator
A theoretical object that is a perfect absorber of all energy that strikes its surface, and that is an ideal emitter of energy whose spectral power distribution curve is based on its temperature

Candela (cd)
Unit of luminous intensity, describing the intensity of a light source in a specific direction

Candlepower (cp)
An obsolete measure of luminous intensity of a light source in a specific direction. It has been replace by the candela. 1 cp = .98 cd

Candlepower Distribution Curve
A curve, plotted on polar coordinates, illustrating the distribution of luminous intensity of a lamp or luminaire in a plane through the light center

Chroma
The saturation or purity of a color

Chromatic Adaptation
The visual system's process of adjusting perceived color based on target and surround colors

Chromaticity
Refers to the color of a light source independent of its brightness

Circadian
Variations with a cycle of approximately 24 hours

Clerestory
The upper portion of a wall containing openings to admit daylight into a building

Coefficient of Utilization (CU)
The fraction of lamp lumens that reach the work plane directly from the source and from inter-reflections

Color
The property possessed by an object of producing different sensations on the eye as a result of the way the object reflects or emits light

Color Consistency
Describes lamp-to-lamp color matching

Color Constancy
See Chromatic Adaptation

Color Gamut
The range of colors that can be created based on the component colors used

Color Rendering Index (CRI)
A measurement of the effect of a light source on the color appearance of an object compared to its color appearance under a reference light source; the evaluation is based on eight color samples, but is calculated mathematically, not visually. It is expressed on a scale of 0 to 100, where 100 indicates no color shift. A low CRI rating suggests that the colors of objects will appear unnatural under that particular light source.

Color Rendering
The effect of a light source on the apparent color of an object

Color Stability
A lamp's ability to continuously emit the same color of light over its entire life

Color Temperature
A numerical indication of the warmth or coolness of white light; specifically, it is the absolute temperature of a blackbody radiator having a chromaticity equal to that of the light source, expressed in Kelvin. Strictly speaking, this applies only to incandescent light sources. Also see Correlated Color Temperature.

Commissioning
The process of setting, refining, and/or resetting a building system's operation; in lighting, this involves setting occupancy and vacancy sensors and control system presets.

Compact Fluorescent
A small fluorescent lamp that is often used as an alternative to incandescent lighting; they are also called CFL, PL, Twin-Tube, or BIAX lamps.

Cones
Retinal photoreceptors that provide color vision and respond to high illuminance levels and that perceive color and detail, so called because their shape resembles a cone

Contrast
The relationship between the luminance or color of an object and its surround

Control Zone
A group of luminaires performing the same task and controlled in unison. Also called a lighting control zone or zone.

Cornea
The clear covering over the iris and pupil; the cornea helps to focus light onto the retina.

Correlated Color Temperature (CCT)
Describes the color temperature of non-incandescent light sources

Cove Lighting
A technique in which a light fixture is set on a shelf or in a recess below the ceiling; light from the fixture is directed out of the recess to reflect off of the ceiling and into the illuminated space.

CRI
See Color Rendering Index

Current
The flow of electricity past a given point. Current is measured in amperes or amps.

Cut-Off Angle
The angle from a fixture's vertical axis at which a reflector, louver, or other shielding device cuts off direct visibility of a lamp

Daylighting
The intentional use of daylight as a significant daytime illuminance source for a building's interior

Daylight Harvesting
An energy-saving technique used in areas with significant daylight contribution in which a dimming system responds to a photocell by reducing the output of the lamps when daylight is present; as daylight levels increase, lamp intensity decreases.

Diffuse
Term describing dispersed light distribution; it refers to the scattering or softening of light.

Diffuser
A translucent piece of glass or plastic that shields the light source in a fixture; the light transmitted throughout the diffuser is redirected and scattered.

Digital Addressable Lighting Interface (DALI)
A communications protocol and network in which each luminaire has a distinct address, receives dimming information, and can report back to the lighting controller

Dimmer
An electrical device that controls lamp intensity by regulating the flow of electricity to the lamp

Direct Distribution
Describes light leaving a fixture and entering the illuminated space without first bouncing off of any architectural elements such as the ceiling or walls

Direct Glare
Glare produced by a direct view of light sources; it is often the result of fixtures with inadequate shielding.

Direct/Indirect
A light distribution pattern or luminaire in which 40–60 percent of the light is directed downward and 40–60 percent of the light is directed upward

Distribution
1. The way light is emitted from a luminaire (upward, downward, etc)

2. The way light is spread over an area or throughout a space

Downlight
A type of ceiling luminaire, usually recessed, from which the light is directed downward

Driver
The electronic device regulating electricity to LEDs; it is also known as a power supply.

Efficacy
Refers to the effectiveness of a device that has different forms of energy in and out; for example, how well lamps receive an input of electricity and convert it to light output is measured as their efficacy.

Efficiency
Refers to the effectiveness of a device that has the same form of energy in and out. For example, how well transformers and ballasts receive an input of electricity, modify the electricity and output electricity is measured as their efficiency.

Electromagnetic Spectrum
A continuous range of electric and magnetic radiation encompassing all wavelengths (or frequencies)

Electronic Ballast
A ballast that uses semi-conductor components to increase the frequency of electricity for fluorescent and HID lamp operation (typically in the 20–40 kHz range); smaller inductive components provide the lamp current control. System efficiency is increased due to high frequency lamp operation.

Field Angle
The angle through the center of the beam where the light level has fallen to 10 percent of the beam's maximum brightness (typically at the center of the beam)

Fixture
See Luminaire

Flange
A horizontal ring at the bottom of a reflector that hides the gap between the ceiling material and the reflector

Fluorescent Lamp
A light source consisting of a glass tube filled with argon, krypton, or other inert gas along with mercury; when electrical current is applied, the arc through the tube causes the mercury to emit ultraviolet radiation that excites the phosphors inside the lamp wall, causing them to radiate visible light.

Foot candle (fc)
The English unit of measurement of the illuminance on a surface; one foot candle is equal to one lumen per square foot.

Foot-Lambert
The English unit of luminance; one foot-lambert is equal to $1/\pi$ candelas per square foot.

Fovea
A small region at the center of the retina that contains only cones and provides the most distinct vision

General Lighting
See Ambient Lighting

Glare
The effect of brightness or differences in brightness within the visual field sufficiently high to cause annoyance, discomfort, or loss of visual performance

Halogen Lamp
An incandescent lamp with a lamp envelope made of quartz and a fill gas of one or more halogens (namely iodine, bromine chlorine, and fluorine), which slow the evaporation of the tungsten; It is also commonly called a quartz lamp or tungsten halogen lamp.

Harmonics
Voltage or current in electrical systems at frequencies that are a multiple of the voltage or current in the conductor. In North American systems of 60 Hz harmonics appear occur at 120 Hz, 180 Hz, 240 Hz, etc. Harmonics are created by most electronic devices and can cause overloading of conductors and transformers, and overheating of equipment.

Heat Sink
A metal component, usually aluminum, used to draw heat away from an LED and dissipate it

High Intensity Discharge (HID)
An electric discharge lamp in which an electric arc through a gas-filled chamber produces light without intermediate steps; also, it is a generic term describing mercury vapor, metal halide, high pressure sodium, and low pressure sodium light sources and luminaires.

High Pressure Sodium Lamp
A high intensity discharge (HID) lamp whose light is produced by radiation from sodium vapor

Hot Restart or Hot Restrike
Restoring the arc in an HID light source after a momentary power loss; hot restart occurs when the arc tube has cooled a sufficient amount.

Housing
The outer enclosure of a luminaire

Hue
The general color attribute of red, blue, yellow, green, etc.

Illuminance
The light incident on a surface or plane; illuminance is commonly referred to as light level or brightness. It is expressed as foot candles or lux.

Index of Refraction
The speed of light in a vacuum divided by the speed of light in a medium

Indirect
A light distribution pattern or luminaire in which all of the light is directed upward to bounce off of the ceiling

Initial Lumens
The light output of a lamp when new

Instant Start
A fluorescent ballast/lamp combination that ignites the lamp instantly with a very high starting voltage from the ballast; instant start lamps have single-pin bases.

Incandescent
A lamp technology that produces light by passing electricity through a tungsten filament, heating it to a high temperature and causing it to emit light

Intensity
The amount of light energy emitted from a light source or delivered to a surface. Commonly referred to as brightness.

Inter reflection
Describes rays of light bouncing off of multiple surfaces within a room

Lamp
Light bulb

Lamp Life
The average life of a lamp, in hours, typically based on an operation cycle of three hours on, then off

Layering
Using more than one lighting technique in a space to achieve multiple goals, create visual interest, and/or give users greater control

Life-Cycle Cost
The total costs associated with purchasing, operating, and maintaining a system over the life of that system

Light
The portion of the electromagnetic spectrum, ranging from about 380 to 770 nanometers, that is capable of exciting the retina and producing visual sensation

Light Emitting Diode (LED)
A solid state lighting device that emits a directional beam of colored light; white LEDs combine blue LEDs and phosphors.

Light Emitting Plasma
A light source in which a halogen gas and metal halides in a quartz capsule are energized to a plasma state by high frequency radio waves

Light Loss Factors (LLFs)
Factors that account for a lighting system's operation at less than initial conditions; these factors are used to calculate maintained light levels. LLFs are divided into two categories, recoverable and nonrecoverable. Examples are lamp lumen depreciation and luminaire surface depreciation.

Light Power Density (LPD)
The watts per square foot of power used by, or allocated to, lighting; energy conservation codes allocate LPDs based on space type or building type.

Light Trespass
Light from one property falling onto an adjacent property; it is often the result of poorly shielded luminaires.

Louver
Generally, a parabolic blade at the aperture of a fluorescent luminaire that is used to control light distribution from a luminaire and to eliminate glare

Low Voltage Lamp
A lamp (typically compact halogen) that operates at lower than 120V, typically 12V, and requires the use of a transformer

Lumen
A unit of light flow, or luminous flux; the lumen rating of a lamp is a measure of the total light output of the lamp.

Luminaire
A complete lighting unit consisting of a lamp or lamps, along with the parts designed to distribute the light, hold the lamps, and connect the lamps to a power source; it is also called a fixture.

Luminance
The brightness of a light source or of light reflected from an illuminated surface. It is expressed as foot-lamberts (English units) or candelas per square meter (metric units).

Lux (lx)
The International System of Units (SI) unit of measure for illuminance of a surface; one lux is equal to one lumen per square meter. One lux equals 0.093 foot candles.

Maintained Illuminance
Refers to the calculated light levels of a space after factoring in light loss factors such as lamp lumen depreciation, luminaire dirt depreciation, and room surface dirt depreciation

Matte
Describes a surface that reflects light, but scatters it in all directions

Mean Lumens
The average light output over the life of a lamp

Mesopic Vision
Vision utilizing both rods and cones; mesopic vision occurs at illuminance levels between .1 and 100 lx.

Metal Halide
A type of high intensity discharge lamp in which light is produced by passing an electric arc through a combination of metal halide and mercury vapors

Metamers
Two or more light sources of the same color but having different spectral power distribution curves

Movement
A change in the intensity, color and/or distribution of light over time

Nadir
A reference direction directly below a luminaire, or "straight down" (0 degree angle)

Occupancy Sensor
A device that automatically turns lights on when motion is detected and automatically turns lights off when motion is no longer detected; it may use ultrasonic, infrared, or both technologies.

Opaque
Describes a material which blocks the passage of light

Optics
A term referring to the components of a light fixture (such as reflectors, refractors, lenses, louvers) or to the light emitting or light controlling performance of a fixture

Organic Light Emitting Diode (OLED)
A light emitting diode in which the light emitting layer is an organic compound between two electrodes, at least one of which is transparent. OLEDs are light emitting sheets of material rather than small chips as with LEDs.

Parabolic Aluminized Reflector (PAR)
A sealed lamp unit having a parabolic shaped reflector, light source (typically incandescent or metal halide), and a lens; PAR lamps are available in a variety of beam angles.

Parabolic Luminaire
A type of fluorescent fixture that has a louver composed of aluminum baffles curved in a parabolic shape; the resulting light distribution produced provides reduced glare and better light control when compared to lay-in fluorescent fixtures.

Pendant
Describes a luminaire hanging from the ceiling

Photocell
A light-sensing device used to control luminaires and dimmers in response to detected light levels

Photometric Report
A set of printed data describing the light distribution, efficiency, and zonal lumen output of a luminaire

Photon
A particle representing a quantum of light or other electromagnetic energy. A photon carries energy but has zero mass.

Photopic Vision
Vision resulting from the cone cells of the retina; generalized as daytime vision, photopic vision occurs at illuminance levels greater than 100 lx.

Preset
A set of light levels saved into the memory of a lighting controller for recall by pressing the associated button on the controller

Primary Color
One of the base colors used to create all other colors, or a color that cannot be created through the mixing of other colors

Program Start
A type of ballast designed to withstand frequent switching. Programmed start ballasts heat the lamp electrodes, but do so in a much more tightly controlled way than rapid start ballasts to preserve the electrodes and extend the life of the lamp

Pupil
The opening of the iris that allows light into the eye

Rapid Start
The most popular fluorescent lamp/ballast combination used today; this ballast quickly and efficiently preheats lamp cathodes to start the lamp. It uses a "bi-pin" base.

Recessed
Describes a luminaire that is installed so that the housing of the luminaire is above the surface of the ceiling, inside a wall, or below the floor

Reflectance
The ratio of light reflected from a surface to the light incident on the surface; reflectances are often used for lighting calculations.

Reflected Glare
The reflection from a specular or semi-specular surface that partially or completely obscures the object being observed

Refraction
The bending of light as it passes between mediums of different densities

Reflector
The part of a luminaire that partially encloses the lamps and redirects some light emitted from them

Reflector Lamp
A lamp in which the outer glass envelope is coated with a reflecting material, also referred to as an R-lamp; variations include the ER and BR. Generically, this may also include other shapes that have reflectors such as MR and PAR.

Refractor
A device used to redirect the light output from a source, primarily by bending the waves of light

Relay
A device that switches an electrical load on or off based on a small input current or voltage

Retina
A membrane lining the inner eye, opposite the pupil, which contains photo-reactive cells that provide vision

Return on Investment (ROI)
The benefit that results from the investment a resource. In construction this generally means the amount of time that will pass before the savings that result from an investment, as in a new energy efficient lighting system, equal the initial investment.

Rods
Retinal photoreceptors that provide vision at low light levels; rods do not provide color vision.

Roof Monitor
The raised section of a building's main roof; the sides of monitors usually contain clerestory windows or louvers to light or ventilate the area below.

Room Cavity Ratio (RCR)
A ratio of room dimensions used to quantify how light will interact with room surfaces; it is a factor used in illuminance calculations.

Schema
A mental framework or concept that helps us interpret and organize new information

Scotopic Vision
Vision that relies only on rods; scotopic vision occurs at illuminance levels below .1 lx.

Secondary Color
An intermediate color created by mixing equal quantities of two primary colors

Semi-Direct
A light distribution pattern or luminaire in which 60 percent or more of the light is directed downward and 40 percent or less of the light is directed upward.

Semi-Indirect
A light distribution pattern or luminaire in which 40 percent or less of the light is directed downward and 60 percent or more of the light is directed upward.

Semi-Recessed
A luminaire that is only partly above the ceiling or within a wall

Semi-Specular
Describes a reflective material that is partially mirror-like. With semi-specular materials light is reflected directionally, but with some amount of scatter.

Shielding Angle
The angle measured from the ceiling plane to the line of sight where the bare lamp in a luminaire becomes visible

Sidelighting
Daylight illumination provided by windows mounted below the ceiling plane

Skyglow
Light that is either emitted directly upward by luminaires or reflected from the ground, and is scattered by dust and gas molecules in the atmosphere, producing a luminous background in the sky. The resulting glow reduces one's ability to view the stars.

Skylight
A window installed in the roof or ceiling

Socket
The part of a luminaire that provides an electrical connection for the lamp and also holds the lamp in the proper position within the luminaire

Solid-State Lighting (SSL)
Refers to LED and OLED light sources

Spacing Criterion
The maximum distance that luminaires may be spaced while still providing uniform illumination on the work plane; the luminaire height above the work plane multiplied by the spacing criterion equals the center-to-center luminaire spacing.

Spectral Colors
The individual colors of the visible spectrum

Spectral Power Distribution Curve
A graphic plot of a light source's radiant power at each wavelength of light

Specular
Describes a mirrored or polished surface. On specular surfaces the angle of incidence is equal to the angle of reflection.

Subtractive Mixing
In light, altering the color of light by using a glass or plastic filter to remove unwanted wavelengths from the beam

Surface Mount
Describes any luminaire installed on the surface of the ceiling, wall, floor, or piece of cabinetry or furniture

Task Lighting
Illumination provided to a specific area, such as a desktop, for the tasks performed there

Thermal Factor
A factor used in lighting calculations that compensates for the change in light output of a fluorescent lamp due to a change in bulb wall temperature; it is applied when the

lamp-ballast combination under consideration is different from that used in the photometric tests.

Toplighting
Daylight illumination provided by skylights

Transformer
A device that increases or decreases electrical pressure; in lighting this typically refers to a device that converts 120V to 12V.

Translucent
Describes a material that diffuses light passing through it so that objects cannot be seen clearly through it

Transmission
The passage of light through a material

Transmittance
The percentage of light that passes through a translucent or diffusing material

Transparent
Describes a material with no diffusion of the light passing through it so that objects are clearly seen through it

Tungsten Halogen Lamp
See Halogen Lamp

Ultraviolet (UV)
Invisible radiation that is shorter in wavelength and higher in frequency than visible violet light (literally beyond the violet light)

Vacancy Sensor
A control device with which lights must be turned on manually, but that automatically turns lights off after the space becomes unoccupied; it may be ultrasonic, infrared, or both.

Value
The relative lightness or darkness of a color

Veiling Reflection
See Reflected Glare

Visual Acuity
The ability to see fine or small details

Visual Task
A vision related activity, such as reading a book, and the details and objects that must be seen for the performance of that activity

Volt
The standard unit of measurement for electrical potential; it defines the "force" or "pressure" of electricity.

Wall Box
Describes a wall mounted switch or dimmer

Wall Grazer
A luminaire set at the top of a wall that directs light down the face of the wall to illuminate it

Wall Washer
A luminaire designed to illuminate a wall. They are usually used in groups and installed +/–3' from the wall.

Watt (W)
The unit for measuring electrical power; it defines the rate of energy consumption by an electrical device when it is in operation.

Wavelength
The distance from crest to crest, or trough to trough, of a wave

Work Plane
The level at which work is done and at which illuminance is specified and measured; for office applications, this is typically a horizontal plane 30 inches above the floor (desk height).

Index